I0010045

Hands-On Neuroevolution with Python

Build high-performing artificial neural network architectures using neuroevolution-based algorithms

Iaroslav Omelianenko

BIRMINGHAM - MUMBAI

Hands-On Neuroevolution with Python

Copyright © 2019 Packt Publishing

All rights reserved. No part of this book may be reproduced, stored in a retrieval system, or transmitted in any form or by any means, without the prior written permission of the publisher, except in the case of brief quotations embedded in critical articles or reviews.

Every effort has been made in the preparation of this book to ensure the accuracy of the information presented. However, the information contained in this book is sold without warranty, either express or implied. Neither the author, nor Packt Publishing or its dealers and distributors, will be held liable for any damages caused or alleged to have been caused directly or indirectly by this book.

Packt Publishing has endeavored to provide trademark information about all of the companies and products mentioned in this book by the appropriate use of capitals. However, Packt Publishing cannot guarantee the accuracy of this information.

Commissioning Editor: Sunith Shetty
Acquisition Editor: Nelson Morris
Content Development Editor: Pratik Andrade
Senior Editor: Ayaan Hoda
Technical Editor: Prachi Sawant
Copy Editor: Safis Editing
Language Support Editor: Safis Editing
Project Coordinator: Anish Daniel
Proofreader: Safis Editing
Indexer: Priyanka Dhadke
Production Designer: Nilesh Mohite

First published: December 2019

Production reference: 1231219

Published by Packt Publishing Ltd.
Livery Place
35 Livery Street
Birmingham
B3 2PB, UK.

ISBN 978-1-83882-491-4

www.packt.com

To my wife, Lucy, for being my dear friend and loving partner throughout our joint life journey.

– Iaroslav

`Packt.com`

Subscribe to our online digital library for full access to over 7,000 books and videos, as well as industry leading tools to help you plan your personal development and advance your career. For more information, please visit our website.

Why subscribe?

- Spend less time learning and more time coding with practical eBooks and Videos from over 4,000 industry professionals

- Improve your learning with Skill Plans built especially for you

- Get a free eBook or video every month

- Fully searchable for easy access to vital information

- Copy and paste, print, and bookmark content

Did you know that Packt offers eBook versions of every book published, with PDF and ePub files available? You can upgrade to the eBook version at `www.packt.com` and as a print book customer, you are entitled to a discount on the eBook copy. Get in touch with us at `customercare@packtpub.com` for more details.

At `www.packt.com`, you can also read a collection of free technical articles, sign up for a range of free newsletters, and receive exclusive discounts and offers on Packt books and eBooks.

Contributors

About the author

Iaroslav Omelianenko occupied the position of CTO and research director for more than a decade. He is an active member of the research community and has published several research papers at arXiv, ResearchGate, Preprints, and more. He started working with applied machine learning by developing autonomous agents for mobile games more than a decade ago. For the last 5 years, he has actively participated in research related to applying deep machine learning methods for authentication, personal traits recognition, cooperative robotics, synthetic intelligence, and more. He is an active software developer and creates open source neuroevolution algorithm implementations in the Go language.

I want to thank all the researchers and developers for sharing their work in a way inspired by open source ideals. Without the open source community, our world would be a different place.

About the reviewers

Alan McIntyre is a principal software architect at CodeReclaimers, LLC, where he provides custom software design and development services for technical computing applications, including computational geometry, computer vision, and machine learning. He has previously worked as a software engineer at General Electric, Microsoft, and multiple start-ups.

Unsal Gokdag has been working full time as a senior data scientist in logistics since 2017, and had previously worked as a research and development engineer in 2013.

He is currently doing his PhD in a comparison of machine learning algorithms for image despeckling and the classification of polarimetric SAR images. His past experience includes work in machine learning, computer vision, and bioinformatics. He was introduced to the NEAT algorithm in this bachelor's thesis and has been interested in evolutionary algorithms since. He is currently residing in Germany.

> *I would like to thank my family for the unconditional love they have given to me. I wouldn't be the person I am without them. To my mother and sister: thank you for all your efforts in my most difficult times. Father, I miss you.*

Packt is searching for authors like you

If you're interested in becoming an author for Packt, please visit authors.packtpub.com and apply today. We have worked with thousands of developers and tech professionals, just like you, to help them share their insight with the global tech community. You can make a general application, apply for a specific hot topic that we are recruiting an author for, or submit your own idea.

Table of Contents

Section 2: Applying Neuroevolution Methods to Solve Classic Computer Science Problems

Section 3: Advanced Neuroevolution Methods

Preface

With conventional deep learning methods almost hitting a wall in terms of their capability, more and more researchers have started looking for alternative approaches to train artificial neural networks.

Deep machine learning is extremely effective for pattern recognition, but fails in tasks that require an understanding of context or previously unseen data. Many researchers, including Geoff Hinton, the father of the modern incarnation of deep machine learning, agree that the current approach to designing artificial intelligence systems is no longer able to cope with the challenges currently being faced.

In this book, we discuss a viable alternative to traditional deep machine learning methods—neuroevolution algorithms. Neuroevolution is a family of machine learning methods that use evolutionary algorithms to ease the solving of complex tasks such as games, robotics, and the simulation of natural processes. Neuroevolution algorithms are inspired by the process of natural selection. Very simple artificial neural networks can evolve to become very complex. The ultimate result of neuroevolution is the optimal topology of a network, which makes the model more energy-efficient and more convenient to analyze.

Throughout this book, you will learn about various neuroevolution algorithms and get practical skills in using them to solve different computer science problems—from classic reinforcement learning to building agents for autonomous navigation through a labyrinth. Also, you will learn how neuroevolution can be used to train deep neural networks to create an agent that can play classic Atari games.

This book aims to give you a solid understanding of neuroevolution methods by implementing various experiments using step-by-step guidance. It covers practical examples in areas such as games, robotics, and the simulation of natural processes, using real-world examples and datasets to help you better understand the concepts explored. After reading this book, you will have everything you need to apply neuroevolution methods to other tasks similar to the experiments presented.

In writing this book, my goal is to provide you with knowledge of cutting-edge technology that is a vital alternative to traditional deep learning. I hope that the application of neuroevolution algorithms in your projects will allow you to solve your currently intractable problems in an elegant and energy-efficient way.

Who this book is for

This book is for machine learning practitioners, deep learning researchers, and AI enthusiasts who are looking to implement neuroevolution algorithms from scratch. You will learn how to apply these algorithms to various sets of real-world problems. You will learn how neuroevolution methods can optimize the process of training artificial neural networks. You will become familiar with the core concepts of neuroevolution and get the necessary practical skills to use it in your work and experiments. A working knowledge of Python and deep learning and neural network basics is mandatory.

What this book covers

Chapter 1, *Overview of Neuroevolution Methods*, introduces the core concepts of genetic algorithms, such as genetic operators and genome encoding schemes.

Chapter 2, *Python Libraries and Environment Setup*, discusses the practical aspects of neuroevolution methods. This chapter provides the pros and cons of popular Python libraries that provide implementations of the NEAT algorithm and its extensions.

Chapter 3, *Using NEAT for XOR Solver Optimization*, is where you start experimenting with the NEAT algorithm by implementing a solver for a classical computer science problem.

Chapter 4, *Pole-Balancing Experiments*, is where you continue with experiments related to the classic problems of computer science in the field of reinforcement learning.

Chapter 5, *Autonomous Maze Navigation*, is where you continue your experiments with neuroevolution through an attempt to create a solver that can find an exit from a maze. You will learn how to implement a simulation of a robot that has an array of sensors to detect obstacles and monitor its position within the maze.

Chapter 6, *Novelty Search Optimization Method*, is where you use the practical experience gained during the creation of a maze solver in the previous chapter to embark on the path of creating a more advanced solver.

Chapter 7, *Hypercube-Based NEAT for Visual Discrimination*, introduces you to advanced neuroevolution methods. You'll learn about the indirect genome encoding scheme, which uses **Compositional Pattern Producing Networks** (**CPPNs**) to aid with the encoding of large-phenotype ANN topologies.

Chapter 8, *ES-HyperNEAT and the Retina Problem*, is where you will learn how to select the substrate configuration that is best suited for a specific problem space.

`Chapter 9`, *Co-Evolution and the SAFE Method*, is where we discuss how a co-evolution strategy is widely found in nature and could be transferred into the realm of the neuroevolution.

`Chapter 10`, *Deep Neuroevolution*, presents you with the concept of Deep Neuroevolution, which can be used to train **Deep Artificial Neural Networks** (**DNNs**).

`Chapter 11`, *Best Practices, Tips, and Tricks*, teaches you how to start working with whatever problem is at hand, how to tune the hyperparameters of a neuroevolution algorithm, how to use advanced visualization tools, and what metrics can be used for the analysis of algorithm performance.

`Chapter 12`, *Concluding Remarks*, summarizes everything you have learned in this book and provides further directions for you to continue your self-education.

To get the most out of this book

A practical knowledge of the Python programming language is essential to work with the examples presented in this book. For better source code understanding, it is preferable to use an IDE that supports Python syntax highlighting and code reference location. If you don't have one installed, you can use Microsoft Visual Studio Code. It is free and cross-platform, and you can download it here: `https://code.visualstudio.com`.

Python and most of the libraries we discuss in this book are cross-platform, and compatible with Windows, Linux, and macOS. All experiments described in the book are executed from the command line, so make yourself familiar with the terminal console application installed on the OS of your choice.

To complete the experiment described in `Chapter 10`, *Deep Neuroevolution*, you need to have access to a modern PC with Nvidia graphics accelerator GeForce GTX 1080Ti or better. This experiment is also better to run in an Ubuntu Linux environment. Ubuntu is a modern Linux-based OS that is free and powerful. Making yourself familiar with it will help you a lot.

Download the example code files

You can download the example code files for this book from your account at `www.packt.com`. If you purchased this book elsewhere, you can visit `www.packtpub.com/support` and register to have the files emailed directly to you.

You can download the code files by following these steps:

1. Log in or register at www.packt.com.
2. Select the **Support** tab.
3. Click on **Code Downloads**.
4. Enter the name of the book in the **Search** box and follow the onscreen instructions.

Once the file is downloaded, please make sure that you unzip or extract the folder using the latest version of:

- WinRAR/7-Zip for Windows
- Zipeg/iZip/UnRarX for Mac
- 7-Zip/PeaZip for Linux

The code bundle for the book is also hosted on GitHub at https://github.com/ PacktPublishing/Hands-on-Neuroevolution-with-Python. In case there's an update to the code, it will be updated on the existing GitHub repository.

We also have other code bundles from our rich catalog of books and videos available at https://github.com/PacktPublishing/. Check them out!

Download the color images

We also provide a PDF file that has color images of the screenshots/diagrams used in this book. You can download it here: https://static.packt-cdn.com/downloads/ 9781838824914_ColorImages.pdf.

Conventions used

There are a number of text conventions used throughout this book.

CodeInText: Indicates code words in text, database table names, folder names, filenames, file extensions, pathnames, dummy URLs, user input, and Twitter handles. Here is an example: "You can start an experiment from the Chapter10 directory by executing the following command."

A block of code is set as follows:

```
if indices is None:
            indices = np.arange(self.batch_size)
```

Any command-line input or output is written as follows:

```
$ conda create -n deep_ne python=3.5
```

Bold: Indicates a new term, an important word, or words that you see onscreen. For example, words in menus or dialog boxes appear in the text like this. Here is an example: "Select **System info** from the **Administration** panel."

Warnings or important notes appear like this.

Tips and tricks appear like this.

Get in touch

Feedback from our readers is always welcome.

General feedback: If you have questions about any aspect of this book, mention the book title in the subject of your message and email us at customercare@packtpub.com.

Errata: Although we have taken every care to ensure the accuracy of our content, mistakes do happen. If you have found a mistake in this book, we would be grateful if you would report this to us. Please visit www.packtpub.com/support/errata, selecting your book, clicking on the Errata Submission Form link, and entering the details.

Piracy: If you come across any illegal copies of our works in any form on the Internet, we would be grateful if you would provide us with the location address or website name. Please contact us at copyright@packt.com with a link to the material.

If you are interested in becoming an author: If there is a topic that you have expertise in and you are interested in either writing or contributing to a book, please visit authors.packtpub.com.

Reviews

Please leave a review. Once you have read and used this book, why not leave a review on the site that you purchased it from? Potential readers can then see and use your unbiased opinion to make purchase decisions, we at Packt can understand what you think about our products, and our authors can see your feedback on their book. Thank you!

For more information about Packt, please visit `packt.com`.

Section 1: Fundamentals of Evolutionary Computation Algorithms and Neuroevolution Methods

This section introduces core concepts of evolutionary computation and discusses particulars of neuroevolution-based algorithms and which Python libraries can be used to implement them. You will become familiar with the fundamentals of neuroevolution methods and will get practical recommendations on how to start your experiments. This section provides a basic introduction to the Anaconda package manager for Python as part of your environment setup.

This section comprises the following chapters:

- Chapter 1, *Overview of Neuroevolution Methods*
- Chapter 2, *Python Libraries and Environment Setup*

Overview of Neuroevolution Methods 1

The concept of **artificial neural networks** (**ANN**) was inspired by the structure of the human brain. There was a strong belief that, if we were able to imitate this intricate structure in a very similar way, we would be able to create artificial intelligence. We are still on the road to achieving this. Although we can implement Narrow AI agents, we are still far from creating a Generic AI agent.

This chapter introduces you to the concept of ANNs and the two methods that we can use to train them (the gradient descent with error backpropagation and neuroevolution) so that they learn how to approximate the objective function. However, we will mainly focus on discussing the neuroevolution-based family of algorithms. You will learn about the implementation of the evolutionary process that's inspired by natural evolution and become familiar with the most popular neuroevolution algorithms: NEAT, HyperNEAT, and ES-HyperNEAT. We will also discuss the methods of optimization that we can use to search for final solutions and make a comparison between objective-based search and Novelty Search algorithms. By the end of this chapter, you will have a complete understanding of the internals of neuroevolution algorithms and be ready to apply this knowledge in practice.

In this chapter, we will cover the following topics:

- Evolutionary algorithms and neuroevolution-based methods
- NEAT algorithm overview
- Hypercube-based NEAT
- Evolvable-Substrate HyperNEAT
- Novelty Search optimization method

Evolutionary algorithms and neuroevolution-based methods

The term artificial neural networks stands for a graph of nodes connected by links where each of the links has a particular weight. The neural node defines a kind of threshold operator that allows the signal to pass only after a specific activation function has been applied. It remotely resembles the way in which neurons in the brain are organized. Typically, the ANN training process consists of selecting the appropriate weight values for all the links within the network. Thus, ANN can approximate any function and can be considered as a universal approximator, which is established by the Universal Approximation Theorem.

For more information on the proof of the Universal Approximation Theorem, take a look at the following papers:

- Cybenko, G. (1989) *Approximations by Superpositions of Sigmoidal Functions*, Mathematics of Control, Signals, and Systems, 2(4), 303–314.
- Leshno, Moshe; Lin, Vladimir Ya.; Pinkus, Allan; Schocken, Shimon (January 1993). *Multilayer feedforward networks with a nonpolynomial activation function can approximate any function.* Neural Networks. 6 (6): 861–867. doi:10.1016/S0893-6080(05)80131-5. (https://www.sciencedirect.com/science/article/abs/pii/S0893608005801315?via%3Dihub)
- Kurt Hornik (1991) *Approximation Capabilities of Multilayer Feedforward Networks*, Neural Networks, 4(2), 251–257. doi:10.1016/0893-6080(91)90009-T (https://www.sciencedirect.com/science/article/abs/pii/089360809190009T?via%3Dihub)
- Hanin, B. (2018). *Approximating Continuous Functions by ReLU Nets of Minimal Width.* arXiv preprint arXiv:1710.11278. (https://arxiv.org/abs/1710.11278)

Over the past 70 years, many ANN training methods have been proposed. However, the most popular technique that gained fame in this decade was proposed by Jeffrey Hinton. It is based on the backpropagation of prediction error through the network, with various optimization techniques built around the gradient descent of the loss function with respect to connection weights between the network nodes. It demonstrates the outstanding performance of training deep neural networks for tasks related mainly to pattern recognition. However, despite its inherent powers, it has significant drawbacks. One of these drawbacks is that a vast amount of training samples are required to learn something useful from a specific dataset. Another significant disadvantage is the fixed network architecture that's created manually by the experimenter, which results in inefficient use of computational resources. This is due to a significant amount of network nodes not participating in the inference process. Also, backpropagation-based methods have problems with transferring the acquired knowledge to other similar domains.

Alongside backpropagation methods, there are very promising evolutionary algorithms that can address the aforementioned problems. These bio-inspired techniques draw inspiration from Darwin's theory of evolution and use natural evolution abstractions to create artificial neural networks. The basic idea behind neuroevolution is to produce the ANNs by using stochastic, population-based search methods. It is possible to evolve optimal architectures of neural networks, which accurately address the specific tasks using the evolutionary process. As a result, compact and energy-efficient networks with moderate computing power requirements can be created. The evolutionary process is executed by applying genetic operators (*mutation, crossover*) to the population of chromosomes (genetically encoded representations of ANNs/solutions) over many generations. The central belief is that since this is in biological systems, subsequent generations will be suited to withstand the generational pressure that's expressed by the objective function, that is, they will become better approximators of the objective function.

Next, we will discuss the basic concepts of genetic algorithms. You will need to have a moderate level of understanding of genetic algorithms.

Genetic operators

Genetic operators are at the very heart of every evolutionary algorithm, and the performance of any neuroevolutionary algorithm depends on them. There are two major genetic operators: mutation and crossover (recombination).

In this chapter, you will learn about the basics of genetic algorithms and how they differ from conventional algorithms, which use error backpropagation-based methods for training the ANN.

Mutation operator

The *mutation* operator serves the essential role of preserving the genetic diversity of the population during evolution and prevents stalling in the local minima when the chromosomes of organisms in a population become too similar. This mutation alters one or more genes in the chromosome, according to the mutation probability defined by the experimenter. By introducing random changes to the solver's chromosome, mutation allows the evolutionary process to explore new areas in the search space of possible solutions and find better and better solutions over generations.

The following diagram shows the common types of mutation operators:

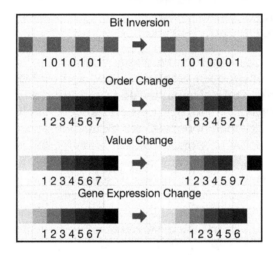

Types of mutation operators

The exact type of mutation operator depends on the kind of genetic encoding that's used by a specific genetic algorithm. Among the various mutation types we come across, we can distinguish the following:

- **Bit inversion**: The randomly selected bit, which is inverted (*binary encoding*).
- **Order change**: Two genes are randomly selected and their position is flipped in the genome (*permutation encoding*).
- **Value change**: A small value is added to the expressed gene at a random position (*value encoding*).
- **Gene expression change**: A random gene is selected and added/removed from the genotype (*structural encoding*).

Genotypes can be encoded using genetic encoding schemes with fixed and variable chromosomal lengths. The first three mutations can be applied to both types of encoding schemes. The last mutation can only be expressed in genotypes that have been encoded using a variable-length encoding.

Crossover operator

The *crossover* (recombination) operator allows us to stochastically generate new generations (solutions) from existing populations by recombining genetic information from two parents to generate offspring. Thus, the portions of good solutions from parent organisms can be combined and can potentially lead to better offspring. Typically, after a crossover, the produced offspring are mutated before being added to the population of the next generation.

The following diagram shows the various crossover operators:

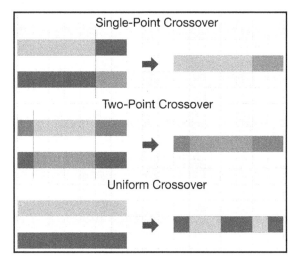

Types of crossover operators

The different types of crossover operators also depend on the genetic encoding that's used by particular algorithms, but the following are the most common:

- **Single-point crossover**: The random crossover point is selected, the genome part from the beginning to the crossover point is copied to the offspring from one parent, and the rest are copied from another parent.

- **Two-point crossover**: The two crossover points are chosen randomly, the part of the genome from the beginning to the first point is copied from the first parent, the part between the first and second crossover point is copied from the second parent, and the rest are copied from the first parent.
- **Uniform crossover**: The genes are copied from the first or second parent randomly.

Genome encoding schemes

One of the most crucial choices when designing the neuroevolution algorithm is to determine the genetic representation of the neural network, which can be evolved in the following ways

- Standard mutation (see the preceding *Mutation operator* subsection)
- Combination operators (see the preceding *Crossover operator* subsection)

At the moment, two major schemes for genome encoding exist: direct and indirect. Let's consider each schema in more detail.

Direct genome encoding

Direct genome encoding attempts were used in neuroevolution methods to create ANNs that were related to neural networks with a fixed topology; that is, the network topology was determined solely by the experimenter. Here, genetic encoding (*genotype*) is implemented as a vector of real numbers, representing the strength (*weights*) of the connections between the network nodes.

The evolutionary operators modify the values of the weights vector with the mutation operator and combine the vectors of the parent organisms with the recombination (crossover) operator to produce offspring. While allowing evolutionary operators to be applied with ease, the described encoding method has some significant drawbacks. One of its main drawbacks is that the network topology is determined by the experimenter from the very beginning and fixed through all the generations during the execution of the algorithm. This approach contradicts the natural evolutionary process, in which not only the properties but also the physical structure of the organisms change during the evolutionary process. This allows us to explore the broadest possible search space and find optimal solutions.

The following diagram shows the evolutionary process:

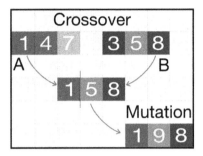

The evolutionary process

To address the drawbacks of the fixed topology methods, Kenneth O. Stanley proposed the **NeuroEvolution of Augmenting Topologies (NEAT)** method. The primary idea behind this algorithm is that the evolutionary operators are applied not only to the vector with the weights of all the connections but also to the topology of the created neural network. Thus, through generating the populations of the organisms, various topologies with a variety of connection weights are tested. We will discuss the particulars of the NEAT algorithm later in this chapter.

The NEAT algorithm demonstrates outstanding performance in a variety of tasks – from traditional reinforcement learning to the control of sophisticated non-player characters in computer games – and has become one of the most popular neuroevolution algorithms ever. However, it belongs to the family of direct encoding algorithms, which limits its use to evolving only modest-sized ANNs, where parameter space is limited to a maximum of thousands of connections. This is because each connection is directly encoded in the genotype, and with a large number of encoded connections, the computational requirements increase significantly. This makes it impossible to use the algorithm to evolve large neural networks.

Indirect genome encoding

To overcome size issues with direct encoding, Kenneth O. Stanley proposed an *indirect* encoding method, which is inspired by how the phenotype is encoded by the genome in the DNA. It is based on the fact that the physical world is built around geometry and regularities (structural patterns), where natural symmetries are found everywhere. Thus, the encoding size of any physical process can be significantly reduced through the reuse of a specific set of encoding blocks for the same structure that repeats many times. The proposed method, called **Hypercube-based NeuroEvolution of Augmenting Topologies (HyperNEAT)**, is designed to build large-scale neural networks by exploiting geometrical regularities. HyperNEAT employs a connective **Compositional Pattern Producing Network (CPPN)** to represent node connections as a function of Cartesian space. We will discuss HyperNEAT in more detail later in this chapter.

Coevolution

In nature, populations of different species often simultaneously evolve in mutual interaction with each other. This type of inter-species relationship is called **coevolution**. Coevolution is a powerful tool of natural evolution, and it is no surprise that it attracted the attention of the neuroevolution community. There are three main types of coevolution:

- **Mutualism**, which is when two or more species coexist and mutually benefit from each other.
- **Competitive coevolution**:
    - **Predation**, which is when one organism kills another and consumes its resources.
    - **Parasitism**, which is when one organism exploits the resources of another but does not kill it.
- **Commensalism**, which is when the members of one species gain benefits without causing harm or gaining benefits from other species.

The preceding coevolution strategies were explored by researchers and their pros and cons were revealed. In this book, we will introduce a neuroevolution algorithm that employs the commensalistic principle to maintain two coevolving populations: the population of candidate solutions and the population of candidate objective functions. We will discuss the **Solution and Fitness Evolution (SAFE)** algorithm later in Chapter 9, *Co-Evolution and the SAFE Method*.

Modularity and hierarchy

Another crucial aspect of how natural cognitive systems are organized is modularity and hierarchy. While studying the human brain, neuroscientists have found that it is not a monolithic system with a uniform structure, but rather a complex hierarchy of modular structures. Also, due to the speed limitations of signal propagation in the biological tissues, the structure of the brain enforces the principle of locality when related tasks are processed by geometrically adjacent structures in the brain. This aspect of natural systems did not escape the attention of researchers of neuroevolution and they are implemented in many evolutionary algorithms. We will discuss how modular ANNs can be created using a neuroevolution-based algorithm in `Chapter 8`, *ES-HyperNEAT and the Retina Problems*.

NEAT algorithm overview

The method of NEAT for evolving complex ANNs was designed to reduce the dimensionality of the parameter search space through the gradual elaboration of the ANN's structure during evolution. The evolutionary process starts with a population of small, simple genomes (seeds) and gradually increases their complexity over generations.

The seed genomes have a very simple topology: only input, output, and bias neurons are expressed. No hidden nodes are introduced into the seed from the beginning to guarantee that the search for a solution starts in the lowest-dimensional parameter space (connection weights) possible. With each new generation, additional genes are introduced, expanding the solution search space by presenting a new dimension that previously did not exist. Thus, evolution begins by searching in a small space that can be easily optimized and adds new dimensions when necessary. With this approach, complex phenotypes (solutions) can be discovered gradually, step by step, which is much more efficient than launching the search directly in the vast space of the final solutions. Natural evolution utilizes a similar strategy by occasionally adding new genes that make phenotypes more complex. In biology, this process of incremental elaboration is called **complexification**.

The primary goal of the NEAT method is to minimize the complexity of the genome structure – not only the final product, but of all the intermediate generations of the organisms as well. Thus, the evolution of the network topology results in a significant performance advantage by reducing the overall solutions for the search space. For example, the high-dimensional space of the final solution is only encountered at the end of the evolutionary process. Another essential feature of the algorithm is that each structure that's introduced to the genome is the subject of subsequent fitness evaluations in the future generations. Also, only useful structures will survive during the evolutionary process. In other words, the structural complexity of the genome is always goal-justified.

NEAT encoding scheme

The genetic encoding scheme of NEAT is designed to allow easy matching between corresponding genes during the mating process when a crossover operator is applied to the two parent genomes. The NEAT genome is a linear representation of the connectivity pattern of the encoded neural network, as shown in the following NEAT genome scheme:

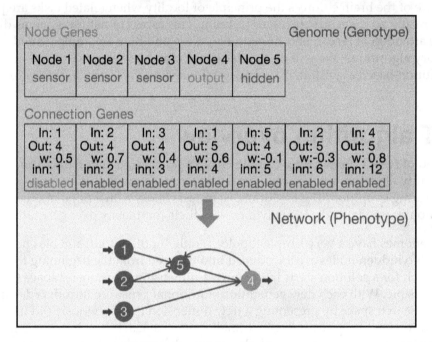

The NEAT genome scheme

Each genome is represented as a list of connection genes that encode connections between the nodes of the neural network. Also, there are node genes that encode information about network nodes, such as the node identifier, node type, and type of activation function. The connection gene encodes the following connection parameters of the network link:

- The identifier of the input network node
- The identifier of the output network node
- The strength (weight) of the connection
- A bit, which indicates whether the connection is enabled (expressed) or not
- An innovation number, which allows matching genes during recombination

The bottom part of the preceding diagram represents a scheme of the same genome in the form of a directed graph.

Structural mutations

The mutation operator that's specific to NEAT can change a connection's strength (weight) and the network's structure. There are two main types of structural mutations:

- Adding a new connection between nodes
- Adding a new node to the network

The following diagram shows the structural mutations of the NEAT algorithm:

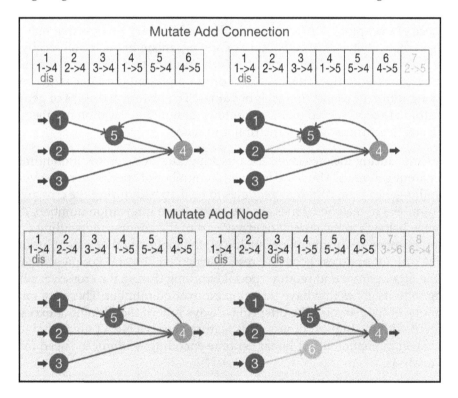

The structural mutations of the NEAT algorithm

When the mutation operator is applied to the NEAT genome, the newly added gene (connection gene or node gene) is assigned with an increasingly incremented innovation number. During the evolutionary process, the genomes of organisms within the population gradually get larger and genomes of varying sizes are produced. This process results in different connection genes being in the same positions within a genome, making the matching process between same-origin genes extremely complicated.

Crossover with an innovation number

There is a piece of unexploited information in the evolutionary process that tells us exactly which genes to match between the genomes of any organism in the topologically diverse population. This is where each gene tells us which ancestor that gene was derived from. The connection genes with the same historical origin represent the same structure, despite possibly having different connection weight values. The historical origins of genes in the NEAT algorithm are represented by incrementally assigned innovation numbers, which allow us to track the chronology of structural mutations.

At the same time, during the crossover, the offspring inherit the innovation numbers of genes from parent genomes. Thus, the innovation number of specific genes never change, allowing similar genes from different genomes to be matched during the crossover. The innovation numbers of matched genes are the same. If the innovation numbers do not match, the gene belongs to the *disjoint* or *excess* part of the genome, depending on whether its innovation number lies inside of, or outside of, the range of other parent innovation numbers. The disjoint or excess genes represent structures that are not present in the genome of the other parent and require special handling during the crossover phase. Thus, the offspring inherits genes that have the same innovation number. These are randomly chosen from one of the parents. The offspring always inherit the disjoint or excess genes from the parent with the highest fitness. This feature allows a NEAT algorithm to efficiently perform gene recombination using linear genome encoding, without the need for complex topological analysis.

The following diagram shows the crossover (recombination) in the NEAT algorithm:

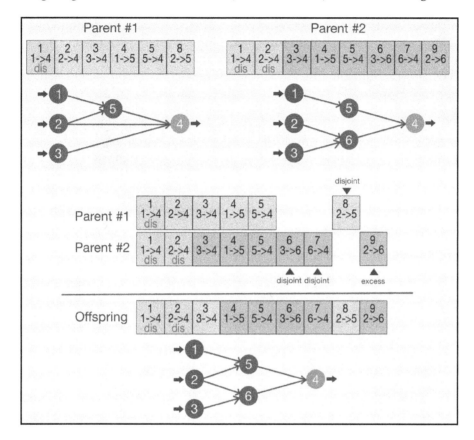

Crossover (recombination) in the NEAT algorithm

The preceding diagram shows an example of a crossover between two parents using the NEAT algorithm. The genomes of both parents are aligned using the innovation numbers (the number at the top of the connection gene cell). After that, the offspring is produced by randomly choosing connection genes from either of parents when the innovation numbers are the same: the genes with innovation numbers from one to five. Finally, the disjoint and excess genes are added from either of the parents unconditionally and ordered by innovation number.

Speciation

In the evolutionary process, organisms can create diverse topologies through generations, but they fail to produce and maintain topological innovations of their own. The smaller network structures optimize faster than larger ones, which artificially reduces the chances of survival of a descendant genome after adding a new node or connection to it. Thus, the freshly augmented topologies experience negative evolutionary pressure due to the temporary decrease of fitness of the organisms within the population. At the same time, novel topologies can introduce innovations that lead to a winning solution in the long run. To address the temporal drop of fitness, the concept of speciation was introduced in the NEAT algorithm. The speciation limits the range of organisms that can mate by introducing narrow niches where only organisms that belong to the same niche compete with each other during the crossover, instead of competing with all the organisms in the population. Speciation is implemented by dividing the population so that organisms with a similar topology belong to the same species.

Let's refer to the following speciation algorithm:

Algorithm 1: Clustering Genomes into Species

Input: A *Population* of organisms and known *Species*
Result: Organisms will be clustered among *Species*. New *Species* will be created as appropriate.

foreach *genome* $\in$ *Population* **do**
  foreach $S \in$ *Species* **do**
    if *genome*.IsCompatible(S) **then**
      // Add compatible Genome to the current species
      S.AddGenome(*genome*);
    else if S *is the last known species* **then**
      // Create new species for a given genome
      $S_{new} \longleftarrow$ *create_new_species*(*genome*) ;
      // Add new species to the list of known Species
      Species $\longleftarrow$ *Species* $\cup S_{new}$;

The speciation algorithm

The NEAT method permits the creation of complex ANNs that are capable of solving a variety of control optimization problems, as well as other unsupervised learning problems. Due to the introduced specifics of ANN topology augmentation through complexification and speciation, the solutions tend to optimize the performance of training and inference. The resulting ANN topology grows to match the problem that needs to be solved, without any excess layers of hidden units being introduced by the conventional methods of ANN's topology design for backpropagation-based training.

More details about the NEAT algorithm can be found in the original paper: `http://nn.cs.utexas.edu/downloads/papers/stanley.phd04.pdf`.

Hypercube-based NEAT

Intelligence is a product of the brain, and the human brain as a structure is itself a product of natural evolution. Such an intricate structure has evolved over millions of years, under pressure from harsh environments, and while competing with other living beings for survival. As a result, an extremely complex structure has evolved, with many layers, modules, and trillions of connections between neurons. The structure of the human brain is our guiding star and is aiding our efforts in creating artificial intelligence systems. However, how can we address all the complexity of the human brain with our imperfect instruments?

By studying the human brain, neuroscientists have found that its spatial structure plays an essential role in all perceiving and cognitive tasks – from vision to abstract thinking. Many intricate geometric structures have been found, such as the grid cells that help us with inertial navigation, and the cortical columns that are connected to the eye's retina to process visual stimuli. It has been demonstrated that the structure of the brain allows us to effectively respond to the patterns in signals that are received from the sensorium by using designated neural structures that are activated by specific patterns in the inputs. This feature of the brain allows it to use an extremely efficient way of representing and processing the entire diversity of the input data that's obtained from the environment. Our brains have evolved to be effective pattern recognition and pattern processing engines that actively reuse specific neural modules to process particular patterns, thus dramatically reducing the number of different neural structures required. This only became possible due to the complex modular hierarchy and the spatial integration of its various parts.

As we mentioned previously, the biological brain incorporates complex hierarchical and spatially-aware data processing routines. This has inspired the researchers of neuroevolution to introduce similar data processing methods in the field of artificial neural networks. When designing such systems, it is necessary to address the following problems:

- The vast number of input features and training parameters that require large-scale ANNs
- The effective representation of natural geometrical regularities and symmetries that are observed in the physical world

- The effective processing of input data through the introduction of the locality principle, that is, when spatially/semantically adjacent data structures are processed by the modules of interconnected neural units, which occupy the same compact area of the entire network structure

In this section, you learned about the **Hypercube-based NeuroEvolution of Augmenting Topologies** (**HyperNEAT**) method, which was proposed by Kenneth O. Stanley to solve various problems by exploiting geometrical regularities. In the next section, we will look at **Compositional Pattern Producing Networks** (**CPPNs**).

Compositional Pattern Producing Networks

HyperNEAT extends the original NEAT algorithm by introducing a new type of indirect genome encoding scheme called CPPNs. This type of encoding makes it possible to represent the connectivity patterns of a phenotype's ANN as a function of its geometry.

HyperNEAT stores the connectivity pattern of the phenotype neural network as a four-dimensional hypercube, where each point encodes the connection between two nodes (that is, the coordinates of the source and target neurons) and the connective CPPN paints various patterns within it. In other words, CPPN computes the four-dimensional function, which is defined as follows:

$$w = CPPN(x_1, y_1, x_2, y_2)$$

Here, the source node is at (x_1, y_1) and the target node is at (x_2, y_2). At this stage, CPPN returns a weight for every connection between every node in the phenotype network, which is represented as a grid. By convention, the connection between the two nodes is not expressed if the magnitude of the connection weight that's computed by CPPN is less than a minimum threshold (w_{min}). That way, the connectivity pattern that's produced by CPPN can represent any network topology. The connectivity pattern can be used to encode large-scale ANNs by discovering regularities in the training data and can reuse the same set of genes to encode repetitions. By convention, the connectivity pattern that's produced by CPPN is called the **substrate**.

The following diagram shows the interpretation of the Hypercube-based Geometric Connectivity Pattern:

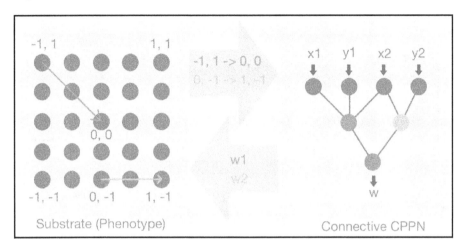

Hypercube-based Geometric Connectivity Pattern interpretation

Unlike traditional ANN architectures, CPPN employs a set of various activation functions for its hidden nodes to explore a variety of geometrical regularities. For example, the trigonometric sine can be used to represent repetitions, while Gaussian can be used to enforce locality at a specific part of the network (that is, symmetry along the coordinate axis). Thus, the CPPN encoding scheme can represent patterns with different geometrical regularities such as symmetry, repetition, repetition with regularities, and so on in a compact manner.

Substrate configuration

The layout of the network nodes in the substrate that CPPN connects to can take various forms, which are best suited to different kinds of problems. It is the responsibility of the experimenter to select the appropriate layout to achieve optimal performance. For example, the output nodes that control a radial entity such as a six-leg crawler may be best laid out with radial geometry so that a connectivity pattern can be expressed with polar coordinates.

The following diagram shows some examples of substrate layout configurations:

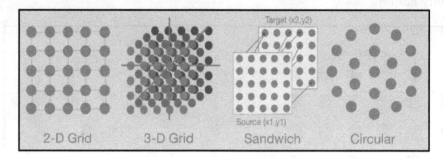

Examples of substrate layout configurations

There are several common types of substrate layout that are typically used with HyperNEAT (see the preceding diagram), some of which are as follows:

- **Two-dimensional grid**: A regular grid of network nodes in a two-dimensional Cartesian space centered at (0, 0)
- **Three-dimensional grid**: A regular grid of network nodes in a three-dimensional Cartesian space centered at (0, 0, 0)
- **State-Space Sandwich**: Two 2D planar grids with source and target nodes in which one layer can send connections in the direction of the other one
- **Circular**: The regular radial structure, which is suited to define regularities in radial geometry-based polar coordinates

Evolving connective CPPNs and the HyperNEAT algorithm

The method is called **HyperNEAT** because it uses a modified NEAT to evolve CPPNs that represent spatial patterns in the hyperspace. Each expressed point of the pattern, which is bounded by a hypercube, represents a connection between two nodes in the lower-dimensional graph (substrate). Thus, the dimensionality of the hyperspace is twice as big as the dimensionality of the underlying lower-dimensional graph. Later in Chapter 8, *ES-HyperNEAT and the Retina Problem*, we will look at some examples that use two-dimensional connectivity patterns.

The HyperNEAT algorithm can be seen in the following diagram:

Algorithm 2: The general form of the HyperNEAT algorithm

---

begin
    1. Choose desired *Substrate* configuration (nodes layout and input/output assignments);
    2. Initialize *Population* of minimal CPPNs with random weights;
    repeat
        foreach *organism* ∈ *Population* **do**
            3. Query the CPPN of the *organism* for the weight of each possible connection in the *Substrate* representing its phenotype. If the absolute value of the output exceeds a threshold magnitude, create the connection with a weight scaled proportionally to the output value.;
            4. Run the *Substrate* as a phenotype ANN in the task domain to evaluate the fitness of found solutions.;
        5. Reproduce CPPNs of the organisms in the *Population* with NEAT;
    until *solution is found*;

The general form of the HyperNEAT algorithm

Any connection gene or node gene that's added to the connective CPPN during its evolution leads to the discovery of a new global dimension of variation in the connectivity patterns across the phenotype substrate (novel traits). Each modification that's made to the CPPN genome represents a new way that an entire connectivity pattern can vary. Also, previously evolved connective CPPNs can be queried to produce connectivity patterns for the substrate at a higher resolution than what was used for its training. This allows us to produce a working solution to the same problem at any resolution, potentially without an upper limit. Thus, the aforementioned properties have made HyperNEAT a powerful instrument in evolving large-scale bio-inspired artificial neural networks.

 For more information on the HyperNEAT method, you can refer to the following link: `https://eplex.cs.ucf.edu/papers/stanley_alife09.pdf`.

Evolvable-Substrate HyperNEAT

The HyperNEAT method exposes the fact that geometrical regularities of the natural world can be adequately represented by artificial neural networks with nodes placed at specific spatial locations. That way, the neuroevolution gains significant benefits and it allows large-scale ANNs to be trained for high dimensional problems, which was impossible with the ordinary NEAT algorithm. At the same time, the HyperNEAT approach is inspired by the structure of a natural brain, which still lacks the plasticity of the natural evolution process. While allowing the evolutionary process to elaborate on a variety of connectivity patterns between network nodes, the HyperNEAT approach exposes a hard limitation on where the network nodes are placed. The experimenter must define the layout of the network nodes from the very beginning, and any incorrect assumption that's made by the researcher will lower the performance of the evolutionary process.

By placing the network node at a specific location in the substrate, the experimenter creates an unintentional constraint on the pattern of weights that are produced by the CPPN. This restriction then interferes with the CPPN when it attempts to encode the geometrical regularities of the natural world into the topography of solution-producing ANN (phenotype). Here, the connectivity pattern produced by CPPN must perfectly align with the layout of the substrate that is defined by the experimenter; connections only are possible between given network nodes. Such limitation leads to unnecessary approximation errors, which spoil the outcome. It may be more effective for the CPPN to elaborate connectivity patterns over nodes that have been placed at slightly different locations.

Information patterns in the hypercube

Why should such limitations on the location of nodes be imposed in the first place? Wouldn't it be nice if the implicit clues that had been drawn from the connectivity patterns became the guidelines of where to place the next node to represent the natural regularities of the physical world better?

The areas with uniform connection weights encode a small amount of information and hence have little functional value. At the same time, the areas with vast gradients of weight values are extremely information-intensive. Such areas can benefit from additional network nodes being placed to represent a much finer encoding of the natural process. As you may recall from our discussion of the HyperNEAT algorithm, it is possible to represent the connection between two nodes in the substrate as a point in a four-dimensional hypercube. Thus, the main feature of the proposed ES-HyperNEAT algorithm is to express more hyper-points in the areas of the hypercube, where the high variation of connection weights are detected. At the same time, the fewer hyper-points are placed in the areas with a lower variation of connection weights.

The placement of nodes and the exposed connections between them can be dictated by the variation in the weights of connections that are produced by the evolving CPPN for a given region of a substrate. In other words, there is no need for additional information to decide on the next node placement in the substrate, other than what we are already receiving from the CPPN that encodes the connectivity patterns of the network. Information density becomes the main guiding principle for the algorithm to determine the topography of the substrate.

Node placement in the phenotype ANN signifies where the information is encoded in the connectivity patterns that are created by the CPPN.

Quadtree as an effective information extractor

To represent hyper-points that are encoding connection weights within the hypercube, the ES-HyperNEAT algorithm employs a *quadtree*. A quadtree is a tree data structure in which each internal node has exactly four children nodes. This data structure was selected due to its inherent properties, allowing it to represent two-dimensional areas at different levels of granularity. With a quadtree, it is possible to organize an effective search through the two-dimensional space by splitting any area of interest into four subareas, and each of them becomes a leaf of the tree, with root (parent) node representing the original (decomposed) region.

Using the quadtree-based information extraction method, the ES-HyperNEAT approach iteratively looks for new connections between nodes in the two-dimensional space of the substrate ANN, starting from the input and output nodes that have been predefined by the experimenter. This method is much more computationally effective than searching directly in the four-dimensional hypercube space.

The following diagram shows an example of extracting information using quadtree data structures:

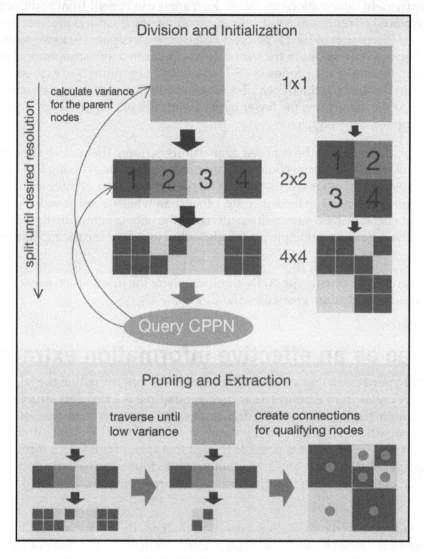

Quadtree information extraction example

The quadtree-based search algorithm operates in two main stages:

1. **Division and initialization**: At this stage, the quadtree is created by recursively subdividing the initial substrate space occupying the area from (-1, -1) to (1, 1). The subdivision stops when the desired tree depth is reached. This implicitly determines how many subspaces fit into the initial space of the substrate (initialization resolution). After that, for every quadtree node with the center at (a, b), the CPPN is queried with (a, b, x_i, y_i) arguments to find connection weights. When connection weights for k leaf nodes of a particular quadtree node p are found, the variance of this node can be calculated by the following formula:

$$\sigma^2 = \sum_{i=1}^{k} (\bar{w} - w_i)^2$$

   Here $\bar{w}$ is the mean connection weight among k leaf nodes and w_i is a connection weight to a specific leaf node. The calculated variance value is a heuristic indicator of the presence of information in the specific substrate area. If this value is higher than the particular division threshold (defining desired information density), then the division stage can be repeated for the corresponding square of the substrate. This way, the desired information density can be enforced by the algorithm. Take a look at the top part of the preceding diagram for a visual insight into how division and initialization are done using the quadtree data structures.

2. **Pruning and extraction**: To guarantee that more connections (and nodes in the substrate) become expressed in the regions with high information density (high weights variance), the pruning and extraction procedure is executed over the quadtree that was generated during the previous stage. The quadtree traverses depth-first until the variance of the current node is smaller than a variance threshold σ_t^2 or until the node has no children (the zero variance). For every qualified node, the connection is expressed between its center (x, y) and each parent node is already defined, either by the experimenter or found at the previous run of these two stages (that is, from hidden nodes that have already been created by ES-HyperNEAT method). Refer to the bottom part of the preceding diagram for a visual insight into how the pruning and extraction phase works.

ES-HyperNEAT algorithm

The ES-HyperNEAT algorithm starts with user-defined input nodes and elaborates on exploring connections from them and sending them to the newly expressed hidden nodes. The expression of outgoing connectivity patterns and hidden nodes placement within the substrate space is done using the quadtree information extraction method, which we described previously. The information extraction process is iteratively applied until the desired level of information expression density is achieved, or until no more information can be discovered in the hypercube. After that, the resulting network is connected to the user-defined output nodes by expressing the incoming connectivity patterns to the outputs. We use quadtree information extraction for this as well. Only those hidden nodes are kept in the final network, which has a path to both the input and output nodes.

Now, we have defined a multitude of nodes and connections within the substrate of the phenotype ANN. It can be beneficial to remove some nodes from the network by introducing an additional band pruning processing stage. At this stage, we keep only the points within a specific band and remove points on the edge of the band. By making bands broader or narrower, the CPPN can manage the density of the encoded information. For more details about band pruning, please refer to the *ES-HyperNEAT paper* (`https://eplex.cs.ucf.edu/papers/risi_alife12.pdf`).

Take a look at the following ES-HyperNEAT algorithm:

Algorithm 3: ES-HyperNEAT Algorithm

Parameters: initialDepth, maxDepth, varianceThreshold, bandThreshold, iterationLevel,
          divisionThreshold

Input   : CPPN, InputPositions, OutputPositions

Output   : Connections, HiddenNodes

begin
```
  // Input-to-hidden node connections
  foreach input ∈ InputPositios do
      // Analyze outgoing connectivity pattern from input
      root ⟵ DivisionAndInitialization(input.x, input.y, true);
      // Traverse quadtree and store qualified connections
      PruningAndExtraction(input.x, input.y, inputConnections, root, true);
      foreach c ∈ inputConnections do
          node ⟵ Node(c.x2, c.y2);
          if node ∉ HiddenNodes then
              HiddenNodes ⟵ HiddenNodes ∪ node;

  // Hidden-to-hidden node connections
  UnexploredHiddenNodes ⟵ HiddenNodes;
  for i ⟵ 1 to iterationLevel do
      foreach hidden ∈ UnexploredHiddenNodes do
          root ⟵ DivisionAndInitialization(hidden.x, hidden.y, true);
          PruningAndExtraction(hidden.x, hidden.y, hidnConnections, root, true);
          foreach c ∈ hidnConnections do
              node ⟵ Node(c.x2, c.y2);
              if node ∉ HiddenNodes then
                  HiddenNodes ⟵ HiddenNodes ∪ node;
          // Remove explored nodes
          UnexploredHiddenNodes ⟵ HiddenNodes − UnexploredHiddenNodes;

  // Hidden-to-output node connections
  foreach ouput ∈ OutputPositions do
      // Analyze incoming connectivity to the output
      root ⟵ DivisionAndInitialization(output.x, output.y, false);
      PruningAndExtraction(output.x, output.y, outputConnections, root, false);
      /* No new nodes created here because all hidden nodes that connected
         to input/output already expressed                                */
  connections ⟵ inputConnections ∪ hidnConnections ∪ outputConnections;
```
Remove nodes and their connections that do not have a path to input and output nodes.

The ES-HyperNEAT algorithm

The ES-HyperNEAT algorithm takes all the advantages of the NEAT and HyperNEAT methods and introduces even more powerful new features, including the following:

- Automatic placement of the hidden nodes within the substrate to precisely match the connectivity patterns that are expressed by evolved CPPNs.
- Allows us to produce modular phenotype ANNs much more easily due to its inherent capabilities to start the evolutionary search with a bias toward locality (by the specific design of the initial CPPN architectures).
- With ES-HyperNEAT, it is possible to elaborate on the existing phenotype ANN structure by increasing the number of nodes and connections in the substrate during evolution. This is the opposite of HyperNEAT, where the number of substrate nodes is predefined.

The ES-HyperNEAT algorithm allows us to use the original HyperNEAT architecture without altering the genetic structure of the NEAT part. It allows us to address problems that are hard to solve with the HyperNEAT algorithm due to difficulties with creating an appropriate substrate configuration in advance.

 More details about the ES-HyperNEAT algorithm and the motivations behind it can be found at `https://eplex.cs.ucf.edu/papers/risi_alife12.pdf`.

Novelty Search optimization method

Most of the machine learning methods, including evolutionary algorithms, base their training on the optimization of the objective function. The main focus underlying the methods of optimization of the objective function is that the best way to improve the performance of a solver is to reward them for getting closer to the goal. In most evolutionary algorithms, the closeness to the goal is measured by the fitness of the solver. The measure of an organism's performance is defined by the fitness function, which is a metaphor for evolutionary pressure on the organism to adapt to its environment. According to that paradigm, the fittest organism is better adapted to its environment and best suited to find a solution.

While direct fitness function optimization methods work well in many simple cases, for more complex tasks, it often falls victim to the local optima trap. Convergence to the local optima means that no local step in the search space provides any improvements during the fitness function optimization process. The traditional genetic algorithms use mutation and island mechanisms to escape from such local optima. However, as we will find out by doing experiments later in this book, it may not always help with deceptive problems, or it can take too long to find a successful solution.

Many real-world problems have such deceptive fitness function landscapes that cannot be solved by an optimization process that is based solely on measuring how close the current solution is to the goal. As an example, we can consider the task of navigating through an unknown city with an irregular street pattern. In such a task, heading toward the destination often means traveling along deceptive roads that move you further away, only to bring you to the destination after several twists. But if you decide to start with roads that have been aligned in direction to the destination, it often leads you to a dead end, while the destination is just behind the wall but unreachable.

Novelty Search and natural evolution

By looking at how natural selection works in the physical world, we can see that the enabling force behind evolutionary diversity is a search for novelty. In other words, any evolving species gains immediate evolutionary advantages over its rivals by finding new behavior patterns. This allows them to exploit the environment more efficiently. The natural evolution has no defined goals, and it broadens the solution search space by rewarding the exploration and exploitation of novel behaviors. This novelty can be considered as a proxy for many hidden creative forces in the natural world, which allows evolution to elaborate on even more complex behaviors and biological structures.

Taking inspiration from the natural evolution, *Joel Lehman* proposed a new method of search optimization for an artificial evolutionary process called **Novelty Search**. With this method, no particular fitness function is defined or used for solution search; instead, the novelty of each found solution is directly rewarded during the neuroevolution process. Thus, the novelty of the solutions that are found guide the neuroevolution toward the final goal. Such an approach gives us a chance to exploit the creative forces of evolution independent of the adaptive pressure to fit the solution into a particular niche.

The effectiveness of a Novelty Search can be demonstrated with the *maze navigation* experiment, where an objective-based search finds the solution for the simple maze in many more steps (generations) than a Novelty Search. Furthermore, for the hard maze with deceptive configuration, the objective-based search fails to find any solution at all. We will discuss maze navigation experiments later in `Chapter 5`, *Autonomous Maze Navigation*.

Novelty metric

The Novelty Search method employs a novelty metric for tracking the uniqueness of the behavior of each new individual. That is, the novelty metric is a measure of how far the new organism is from the rest of the population in the behavior space. An effective novelty metric implementation should allow us to compute sparseness at any point of the behavior space. Any area with a denser cluster of visited points is less novel and produces less evolutionary rewards.

The most straightforward measure of sparseness at a point is an average distance to the k-nearest neighbors of that point in the behavior space. When this distance is high, the point of interest is in the sparse area. At the same time, the denser areas are marked by lower values of distance. Thus, sparseness ρ at the point x is given by the following formula:

$$\rho(x) = \frac{1}{k} \sum_{i=0}^{k} dist(x, \mu_i)$$

Here, μ_i is the i-th nearest neighbor of x, as calculated by the distance metric $dist(x, \mu_i)$. The distance metric is a domain-specific measure of the behavioral difference between the two individuals.

The candidate individuals from sparse areas receive higher novelty scores. When this score exceeds some minimum threshold ρ_{min}, the individual at that location is added to the archive of best performers that characterize the distribution of prior solutions in the behavior space. The current generation of the population, combined with the archive, defines where the search has already been and where it is now. Thus, by maximizing the novelty metric, the gradient of search is directed toward new behavior, without any explicit objective. However, Novelty Search is still driven by meaningful information because exploring new behaviors requires comprehensive exploitation of the search domain.

The following image shows the Novelty Search algorithm:

Algorithm 4: The Novelty Search Method

Parameters: noveltyThreshold
Input   : Population, NoveltyArchive
Results   : Each organism in a population will be evaluated with novelty metric against *NoveltyArchive* and other organisms in *Population*. If its novelty score exceeds *noveltyThreshold*, it would be added to the *NoveltyArchive*. The *Fitness* value of each organism will be updated with its novelty scores. Later the fitness scores of organisms can be used by evolutionary algorithms to decide what organisms suitable for reproduction.

begin
    foreach *organism* ∈ *Population* **do**
        `// Calculate novelty score for` *organism* `among`
        `//` *Population* `combined with` *NoveltyArchive*
        novelty ⟵ AvgKnnDistance(*organism*. *Population*. *NoveltyArchive*);
        if *novelty* > *noveltyThreshold* **then**
            `// Add` *organism* `to the` *NoveltyArchive*
            NoveltyArchive ⟵ *NoveltyArchive* ∪ *organism*;
            `// Remove from novelty archive records with lowest`
            `// novelty scores to maintain its size.`
            PurgeNoveltyArchive(*NoveltyArchive*)
        `/* Set fitness value of` *organism* `to the` *novelty* `score to be used on the next stage of evolutionary algorithm, such as reproduction, where most fit organisms have a chance to produce offspring.      */`
        organism.Fitness ⟵ *novelty*

The Novelty Search algorithm

The Novelty Search optimization method allows evolution to search for solutions in any deceptive space and find optimal solutions. With this method, it is possible to implement divergent evolution when the population is forced not to converge in a particular niche solution (local optima) and have to explore the whole solution space. It seems like a very effective search optimization method, despite its counterintuitive approach, which completely ignores the explicit objective during the search. Moreover, it can find the final solution in most cases even faster than a traditional objective-based search that's measuring fitness as a distance from the final solution.

 For more details, you can refer to the following link: `http://joellehman.com/lehman-dissertation.pdf`.

Summary

In this chapter, we began by discussing the different methods that are used to train artificial neural networks. We considered how traditional gradient descent-based methods differ from neuroevolution-based ones. Then, we presented one of the most popular neuroevolution algorithms (NEAT) and the two ways we can extend it (HyperNEAT and ES-HyperNEAT). Finally, we described the search optimization method (Novelty Search), which can find solutions to a variety of deceptive problems that cannot be solved by conventional objective-based search methods. Now, you are ready to put this knowledge into practice after setting up the necessary environment, which we will discuss in the next chapter.

In the next chapter, we will cover the libraries that are available so that we can experiment with neuroevolution in Python. We will also demonstrate how to set up a working environment and what tools are available to manage dependencies in the Python ecosystem.

Further reading

For a deeper understanding of the topics that we discussed in this chapter, take a look at the following links:

- **NEAT**: http://nn.cs.utexas.edu/downloads/papers/stanley.phd04.pdf
- **HyperNEAT**: https://eplex.cs.ucf.edu/papers/stanley_alife09.pdf
- **ES-HyperNEAT**: https://eplex.cs.ucf.edu/papers/risi_alife12.pdf
- **Novelty Search**: http://joellehman.com/lehman-dissertation.pdf

2
Python Libraries and Environment Setup

This chapter introduces the Python libraries that we can use in order to implement the neuroevolution algorithms we described in the previous chapter. We will also discuss the strengths and weaknesses of each library that's presented. In addition to this, we will provide basic usage examples. Then, we will consider how to set up the environment for the experiments that we will perform later in this book and examine common ways to do this in the Python ecosystem. Finally, we will demonstrate how to set up a working environment using Anaconda Distribution, which is a popular tool for managing Python dependencies and virtual environments among data scientists. In this chapter, you will learn how to start using Python to experiment with the neuroevolution algorithms that will be covered in this book.

In this chapter, we will cover the following topics:

- Suitable Python libraries for neuroevolution experiments
- Environment setup

Suitable Python libraries for neuroevolution experiments

The Python programming language is one of the most popular languages for activities related to machine learning and research and development in the field of artificial intelligence. The most prominent frameworks are either written in Python or provide corresponding interfaces. Such popularity can be explained by Python's short learning curve and its nature as a scriptable language, which allows experiments to take place quickly. Thus, following a general trend in the machine learning community, several libraries were written in Python with the support for neuroevolution, and the number of libraries continues to grow over time. In this section, we will look at the most stable Python libraries for experiments in the field of evolutionary algorithms.

NEAT-Python

As its name suggests, this is the NEAT algorithm's implementation through the Python programming language. The NEAT-Python library provides the implementation of the standard NEAT methods for the genetic evolution of the genomes of organisms in a population. It implements utilities to convert the genotype of the organism into its phenotype (an artificial neural network) and provides convenient methods to load and save the genome configurations, along with the NEAT parameters. Additionally, it implements useful routines so that it can collect statistics about evolutionary process execution and a way to save/load intermediate checkpoints. Checkpoints allow us to save the state of the evolutionary process periodically and restore the process's execution from the saved checkpoint data later.

The pros of the NEAT-Python algorithm are as follows:

- It has a stable implementation.
- It is comprehensively documented.
- It is available through the PIP package manager for easy installation.
- It has a built-in statistics collection and support for storing execution checkpoints, as well as restoring execution from a given checkpoint.
- It provides multiple types of activation functions.
- It supports the continuous-time recurrent neural network phenotypes.
- It can be easily extended to support various NEAT modifications.

The cons of the NEAT-Python algorithm are as follows:

- Only the NEAT algorithm is implemented by default.
- It is in a maintenance-only state right now and no active development has been done recently.

NEAT-Python usage example

The following is a general example of how to use the NEAT-Python library, without any particular problem in mind. It describes the typical steps to be taken and how to obtain the necessary results. We will use this library extensively throughout this book. You can skip to the next chapter for the concrete usage example, but you should follow through to the end of this chapter to learn more about alternative libraries. Let's get started:

1. Load the NEAT settings and the initial genome configuration:

   ```
   config = neat.Config(neat.DefaultGenome, neat.DefaultReproduction,
   neat.DefaultSpeciesSet, neat.DefaultStagnation, config_file)
   ```

   Here, the `config_file` parameter points to the file that contains the NEAT-Python library settings and the default configuration of the initial genome.

2. Create a population of organisms from the configuration data:

   ```
   p = neat.Population(config)
   ```

3. Add the statistics reporter and checkpoints collector:

   ```
   # Output progress to the stdout
   p.add_reporter(neat.StdOutReporter(True))
   stats = neat.StatisticsReporter()
   p.add_reporter(stats)
   p.add_reporter(neat.Checkpointer(5))
   ```

4. Run the evolution process over a specific number of generations (300, in our case):

   ```
   winner = p.run(eval_genomes, 300)
   ```

   Here, `eval_genomes` is a function that's used to evaluate the genomes of all the organisms in the population against a particular fitness function and `winner` is the best performing genotype found.

5. The phenotype ANN can be created from a genome as follows:

```
winner_ann = neat.nn.FeedForwardNetwork.create(winner, config)
```

6. After that, the ANN can be queried with input data to calculate the results:

```
for xi in xor_inputs:
    output = winner_ann.activate(xi)
    print(xi, output) # print results
```

The library is available at
https://github.com/CodeReclaimers/neat-python.

The preceding source code is to give you a feeling of the library. The full code examples will be provided in the chapters that follow.

PyTorch NEAT

This library is built around the NEAT-Python library. It provides easy integration for artifacts that have been produced by the NEAT-Python library with the *PyTorch* platform. As a result, it becomes possible to convert the NEAT genome into a phenotype ANN, which is based on the PyTorch implementation of recurrent neural networks. Also, it allows us to represent **Compositional Pattern Producing Networks** (**CPPNs**) as PyTorch structures, which are the primary building blocks of the HyperNEAT method. The main advantage of integration with PyTorch is that it allows us to utilize GPUs for computing, potentially accelerating the evolutionary process due to the increased rate of evaluation of the genomes of organisms in the evolving population.

The pros of PyTorch NEAT are as follows:

- It is built around a stable NEAT-Python library, which makes it possible for us to use all of its benefits.
- Integration with the PyTorch framework.
- It is GPU accelerated for the evaluation of NEAT genomes.
- It includes CPPN implementation, which is a building block of the HyperNEAT algorithm.
- Integration with the OpenAI GYM environment.

The cons of PyTorch NEAT are as follows:

- Only the NEAT algorithm is fully implemented.
- It provides only partial support for the HyperNEAT algorithm's implementation.

 For more details about OpenAI GYM, go to `https://gym.openai.com`.

PyTorch NEAT usage example

The following is an example of using the PyTorch NEAT library to implement a cartpole balancing controller. This is only being presented as an overview. Later in this book, we will dive deeper into the pole balancing problem in more detail. Let's get started:

1. Load the NEAT settings and seed genome configuration:

```
config = neat.Config(neat.DefaultGenome, neat.DefaultReproduction,
        neat.DefaultSpeciesSet, neat.DefaultStagnation, config_file)
```

Here, the `config_file` file stores the NEAT algorithm settings, along with the default genome configuration.

2. Create a population of organisms from the configuration data:

```
pop = neat.Population(config)
```

3. Prepare the multi-environment genome evaluator based on PyTorch and OpenAI GYM:

```
def make_env():
    return gym.make("CartPole-v0")

def make_net(genome, config, bs):
    return RecurrentNet.create(genome, config, bs)

def activate_net(net, states):
    outputs = net.activate(states).numpy()
    return outputs[:, 0] > 0.5

evaluator = MultiEnvEvaluator(
    make_net, activate_net, make_env=make_env,
    max_env_steps=max_env_steps
)
```

```
def eval_genomes(genomes, config):
    for _, genome in genomes:
        genome.fitness = evaluator.eval_genome(genome, config)
```

Here, the call to the `gym.make("CartPole-v0")` function is the call to the OpenAI GYM framework to create a single-pole balancing environment.

4. Add the statistics and log reporter:

```
stats = neat.StatisticsReporter()
pop.add_reporter(stats)
reporter = neat.StdOutReporter(True)
pop.add_reporter(reporter)
logger = LogReporter("neat.log", evaluator.eval_genome)
pop.add_reporter(logger)
```

5. Run the evolution process over a specific number of generations (`100`, in our case):

```
winner = pop.run(eval_genomes, 100)
```

Here, `eval_genomes` is a function for evaluating the genomes of all the organisms in a population against a certain fitness function, and the `winner` is the best performing genotype found.

6. The phenotype ANN can be created from a genome, as shown in the following code:

```
winner_ann = RecurrentNet.create(genome, config, bs)
```

Here, the `genome` is the NEAT genome configuration, `config` is an object that encapsulates the NEAT settings, and `bs` is a parameter that indicates the desired batch size.

7. After that, the ANN can be queried with the input data to obtain the results:

```
action = winner_ann.activate(states).numpy()
```

Here, `action` is the action specifier to be used in the simulation and `states` is the tensor that includes the current state of the environment that was obtained from the simulator.

The library's source code is available at https://github.com/uber-research/PyTorch-NEAT.

The preceding source code is to give you a feeling of the library. The full code examples will be provided in the chapters that follow.

MultiNEAT

MultiNEAT is the most universal library among the libraries we will discuss in this book since it supports the standard NEAT algorithm and two crucial extensions: HyperNEAT and ES-HyperNEAT. Also, the MultiNEAT library provides an implementation of a Novelty Search optimization method. The library is written in the C++ programming language but provides a comprehensive Python interface. The MultiNEAT Python wheel is also available through the Anaconda package manager, which makes it easy to install and use in any OS.

The pros of the MultiNEAT library are as follows:

- Stable implementation
- Implements a multitude of algorithms from the NEAT family, such as the following:
    - NEAT
    - HyperNEAT
    - ES-HyperNEAT
- Provides an implementation of the Novelty Search optimization method
- Supports plastic neural networks through Hebbian learning
- Provides visualization of genotypes and phenotypes through OpenCV in Python
- Integration with the OpenAI GYM environment
- Comprehensive documentation

The cons of the MultiNEAT library are as follows:

- No GPU support
- Does not support checkpoints

MultiNEAT usage example

The following is an example of using the MultiNEAT library to implement the XOR solver using neuroevolution. This is just an overview, without the implementation of the XOR fitness score evaluator (`evaluate_xor`), which will be discussed in the next chapter. Let's get started:

1. Create the NEAT configuration settings:

```
params = NEAT.Parameters()
params.PopulationSize = 100
# The rest of the settings omitted for brevity
```

2. Create a minimal genome configuration and spawn a population of organisms from this genome:

```
g = NEAT.Genome(0, 3, 0, 1, False,
        NEAT.ActivationFunction.UNSIGNED_SIGMOID,
        NEAT.ActivationFunction.UNSIGNED_SIGMOID, 0, params, 0)
pop = NEAT.Population(g, params, True, 1.0, i)
```

3. Run the evolution process over `1000` generations or until the winner is found:

```
for generation in range(1000):
    # Evaluate genomes
    genome_list = NEAT.GetGenomeList(pop)
    fitnesses = EvaluateGenomeList_Serial(genome_list,
                            evaluate_xor, display=False)
    [genome.SetFitness(fitness) for genome, fitness in
zip(genome_list, fitnesses)]
    # Evaluate fitness value against specific threshold
    best = max(fitness_list)
    if best > 15.0:
        # get the phenotype of a best organism
        net = NEAT.NeuralNetwork()
        pop.Species[0].GetLeader().BuildPhenotype(net)
        # return the fitness and phenotype ANN of the winner
        return (best, net)

    # Next epoch
    pop.Epoch()
```

4. The following is the query winner phenotype ANN, along with some inputs to get results:

```
net.Input( [ 1.0, 0.0, 1.0 ] )
net.Activate()
output = net.Output()
```

You can find this library at `https://github.com/peter-ch/MultiNEAT`.

The preceding source code is to give you a feeling of the library. The full code examples will be provided in the chapters that follow.

Deep Neuroevolution

Deep Neural Networks (**DNNs**) demonstrate outstanding performance improvements in tasks related to pattern recognition and reinforcement learning by utilizing the parallel processing capabilities of modern GPUs. In the context of neuroevolution, it is particularly interesting to explore how conventional **deep reinforcement learning** (**deep RL**) methods can be compared to the ones based on Deep Neuroevolution. To answer this question, the research team from UberAI labs created and released the corresponding library in the Python programming language, which uses the TensorFlow framework to handle computations related to neural network training on GPU devices.

The library provides an implementation of the simple **genetic algorithm** (**GA**) and the Novelty Search optimization method. It also provides an implementation of the Evolution Strategies method, which is another kind of evolutionary algorithm.

You can find more details about the Evolution Strategies method at Hans-Georg Beyer, *The Theory of Evolution Strategies*. Springer April 27, 2001.

The pros of Deep Neuroevolution are as follows:

- Stable implementation
- GPU-enabled through integration with TensorFlow
- The ability to work directly with high-dimensional problems, such as learning to act directly from pixels
- Provides an implementation of the Novelty Search optimization method
- Gradient-free method to optimize DNNs
- Provides visualization of the learning process through the **Visual Inspector for Neuroevolution** (**VINE**)
- Provides integration with the OpenAI GYM environment
- Provides integration with the Atari games environment

The disadvantage of Deep Neuroevolution is that it does not provide an implementation of the NEAT family of neuroevolution algorithms, that is, NEAT, HyperNEAT, and ES-HyperNEAT.

The genetic algorithm that's implemented in the Deep Neuroevolution library controls the evolution of a population of organisms that have genomes encoding a vector of learning parameters (connection weights) for a deep neural network. At every generation, each genotype is evaluated and produces a fitness score. After that, the specific number of organisms are selected uniformly at random from the top best-fit individuals to become parents of the next generation. The genotype of each selected parent organism is then mutated by adding Gaussian noise. Also, the algorithm uses the notion of elitism, in which the specific number of best-fit organisms from the previous generation are added to the next without any modifications being made. The crossover operator is not applied during the evolutionary process to simplify the algorithm. The topology of the DNN that's used in this algorithm is fixed and set by experimenters manually.

Let's refer to the following simple genetic algorithm:

Algorithm 5: Simple Genetic Algorithm

Parameters: mutation operator ψ, the size of population N, number of selected organisms T, policy initialization routine ϕ, fitness function F

Output : The *Elite* among populations of organisms in G generations.

begin

  for $g \leftarrow 1, 2 \ldots, G$ *generations* **do**

    for $i \leftarrow 1, \ldots, N$ *in the next generation's population* **do**

      if $g = 1$ **then**

        `// Initialize random DNN with Gaussian`

        $\mathcal{P}_i^{g=1} \leftarrow \phi(\mathcal{N}(0, I))$

      else

        `// Select parents for next generation`

        $k \leftarrow \texttt{uniformRandom}(1, T)$

      `// Evaluate fitness of the organism`

      $\mathcal{F}_i \leftarrow F(\mathcal{P}_i^g)$

    Sort $\mathcal{P}_i^g$ with descending order by $\mathcal{F}_i$

    `// Find elite candidates for the next generation`

    if $g = 1$ **then**

      `// Get top ten organisms from population`

      `// (the population is in descending order by fitness)`

      $C \leftarrow \mathcal{P}_{1 \ldots 10}^{g=1}$

    else

      `// Get top nine organisms from the population joined with current`
      `   elite`

      $C \leftarrow \mathcal{P}_{1 \ldots 9}^g \cup Elite$

    `/* The selected elite candidates `C` then evaluated on 30 additional`
    `   episodes to reliably select the `*true*` elite                    */`

    $Elite \leftarrow \arg \max_{\Theta \in C} \frac{1}{30} \sum_{j=1}^{30} F(\Theta)$

    `// Copy `*Elite*` to the population of next generation`

    $\mathcal{P}^g \leftarrow Elite \cup (\mathcal{P}^g - Elite)$ `// To include the `*Elite*` only once`

  Return : *Elite*

The simple genetic algorithm

 More details about the implementation of Deep Neuroevolution is available at `https://github.com/uber-research/deep-neuroevolution`.

Comparing Python neuroevolution libraries

The following table provides a quick comparison between the Python libraries we've discussed in this chapter:

	NEAT-Python	PyTorch NEAT	MultiNEAT	Deep Neuroevolution
NEAT	Yes	Yes	Yes	No
HyperNEAT	No	Partial (CPPN only)	Yes	No
ES-HyperNEAT	No	No	Yes	No
Novelty Search	No	No	Yes	Yes
OpenAI GYM	No	Yes	Yes	Yes
Visualization	No	No	Yes	Yes
GPU support	No	Yes	No	Yes
PIP	Yes	No	No	No
Anaconda	No	No	Yes	No
Checkpoints	Yes	Yes	No	Yes

The NEAT-Python library provides excellent visualization integration and is easy to use. However, it has a significant drawback in that it is implemented solely in Python and, as a result, has a very slow execution speed. It is only suitable for simple problems.

The MultiNEAT Python library has core implemented in C++, which gives it slightly better performance compared to the NEAT-Python library. It can be used for solving more complex tasks requiring the creation of larger phenotype ANNs. Also, it provides the implementation of the HyperNEAT and ES-HyperNEAT methods, which makes it the right choice for tasks related to training large-scale ANNs.

The Deep Neuroevolution library is the most advanced neuroevolution implementation and allows us to employ the powers of GPUs to handle training tasks with millions of trainable parameters. This can be found in the visual imagery processing domain.

Later in this book, we will get to know each Python library better and put them into practice.

Environment setup

When working with Python libraries, it is essential to set up a working environment properly. There are a lot of dependencies, including the Python language version and the binaries that are available in the system; all of these must be aligned and have compatible versions. As a result of this process, the conflicting configurations of libraries and language versions can be easily created, adding to the frustration and hours of debugging and bug fixes. To solve this problem, the concept of the virtual environment was introduced in the Python programming language. A virtual environment allows us to create isolated Python environments that contain all the necessary dependencies and executables that are used in a particular Python project. Such a virtual environment can be easily created and deleted after it is no longer needed, without leaving any remains in the system.

Among the most popular tools for working with Python virtual environments, we can highlight the following:

- Pipenv
- Virtualenv
- Anaconda

Pipenv

Pipenv is a tool that combines package manager with the virtual environments manager. The main goal is to make it easy for developers to set up a unique working environment for a particular project with all the necessary dependencies included.

It can be installed with PIP (the package installer for Python) using the following command:

```
$ pip install --user pipenv
```

The preceding command installs the pipenv tool into the user space to prevent it from breaking any system-wide packages.

To install all the dependencies and create a new virtual environment (if not present) for your project, change into the project's directory and run the installation process, as follows:

```
$ cd my_project_folder
$ pipenv install <package>
```

This command creates a new virtual environment in `my_project_folder` and installs `<package>` into it. That's it.

It is possible to provide a configuration file (Pipfile) that specifies which packages should be installed, as well as other information that's specific to the build process. When you run `install` for the first time, the Pipfile will be created automatically if it doesn't exist yet.

 More details about the tool can be found at `https://pipenv.kennethreitz.org/en/latest/`.

Virtualenv

Virtualenv is a tool that's used to create isolated Python environments, starting from Python v3.3, and is partially integrated into the standard library under the `venv` module. The major problem that's addressed by this tool is maintaining the unique set of dependencies, versions, and permissions for each Python project independently. Virtualenv handles this by creating a separate environment with its own installation directories for each project. This prevents us from sharing any dependencies and libraries with other projects. Also, it is possible to block access to globally installed libraries.

Virtualenv is a pure virtual environments manager and it doesn't provide any package manager routines. Therefore, it is usually used along with the package manager to manage dependencies of your project, such as PIP. Let's take a look at Virtualenv:

1. Install Virtualenv with PIP as follows:

   ```
   $ pip install virtualenv
   ```

2. Test that the installation was successful:

   ```
   $ virtualenv --version
   ```

3. Create a virtual environment for your project with the following commands:

   ```
   $ cd my_project_folder
   $ virtualenv venv
   ```

   This command creates a new virtual environment in `my_project_folder`. The fresh environment includes a folder with Python executable files inside it, as well as a copy of the PIP library, which is a package manager that allows us to install other dependencies.

4. Before you start using it, you need to activate the virtual environment with the following command, which can be typed into the Terminal application of your choice:

```
$ source /path/to/ENV/bin/activate
```

After the preceding command, all the necessary environment variables will be set to the correct values that are specific to your project, and the current session of the Terminal application will use it for any subsequent commands that are entered.

5. Additional packages can be easily installed into an active environment with PIP:

```
$ pip install sqlite
```

The preceding command installs the SQLite package in the currently active environment.

If no package name is provided after the `pip install` command, the pip manager will look for a `requirements.txt` file in the current directory for the specification of the packages to be installed.

You can find more details at `https://virtualenv.pypa.io/en/latest/`.

Anaconda

Anaconda Distribution is a package and a virtual environment manager that is popular among data scientists and machine learning professionals because it provides easy access to an extensive collection of tailored scientific libraries (over 1,500+) and useful tools. Apart from this, it allows you to write source code and execute scripts in Python and R from one place. With Anaconda, it is possible to easily create, save, load, and switch between virtual environments, as well as install thousands of packages from the repository that have been reviewed and maintained by the Anaconda team into each virtual environment.

To install Anaconda, you need to download the installer that's appropriate to your operating system from `https://www.anaconda.com/distribution/`.

After that, the new environment for your project can be created with the following command:

```
$ cd my_project_folder
$ conda create --name ENV_NAME <package>
```

The preceding command creates a new virtual environment for your project and installs into it the specified package or multiple packages. Additional packages can be easily installed into a fresh environment later, after it's been activated.

All the environments that are available in the system can be listed with the following command:

```
$ conda env list
```

Any existing environment can be activated as follows:

```
$ conda activate ENV_NAME
```

To deactivate the current active environment, use the following command:

```
$ conda deactivate
```

Additional libraries can be installed into the current environment either through standard PIP or by using the conda install command:

```
$ conda install sqlite
```

After the preceding command, SQLite will be installed into the currently active environment.

In this book, we will use Anaconda to manage the dependencies and environments for most of our projects.

 If you are interested in finding out more, please make yourself familiar with all available Anaconda commands at https://docs.conda.io/ projects/conda/en/latest/commands.html.

Summary

In this chapter, we learned about four popular Python libraries that we can use for experiments in the field of neuroevolution. We discussed the strengths and weaknesses of each library that was presented, and reviewed the basic examples of using these libraries in Python. After that, we looked at how to set up the environment for Python-based experiments to avoid the side effects of having multiple versions of the same library in the Python path. We found that the best way to do this is to create isolated virtual environments for each Python project, and considered several popular solutions created by the open source community to help with this task. Finally, we introduced Anaconda Distribution, which includes, among other useful things, the package manager and an environment manager. For the rest of this book, we will use Anaconda to handle setting up the environment in our experiments properly.

In the next chapter, we will discuss how the NEAT algorithm can be used to solve the classic computer science problem. You will write the XOR problem solver using the NEAT-Python library we discussed in this chapter. We will also discuss the hyperparameters that are used to configure the NEAT algorithm and how they can be adjusted to increase the performance of the neuroevolution process.

2
Section 2: Applying Neuroevolution Methods to Solve Classic Computer Science Problems

This section discusses how to apply neuroevolution-based algorithms to solve classic computer science problems. In this section, you will learn the basic techniques and skills you need to use neuroevolutionary algorithms to solve classic computer science problems. This section will prepare you to work with the more advanced techniques discussed in the third section of this book.

This section comprises the following chapters:

- Chapter 3, *Using NEAT for XOR Solver Optimization*
- Chapter 4, *Pole-Balancing Experiments*
- Chapter 5, *Autonomous Maze Navigation*
- Chapter 6, *Novelty Search Optimization Method*

Using NEAT for XOR Solver Optimization

3

In this chapter, you will learn about one of the classic computer science experiments that demonstrates that the NEAT algorithm works and can create a proper network topology. In this chapter, you will get first-hand experience of writing an objective function to guide the XOR problem solver. You will also learn how to select the correct hyperparameters of the NEAT algorithm to assist with solving the XOR problem. This chapter aims to introduce you to the basic techniques of how to apply the NEAT algorithm to solve classic computer science problems.

After completing the experiment and exercises described in this chapter, you will have a solid understanding of the XOR experiment's particulars and get the practical skills you need to write the relevant Python source code using the NEAT-Python library. You will also gain experience in setting up the hyperparameters of the NEAT-Python library and using visualization utilities to visualize the results of an experiment. After that, you will be ready to begin experimenting with the more complex problems that will be discussed later in this book.

In this chapter, we will cover the following topics:

- The XOR problem basics
- How to define the objective function to guide the XOR problem solver
- Hyperparameter selection for the XOR experiment
- Running the XOR experiment

Technical requirements

The following technical requirements should be met to carry out the experiments described in this chapter:

- Windows 8/10, macOS 10.13 or newer, or modern Linux
- Anaconda Distribution version 2019.03 or newer

The code for this chapter can be found at `https://github.com/PacktPublishing/Hands-on-Neuroevolution-with-Python/tree/master/Chapter3`

XOR problem basics

The classic **multilayer perceptron** (**MLP**) or **artificial neural network** (**ANN**) without any *hidden units* in their topology is only capable of solving linearly separable problems correctly. As a result, such ANN configurations cannot be used for pattern recognition or control and `optxor_experiment.pyimization` tasks. However, with more complex MLP architectures that include some hidden units with a kind of non-linear activation function (such as sigmoid), it is possible to approximate any function to the given accuracy. Thus, a non-linearly separable problem can be used to study whether a neuroevolution process can grow any number of hidden units in the ANN of the solver phenotype.

The XOR problem solver is a classic computer science experiment in the field of reinforcement learning that cannot be solved without introducing non-linear execution to the solver algorithm. The solution search space of the problem has a minimum size and can be used to demonstrate that the NEAT algorithm can evolve the topology of the ANN, starting from a very straightforward one and gradually increasing the complexity to finding an appropriate network structure where all the connections are wired correctly. By demonstrating the NEAT algorithm's ability to grow an appropriate topology consistently, the XOR experiment also demonstrates that NEAT can avoid the local maxima of the fitness values landscape. The local maxima is a trap where the solver can get stuck, producing a local champion with the wrong connectivity pattern. After that, a local champion may dominate the population so much that the solver fails to solve a problem.

Here is a table defining the XOR features:

Input 1	Input 2	Output
1	1	0
1	0	1
0	1	1
0	0	0

XOR is a binary logical operator that only returns true if only one of the two inputs is true. The two input signals must be combined by the non-linear hidden unit to produce the correct output signal. There is no linear function for the combination of XOR inputs that are able to separate them into their correct classes correctly.

The NEAT algorithm starts with the initial population, which encodes a very simple phenotype, and gradually evolves the topology of the phenotype until an appropriate ANN is created. The initial structure of the phenotype ANN does not include any hidden units and consists of two input units, one output unit, and one bias unit. The two input nodes and the bias node are connected to the output node, that is, the initial genotype has three connection genes and four node genes. The bias unit is a particular type of input that is always initialized to a specific value greater than 0 (usually, it is 1.0 or 0.5). The bias unit is necessary if we wish to set the activation of the neuron unit (output or hidden)—which is calculated by the related activation function that's applied to a sum of inputs and bias—to a specific non zero value if both inputs have a value of 0.

The initial and the smallest possible XOR phenotypes are shown in the following diagram:

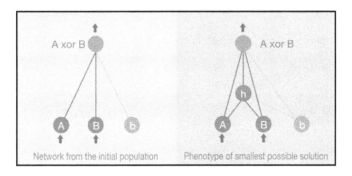

Initial and optimal XOR phenotypes

The ANN of the phenotype becomes more and more complex until the final solution is found by including one or more additional hidden nodes. The smallest possible solver includes only one hidden node, and the NEAT method demonstrates its power by finding an optimal solver configuration among the more complex ones.

The objective function for the XOR experiment

In the XOR experiment, the fitness of the organism in the population is defined as the squared distance between the correct answer and the sum of the outputs that are generated for all four XOR input patterns. It is computed as follows:

1. The phenotype ANN is activated against all four XOR input patterns.
2. The output values are subtracted from the correct answers for each pattern, and the absolute values of the results are then summed.
3. The error value that was found at the previous step is subtracted from the maximal fitness value (4) to calculate organism fitness. The highest fitness value means better solver performance.
4. The calculated fitness is then squared to give proportionally more fitness to the organisms, thereby producing solver ANNs that give closer answers to the correct solution. This approach makes the evolutionary pressure more intense.

Thus, the objective function can be defined as follows:

$$f = (4 - \sum_{i=1}^{4} |y_i - ANN(x1_i, x2_i)|)^2$$

The corresponding Python source code that is based on the NEAT-Python library is as follows:

```
# XOR inputs and expected output values
xor_inputs = [(0.0, 0.0), (0.0, 1.0), (1.0, 0.0), (1.0, 1.0)]
xor_outputs = [ (0.0,), (1.0,), (1.0,), (0.0,)]

def eval_fitness(net):
    error_sum = 0.0
    for xi, xo in zip(xor_inputs, xor_outputs):
        output = net.activate(xi)
        error_sum += abs(output[0] - xo[0])
    # Calculate amplified fitness
    fitness = (4 - error_sum) ** 2
    return fitness
```

Note that there is no need to normalize the fitness value to fit the [0, 1] range (like there is with backpropagation-based methods) because there are no backward gradient calculations involved in the training process. The organisms' fitness scores are compared directly based on their absolute values. Thus, the range of the values doesn't matter.

You can also try different variations of fitness score calculation methods. For example, you can implement a function resembling mean squared error and compare the performance of the algorithm against the different implementations of the objective function. The only requirement is that the objective function should produce higher fitness scores for better solvers.

Hyperparameter selection

The XOR experiment we will discuss in this chapter uses the NEAT-Python library as a framework. The NEAT-Python library defines a set of hyperparameters that are used to control the execution and performance of the NEAT algorithm. The configuration file is stored in a format similar to Windows .INI files; each section starts with a name in square brackets ([*section*]), followed by key-value pairs that are delimited by an equals sign (=).

In this section, we will discuss some hyperparameters of the NEAT-Python library that can be found in each section of the configuration file.

A full list of the hyperparameters in the NEAT-Python library can be found at `https://neat-python.readthedocs.io/en/latest/config_file.html`.

NEAT section

This section specifies parameters that are specific to the NEAT algorithm. This section includes the following parameters:

- `fitness_criterion`: The function that computes the termination criterion from a set of fitness values of all the genomes in the population. The parameter values are the names of standard aggregate functions, such as min, max, and mean. The min and max values are used to terminate the evolution process if the minimal or maximal fitness of the population exceeds the given `fitness_threshold`. When the value is set to mean, the average fitness of the population is used as a termination criterion.

- `fitness_threshold`: The threshold value is compared against the fitness and calculated by the `fitness_criterion` function to test whether evolution must be terminated.

- `no_fitness_termination`: The flag that disables fitness-based termination of the evolutionary process is defined by the preceding parameters. When it's set to `True`, the evolution will be terminated only after the maximum number of generations has been evaluated.

- `pop_size`: The number of individual organisms in each generation.

- `reset_on_extinction`: A flag that controls whether a new random population should be created when all the species in the current generation become extinct due to stagnation. If `False`, `CompleteExtinctionException` will be thrown upon complete extinction.

DefaultStagnation section

This section defines parameters that are specific to the species stagnation routines, as implemented by the `DefaultStagnation` class. This section includes the following parameters:

- `species_fitness_func`: The name of a function that's used to compute species fitness, that is, to calculate the aggregate fitness value of all the organisms belonging to a particular species. The allowed values are max, min, and mean.

- `max_stagnation`: The species that have not shown an improvement in the fitness value calculated by `species_fitness_func` in more than `max_stagnation` number of generations are considered stagnant and are subject to extinction.

- `species_elitism`: The number of species to unconditionally protect from stagnation. It is intended to prevent the total extinction of the population before new species arise. The specified number of species with the highest fitness always survive in the population, despite showing no further fitness improvements.

DefaultReproduction section

This section provides configuration for the reproduction routines that are implemented by the built-in `DefaultReproduction` class. This section includes the following parameters:

- `elitism`: The number of most-fit organisms in each species, which are copied without changes to the next generation. This factor allows us to retain any beneficial mutations that were found in the previous generations.
- `survival_threshold`: The fraction of organisms in each species that are allowed to be parents of the next generation, that is, eligible for sexual reproduction (*crossover*). By adjusting this value, it is possible to define the lowest fitness score of the organism that is allowing it to participate in the reproduction process. This becomes possible because the `survival_threshold` fraction is taken from the sorted list of organisms, ordered by fitness in decreasing order.
- `min_species_size`: The minimum number of organisms per species to keep after the reproduction cycle.

DefaultSpeciesSet section

This section provides the configuration for the speciation process that's implemented by the built-in `DefaultSpeciesSet` class and includes the following parameter:

- `compatibility_threshold`: The threshold to control whether organisms belong to the same species (genomic distance is less than this value) or to a different species. Higher values mean the evolutionary process has less speciation power.

DefaultGenome section

This section defines the configuration parameters that are used to create and maintain the genome, as implemented by the `DefaultGenome` class. This section includes the following parameters:

- `activation_default`: The name of the activation function to use in node genes.
- `activation_mutate_rate`: If the genome supports multiple activation functions (such as for the CPPN genome), then this is the probability of the mutation replacing the activation function of the current node with a new one that's been taken from the list of supported functions (see `activation_options`).

- `activation_options`: A space-separated list of the activation functions that can be used by node genes.
- `aggregation_default`: The name of the default aggregate function to be used by a network node to any aggregate input signals that are received from other nodes before activation.
- `aggregation_mutate_rate`: If multiple aggregate functions are supported by the genome, then this parameter defines the probability of mutation that replaces the aggregate function of the current node with a new one from the list of aggregate functions (see `aggregation_options`).
- `aggregation_options`: A space-separated list of the aggregate functions that can be used by node genes. The supported values are sum, min, max, mean, median, and maxabs.
- `compatibility_threshold`: The threshold to control whether organisms belong to the same species (genomic distance is less than this value) or to different species. Higher values mean that the evolutionary process has less speciation power.
- `compatibility_disjoint_coefficient`: The coefficient that's used during the genomic distance calculation to count how disjoint or excess genes contribute to the calculation result. Higher values of this parameter amplify the significance of the presence of disjoint or excess genes in the genomic distance calculation.
- `compatibility_weight_coefficient`: The coefficient that manages how the genomic distance calculation of the difference between the bias and response attributes of the node genes and the weight attributes of the connection genes contribute to the results.
- `conn_add_prob`: The probability of a mutation that introduces a new connection gene between existing node genes.
- `conn_delete_prob`: The probability of a mutation that removes an existing connection gene from the genome.
- `enabled_default`: The default value for the enabled attribute of the newly created connection genes.
- `enabled_mutate_rate`: The probability of a mutation that toggles the enabled attribute of the connection gene.
- `feed_forward`: Controls the type of phenotype networks to be generated during genesis. If set to `True`, then no recurrent connections are allowed.
- `initial_connection`: Specifies the initial connectivity pattern for the newly created genomes. The allowed values include `unconnected`, `fs_neat_nohidden`, `fs_neat_hidden`, `full_direct`, `full_nodirect`, `partial_direct`, and `partial_nodirect`.

- node_add_prob: The probability of a mutation that adds a new node gene.
- node_delete_prob: The probability of a mutation that removes the existing node gene from the genome and all the connections to it.
- num_hidden, num_inputs, num_outputs: The number of hidden, input, and output nodes in the genomes of the initial population.
- single_structural_mutation: If set to True, then only the structural mutations are allowed in the evolution process, that is, only the addition or removal of nodes or connections.

XOR experiment hyperparameters

The XOR experiment starts with a very straightforward initial genome configuration that has only two input nodes, one output node, and one special input—the bias node. No hidden node is introduced in the initial genome:

```
[DefaultGenome]
# The network parameters
num_hidden = 0
num_inputs = 2
num_outputs = 1

# node bias options
bias_init_mean = 0.0
bias_init_stdev = 1.0
```

The activation function of all the network nodes is a sigmoid and the node inputs are aggregated by the sum function:

```
[DefaultGenome]
# node activation options
activation_default = sigmoid

# node aggregation options
aggregation_default = sum
```

The type of the encoded network is feed-forward fully connected:

```
[DefaultGenome]
feed_forward = True
initial_connection = full_direct
```

During evolution, the new network nodes and connections are added and/or removed with a particular probability:

```
[DefaultGenome]
# node add/remove rates
node_add_prob = 0.2
node_delete_prob = 0.2

# connection add/remove rates
conn_add_prob = 0.5
conn_delete_prob = 0.5
```

All the connections are enabled by default, with a very low probability of becoming disabled due to mutation:

```
[DefaultGenome]
# connection enable options
enabled_default = True
enabled_mutate_rate = 0.01
```

The genomic distance is highly influenced by the excess/disjoint parts of the parent genomes to spur the species' diversity:

```
[DefaultGenome]
# genome compatibility options
compatibility_disjoint_coefficient = 1.0
compatibility_weight_coefficient = 0.5
```

Species stagnation is prolonged to 20 generations, and unique species are partially prevented from extinction:

```
[DefaultStagnation]
species_fitness_func = max
max_stagnation = 20
species_elitism = 2
```

The survival threshold of organisms within a species is set to a low value to narrow the evolutionary process, allowing only the fittest organisms to reproduce (the top 20% of the list of organisms, ordered by fitness). At the same time, elitism is also introduced to unconditionally copy the two fittest individuals to the next generation in each species. The minimal species size also influences speciation, and we leave it as the default value:

```
[DefaultReproduction]
elitism = 2
survival_threshold = 0.2
min_species_size = 2
```

The species compatibility threshold controls the diversity of species in the population. Higher values of this parameter result in a more diverse population. Species diversity should be balanced to keep the evolutionary process going in the desired direction, avoiding the exploration of too many search vectors, but at the same time permitting the exploration of innovation:

```
[DefaultSpeciesSet]
compatibility_threshold = 3.0
```

The population size is set to `150`, which is pretty moderate, but sufficient for such a simple problem as XOR. The termination criterion (`fitness_threshold`) is set to `15.5` to guarantee that evolution terminates when the solution found is maximally close to the goal (the maximal fitness score is `16.0` according to our `fitness` function).

In this task, we are interested in finding the evolution champion that's able to solve the XOR problem, so our termination function (`fitness_criterion`) is the `max` function, which selects the maximal fitness among all the organisms in a population:

```
[NEAT]
fitness_criterion = max
fitness_threshold = 15.5
pop_size = 150
reset_on_extinction = False
```

 The complete configuration file, `xor_config.ini`, is provided in the `Chapter3` directory in the source files repository associated with this chapter.

We have only presented the major hyperparameters that have a high impact on the NEAT algorithm's performance. The values of the hyperparameters were tested to produce a working XOR solver, but feel free to play around and see what happens.

Running the XOR experiment

Before we start working on the XOR experiment, we need to set up our Python environment correctly according to the requirements of the NEAT-Python library, which we chose as the framework for writing our code. The NEAT-Python library is available from PyPI, so we can use the pip command to install it into the virtual environment of the XOR experiment.

Environment setup

Before we start writing the code related to the XOR experiment, the appropriate Python environment should be created, and all the dependencies need to be installed into it. Follow these steps to set up the work environment properly:

1. A Python 3.5 virtual environment for the XOR experiment is created using the `conda` command from the Anaconda Distribution, as follows:

   ```
   $ conda create --name XOR_neat python=3.5
   ```

   Make sure that Anaconda Distribution is installed in your system, as described in `Chapter 2`, *Python Libraries and Environment Setup*.

2. To use the newly created virtual environment, you must activate it:

   ```
   $ conda activate XOR_neat
   ```

3. After that, the NEAT-Python library can be installed into an active environment using the following command:

   ```
   $ pip install neat-python==0.92
   ```

   We use the specific version (`0.92`) of the NEAT-Python library here, which was the most recent at the time of writing.

4. Finally, we need to install the optional dependencies that are used by the visualization utilities. This can be done with the `conda` command, as follows:

   ```
   $ conda install matplotlib
   $ conda install graphviz
   $ conda install python-graphviz
   ```

Now, we are ready to start writing the source code.

XOR experiment source code

To start the experiment, we need to create a directory named `Chapter3` using the `mkdir` command (for Linux and macOS) or `md` (for Windows):

```
$ mkdir Chapter3
```

This directory will save all the source files related to the experiment described in this chapter.

Then, we need to copy the `xor_config.ini` file from the source code repository associated with this chapter into the newly created directory. This file contains the complete configuration of the hyperparameters for the XOR experiment, as we discussed earlier.

The experiments that will be discussed in this book use various utilities to visualize the results to help us understand the internals of the neuroevolution process. The XOR experiment also depends on the specific visualization utilities that are implemented in the `visualize.py` file in this book's source code repository. You need to copy this file into the `Chapter3` directory as well.

The Anaconda Distribution installation includes VS Code, which is a free cross-platform code editor. It is reasonably straightforward in terms of functionality but provides excellent support for Python and makes it easy to switch between virtual environments. You can use it to write the source code for the experiments described in this book.

Finally, create `xor_experiment.py` in the `Chapter3` directory and use your favorite Python source code editor to write the code:

1. First, we need to define the imports that will be used later:

```
# The Python standard library import
import os
# The NEAT-Python library imports
import neat
# The helper used to visualize experiment results
import visualize
```

2. Next, we need to write some fitness evaluation code, as we described earlier:

```
# The XOR inputs and expected corresponding outputs for
# fitness evaluation
xor_inputs = [(0.0, 0.0), (0.0, 1.0), (1.0, 0.0), (1.0, 1.0)]
```

```
xor_outputs = [ (0.0,), (1.0,), (1.0,), (0.0,)]

def eval_fitness(net):
    """
    Evaluates fitness of the genome that was used to generate
    provided net
    Arguments:
        net: The feed-forward neural network generated from genome
    Returns:
        The fitness score - the higher score the means
        the better fit organism. Maximal score: 16.0
    """
    error_sum = 0.0
    for xi, xo in zip(xor_inputs, xor_outputs):
        output = net.activate(xi)
        error_sum += abs(xo[0] - output[0])
    # Calculate amplified fitness
    fitness = (4 - error_sum) ** 2
    return fitness
```

Never miss the opportunity to write comments in the source code that describe the purpose of the function, its input parameters, and the results of execution. It is also advantageous to comment on some interesting/tricky parts of the source code to provide a better understanding of it to the person who will see it later (this could be you!).

3. With the fitness evaluation function, you can write a function to evaluate all the organisms in the current generation and update the fitness of each genome accordingly:

```
def eval_genomes(genomes, config):
    """
    The function to evaluate the fitness of each genome in
    the genomes list.
    The provided configuration is used to create feed-forward
    neural network from each genome and after that created
    the neural network evaluated in its ability to solve
    XOR problem. As a result of this function execution, the
    fitness score of each genome updated to the newly
    evaluated one.
    Arguments:
        genomes: The list of genomes from population in the
                 current generation
        config: The configuration settings with algorithm
                hyper-parameters
    """
    for genome_id, genome in genomes:
```

```
genome.fitness = 4.0
net = neat.nn.FeedForwardNetwork.create(genome, config)
genome.fitness = eval_fitness(net)
```

4. Now that we have implemented the function to evaluate the fitness of the individual genome and the objective function has been defined, it is time to implement the function to run the experiment. The `run_experiment` function loads the hyperparameter configuration from the configuration file and creates the initial genome population:

```
# Load configuration.
config = neat.Config(neat.DefaultGenome,
        neat.DefaultReproduction, neat.DefaultSpeciesSet,
        neat.DefaultStagnation, config_file)

# Create the population, which is the top-level object
# for a NEAT run.
p = neat.Population(config)
```

5. We are interested in the accumulation of statistics to evaluate the experiment and observe the process in real time. It is also essential to save checkpoints, which allows you to restore the execution from a given checkpoint in the case of failure. Thus, two types of reporters (standard output and statistics collector) and a checkpoint collector can be registered as follows:

```
# Add a stdout reporter to show progress in the terminal.
p.add_reporter(neat.StdOutReporter(True))
stats = neat.StatisticsReporter()
p.add_reporter(stats)
p.add_reporter(neat.Checkpointer(5,
                filename_prefix='out/neat-checkpoint-'))
```

6. After that, we are ready to run neuroevolution for 300 generations by providing the `eval_genome` function, which serves to evaluate the fitness scores of each genome in the population of each generation until a solution is found or the process reaches the maximum number of generations:

```
# Run for up to 300 generations.
best_genome = p.run(eval_genomes, 300)
```

7. When the execution of the NEAT algorithm stops due to success or after reaching the maximum number of generations, the most fit genome is returned. It is possible to check whether this genome is a winner, that is, able to solve the XOR problem with a given accuracy:

```
# Check if the best genome is an adequate XOR solver
best_genome_fitness = eval_fitness(net)
if best_genome_fitness > config.fitness_threshold:
    print("\n\nSUCCESS: The XOR problem solver found!!!")
else:
    print("\n\nFAILURE: Failed to find XOR problem solver!!!")
```

8. Finally, the collected statistics and the best-fit genome can be visualized to explore the results of the neuroevolution process and to see how it performed from zero to the maximum number of generations:

```
# Visualize the experiment results
node_names = {-1:'A', -2: 'B', 0:'A XOR B'}
visualize.draw_net(config, best_genome, True,
    node_names=node_names, directory=out_dir)
visualize.plot_stats(stats, ylog=False, view=True,
    filename=os.path.join(out_dir, 'avg_fitness.svg'))
visualize.plot_species(stats, view=True,
    filename=os.path.join(out_dir, 'speciation.svg'))
```

The complete source code of the XOR experiment runner can be found in the xor_experiment.py file at https://github.com/PacktPublishing/Hands-on-Neuroevolution-with-Python/blob/master/Chapter3/xor_experiment.py.

As a result of the preceding code execution, Matplotlib will be used to render graphs with the collected statistics. Also, a network graph of the best-fit genome will be presented.

Running the experiment and analyzing the results

The following command should be issued in the Chapter3 directory to start the experiment:

```
$ python xor_experiment.py
```

Don't forget to activate the XOR_neat virtual environment with $ conda activate XOR_neat. Otherwise, errors about missing a neat package will be raised.

After the preceding command is entered in your Terminal application of choice, the NEAT algorithm starts execution, and the Terminal window starts to show intermediate results in real time. For each generation, the output is as follows:

```
****** Running generation 43 ******
Population's average fitness: 6.01675 stdev: 2.53269
Best fitness: 14.54383 - size: (4, 7) - species 2 - id 5368
Average adjusted fitness: 0.238
Mean genetic distance 2.482, standard deviation 0.991
Population of 151 members in 5 species:
   ID age size fitness adj fit stag
   ==== === ==== ======= ======= ====
    1   43   28    9.0    0.241    0
    2   33   42   14.5    0.274    7
    3   20   39    9.0    0.306    0
    4    4   34    9.0    0.221    0
    5    1    8    8.4    0.149    0
Total extinctions: 0
Generation time: 0.045 sec (0.038 average)
```

The population's average fitness (6.01675) in generation 43, which is quite low compared to the completion criterion set in the configuration file (fitness_threshold =15.5). However, it looks like we have some potential champion species (ID: 2) that are on their way to reaching the target fitness threshold by evolving the champion organism with a fitness score of 14.54383, which encodes an ANN phenotype that consists of four nodes and seven connections (the size is (4, 7)).

The population includes 151 individuals separated into five species with the following properties:

- id is a species identifier.
- age is the age of the species as the number of generations from their creation until now.
- size is the number of individuals belonging to this species.
- fitness is the species fitness score calculated from its individuals (max, in our case).
- adj fit is the fitness of a particular species that's been adjusted to the entire population's fitness scores.
- stag is the stagnation age of a particular species as the number of generations since the species' last fitness improvements.

When an appropriate XOR solver is found by the NEAT algorithm, the following output is presented in the Terminal window. It starts with general statistics about the final genome population and the winner (the successful XOR solver):

```
****** Running generation 44 ******

Population's average fitness: 6.04705 stdev: 2.67702
Best fitness: 15.74620 - size: (3, 7) - species 2 - id 6531

Best individual in generation 44 meets fitness threshold - complexity: (3,
7)
```

From the preceding output, we can see that, in generation 44, the evolution process creates a genome that encodes a phenotype ANN that can solve an XOR problem with a given accuracy. This genome belongs to the organism from species with ID:2, and this species has already championed the evolutionary process over the past seven generations. The champion organism (ID:6531) of generation 44 is a mutation of an individual (ID:5368) in the species with ID:2 from the previous generation that has lost one hidden node and now has three nodes with seven connections (size: (3, 7)).

Then follows the best genome section:

```
Best genome:
Key: 6531
Fitness: 15.74619841601669
Nodes:
  0 DefaultNodeGene(key=0, bias=-3.175506745721987, response=1.0,
activation=sigmoid, aggregation=sum)
  224 DefaultNodeGene(key=224, bias=-2.5796785460461154, response=1.0,
activation=sigmoid, aggregation=sum)
  612 DefaultNodeGene(key=612, bias=-1.626648521448398, response=1.0,
activation=sigmoid, aggregation=sum)
Connections:
  DefaultConnectionGene(key=(-2, 224), weight=1.9454770276940339,
enabled=True)
  DefaultConnectionGene(key=(-2, 612), weight=2.1447044917213383,
enabled=True)
  DefaultConnectionGene(key=(-1, 0), weight=-2.048078253002224,
enabled=True)
  DefaultConnectionGene(key=(-1, 224), weight=3.6675667680178328,
enabled=True)
  DefaultConnectionGene(key=(224, 0), weight=6.1133731818187655,
enabled=True)
  DefaultConnectionGene(key=(612, 0), weight=-2.1334321035742474,
enabled=True)
  DefaultConnectionGene(key=(612, 224), weight=1.5435290073038443,
enabled=True)
```

The best genome section represents the performance statistics of a population champion, along with its genome configuration. Input nodes have the IDs -1 and -2 and are not shown because they are relatively simple, providing us with the means to input values into the network graph. The output node and two hidden nodes have the IDs 0, 224, and 612, respectively. Also, DefaultNodeGene holds the values for bias, the name of the activation function, and the name of the function that's used to aggregate inputs at each node. The connection genes (DefaultConnectionGene), which will be presented later, provide the IDs of the source and target nodes, along with the associated connection weight.

Finally, let's look at the Output section:

```
Output:
input (0.0, 0.0), expected output (0.0,), got [1.268084297765355e-07]
input (0.0, 1.0), expected output (1.0,), got [0.9855287279878023]
input (1.0, 0.0), expected output (1.0,), got [0.9867962503269723]
input (1.0, 1.0), expected output (0.0,), got [0.004176868376596405]
```

The Output section represents the output values that are produced by the ANN of the phenotype of the population champion when receiving four input data pairs. As we can see, the output is close to the expected values within the specified accuracy.

The Output directory also contains a diagram of the ANN graph of the successful XOR solver, which is as follows:

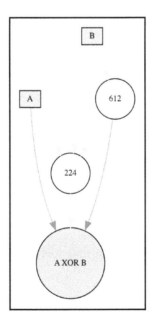

The ANN of the XOR winner phenotype

The ANN of the winner phenotype is close to the optimal configuration we described earlier, but it has one additional hidden node (`ID:612`). The bias node is not shown in the graph since the NEAT-Python library does not allocate a bias to a separate node; instead, it assigns a bias value to each network node as an attribute, which can be seen in the output listing (each `DefaultNodeGene` has a bias attribute).

A plot with the statistics of fitness change over generations of evolution is also saved to the `Output` directory:

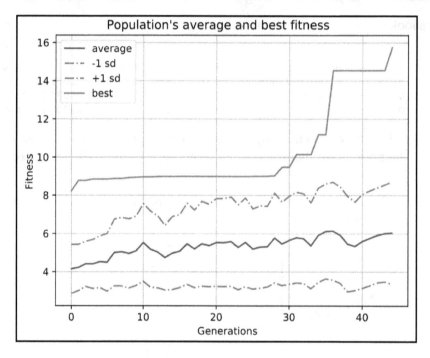

Population's average and best fitness scores changing over generations

The preceding plot visualizes the changes in the best and average fitness scores of the population over generations of evolution. The average fitness of the population has increased slightly. However, due to the speciation feature that was introduced in the NEAT algorithm, some species have demonstrated outstanding performance from the earliest generations (#10), and thanks to the preservation of the beneficial mutation, they finally managed to produce a champion organism that solves the XOR problem with a given accuracy.

The `Output` directory also contains the speciation graph, as follows:

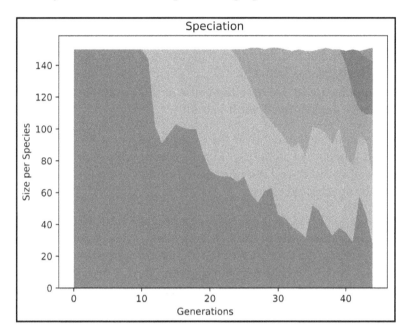

Speciation of the population over generations of evolution

The speciation graph demonstrates how the speciation process has evolved over the generations of the population of organisms. Each separate species is marked with a different color. The evolution began with a single species (`ID:1`), which includes the entire population. Then, the second species (`ID:2`) sprouted around the 10th generation and eventually produced a champion organism. Also, in the later stages of evolution, the population branched into three more species in generations 23, 39, and 42.

Exercises

Now that we have the source code of the neuroevolutionary-based XOR solver, try to experiment by changing NEAT's hyperparameters, which control the evolutionary process.

One of the parameters of particular interest is `compatibility_threshold`, which can be found in the `DefaultSpeciesSet` section of the configuration file:

- Try to increase its value and monitor the speciation of the population. Compare the performance of the algorithm with the new value against the default one (`3.0`). Does it get any better?
- What happens if you decrease the value of this parameter? Compare its performance against the default value.

Another essential parameter that controls the evolutionary process is `min_species_size`, which can be found in the `DefaultReproduction` section. By changing the values of this parameter, you can directly control the minimum number of individuals per species and implicitly control the species' diversity:

1. Set the `compatibility_threshold` parameter value to the default (`3.0`) and try to increase the value of the `min_species_size` parameter in the range `[2, 8]`. Compare the performance of the algorithm against the default value. See how the species' diversity changes over generations. Go through the algorithm's output and check whether any species have stagnated and have been removed from the evolution due to exceeding the stagnation age.
2. Set the `min_species_size` parameter value to extremely high for our population (32) and look for the explosion of the species diversity near the end of the evolution process on the speciation graph. Why does this happen? Check the graph depicting the configuration of the ANN phenotype in `Digraph.gv.svg`. Is this optimal?

Increasing the minimum size of species makes the evolutionary process more elaborate and allows it to keep more beneficial mutations. As a result, we have an increase in the chances of producing the optimal genome that encodes the ANN of the phenotype of the minimal XOR solver.

The graph of the ANN of the minimal XOR solver is as follows:

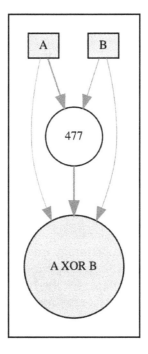

The optimal ANN phenotype with an increased minimum species size

As we already mentioned, the ANN of the minimal XOR solver has only one hidden node, as can be seen in the preceding diagram.

Try to implement some modified code to solve a three XOR (A xor B xor C) problem. Can it be solved with the same hyperparameters that we used in the experiment that we described in this chapter?

Summary

In this chapter, we introduced a classic computer science problem related to the creation of the optimal XOR solver. We discussed the basics of the XOR problem and demonstrated its importance as the first experiment with neuroevolution—it allows you to check whether the NEAT algorithm can evolve a more complex ANN topology, starting with the most straightforward ANN configuration. Then, we defined the objective function for the optimal XOR solver and a detailed description of the NEAT hyperparameters. After that, we used the NEAT-Python library to write the source code of the XOR solver using a defined objective function, and then we experimented.

The results of the experiment we carried out allowed us to conclude the relationship between the number of species in the population, the minimum size of each species, and the performance of the algorithm, as well as the produced ANN topologies.

In the next chapter, we will learn about classic reinforcement learning experiments, which are often used as benchmarks for control strategy implementation. You will learn how to write accurate simulations of real-life physical apparatuses and how to use such simulations to define the objective functions for the NEAT algorithm. You will get first-hand experience of writing the control strategies for various cart-pole balancing controllers using the NEAT-Python library.

Pole-Balancing Experiments

4

In this chapter, you will learn about a classic reinforcement learning experiment, which is also an established benchmark for testing various implementations of the control strategies. In this chapter, we consider three modifications of the cart-pole balancing experiment and develop control strategies that can be used to stabilize the cart-pole apparatuses of given configurations. You will learn how to write accurate simulations of real-life physical systems and how to use them for a definition of the objective function for the NEAT algorithm. After this chapter, you will be ready to apply the NEAT algorithm to implement controllers that can be directly used to control physical appliances.

In this chapter, we will cover the following topics:

- The single-pole balancing problem in reinforcement learning
- Implementation of the simulator of the cart-pole apparatus in Python
- How to define the objective function of a single-pole balancing controller using the simulator
- The peculiarities of the double-pole balancing problem
- Implementation of the simulator of the cart-pole apparatus with two poles in Python
- How to define the objective function for the double-pole balancing controller

Technical requirements

The following technical requirements should be met to execute the experiments described in this chapter:

- Windows 8/10, macOS 10.13 or newer, modern Linux
- Anaconda Distribution version 2019.03 or newer

The code for this chapter can be found at `https://github.com/PacktPublishing/Hands-on-Neuroevolution-with-Python/tree/master/Chapter4`

The single-pole balancing problem

The single-pole balancer (or *inverted pendulum*) is an unstable pendulum that has its center of mass above its pivot point. It can be stabilized by applying external forces under the control of a specialized system that monitors the angle of the pole and moves the pivot point horizontally back and forth under the center of mass as it starts to fall. The single-pole balancer is a classic problem in dynamics and control theory that is used as a benchmark for testing control strategies, including strategies based on reinforcement learning methods. We are particularly interested in the implementation of the specific control algorithm that uses neuroevolution-based methods to stabilize the inverted pendulum for a given amount of time.

The experiment described in this chapter considers the simulation of the inverted pendulum implemented as a cart that can move horizontally with a pivot point mounted on top of it, that is, the cart and pole apparatus. The apparatus is shown in the following diagram:

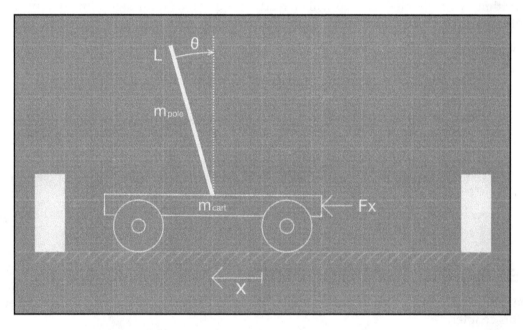

The cart and single-pole apparatus

Before we start writing the source code of the simulator, we need to determine the equation of motion that can be used to estimate the values of the state variables of the pole balancer at any given time.

The equations of motion of the single-pole balancer

The goal of the controller is to exert a sequence of forces, F_x, on the center of mass of the cart such that the pole balanced for a specific (or infinite) amount of time and the cart stays within the track, that is, doesn't hit left or right walls. Taking into account the mechanics described here, we can qualify the pole-balancing task as an *avoidance control problem*, because the state of the cart-pole apparatus must be maintained to avoid certain regions of the state space. No unique solution exists for appropriate state estimation, and any solution of equations of motion that enables the avoidance of certain regions is acceptable.

The learning algorithm needs to receive a minimal amount of knowledge about the task from the environment to train the pole-balancing controller. Such knowledge should reflect how close our controller is to the goal. The goal of the pole-balancing problem is to stabilize an inherently unstable system and keep it balanced for as long as possible. Thus, the reinforcement signal (r_t) received from the environment must reflect the occurrence of a failure. The failure can be caused either by the pole falling past a predefined angle or the cart hitting the boundaries of the track. The reinforcement signal, r_t, can be defined as follows:

$$r_t = \begin{cases} 0 & \text{if } -0.21 \text{ radians} < \theta_t < 0.21 \text{ radians and } -2.4 \text{ m} < x_t < 2.4 \text{ m} \\ -1 & \text{otherwise} \end{cases}$$

In this equation, θ_t is the angle between the pole and vertical positive in a clockwise direction, and x_t is the horizontal position of the cart relative to the track.

Note that the reinforcement signal, r_t, doesn't depend on either the angular pole velocity ($\dot{\theta}$) or the horizontal cart speed ($\dot{x}$). It only provides information on whether the dynamics of the cart-pole system is within defined constraints.

The motion-dynamic equations for the cart-pole system, ignoring friction, are as follows:

$$\ddot{\Theta} = \frac{g \sin\theta + \cos\theta \left(\frac{-F_x - m_p L \dot{\theta}^2 \sin\theta}{m_c + m_p} \right)}{L \left(\frac{4}{3} - \frac{m_p \cos^2\theta_t}{m_c + m_p} \right)}$$

$$\ddot{x} = \frac{F_x + m_p L \left(\dot{\theta}^2 \sin\theta - \ddot{\theta} \cos\theta \right)}{m_c + m_p}$$

In this equation, $\dot{\theta}$ is the angular velocity of the pole, and $\ddot{\theta}$ is the angular acceleration of the pole. Furthermore, $\dot{x}$ is the horizontal velocity of the cart and $\ddot{x}$ is the acceleration of the cart along the x-axis.

In our experiment, the following system parameters are used:

- $m_c = 1.0$ kg is the mass of the cart.
- $m_p = 0.1$ kg is the mass of the pole.
- $L = 0.5$ m is the distance from the center of mass of the pole to the pivot.
- $g = 9.8$ m/s^2 is the acceleration due to gravity.

State equations and control actions

The cart-pole system for the experiment is simulated by numerically approximating the equations of motion using Euler's method with a time step of $\tau = 0.02$ seconds. Thus, the state equations can be defined as follows:

$$x_{t+\tau} = x_t + \tau\dot{x}_t$$

$$\dot{x}_{t+\tau} = \dot{x}_t + \tau\ddot{x}_t$$

$$\theta_{t+\tau} = \theta_t + \tau\dot{\theta}_t$$

$$\dot{\theta}_{t+\tau} = \dot{\theta}_t + \tau\ddot{\theta}_t$$

For a small range of pole angles, as used in our experiment, we can use the linear approximation of the surface that divides the space of all possible states of the system that require different actions (the switching surface). Thus, the action space consists of left and right push actions. The cart-pole controller that we use in our experiment is not designed to produce a zero force. Instead, at each time step, t, it applies a force to the cart's center of mass with equal amplitude, but in the opposite direction. Such a control system has a name (*bang-bang controller*) and can be defined with the following equation:

$$F_x = \begin{cases} 10\text{ N}, & \text{if } a[t] = 1 \\ -10\text{ N}, & \text{if } a[t] = 0 \end{cases}$$

In this equation, $a[t]$ is an action signal received from the solver. Given the action value, the bang-bang controller applies the force, F_x, of the same magnitude (10 Newtons) but in the opposite direction, depending on the action selected.

The interactions between the solver and the simulator

The solver receives scaled values of the state variables described previously at each given time, t. These values serve as inputs to the ANNs created from the phenotypes of the solver genomes and are defined as follows:

$$x_0[t] = 1.0,$$

$$x_1[t] = \frac{1}{4.8}\left(x[t] + 2.4\right),$$

$$x_2[t] = \frac{1}{3}\left(\dot{x}[t] + 1.5\right),$$

$$x_3[t] = \frac{1}{0.42}\left(\theta[t] + 0.21\right),$$

$$x_4[t] = \frac{1}{4}\left(\dot{\theta}[t] + 2\right).$$

In the first equation, x_0 is a constant bias value and $x_1 \cdots x_4$ correspond to the cart's horizontal position, its horizontal speed, the pole angle from vertical, and its angular speed, respectively.

Taking into account the system constraints defined previously (see r_t), the scaled values of x_1 and x_3 are guaranteed to be within the [0,1] range, while the scaled values of x_2 and x_4 mostly fall within the [0,1] range, but can fall outside these bounds eventually. The state variables are scaled to accomplish the two essential goals:

- To remove the learning bias that can arise when terms with predominantly large magnitudes have a more significant impact on the learner due to the rounding effects.
- For this particular task, since the values of state variables are centered around zero, it is possible to find an ANN solver that doesn't need any hidden units. However, we are interested in evolving the topology of neural networks with the NEAT algorithm. The introduced scaling scheme ensures that the neuroevolution process eventually produces phenotypes that encode the hidden units.

The pole-balancing controller takes the scaled inputs and produces an output that is a binary value determining the action to be applied at time *t*, as discussed earlier. The sampling rate of the state variables of the cart-pole system and the rate at which the control force is applied are the same as the simulation rate, $1/\tau = 50\ \text{Hz}$.

Thus, the initial configuration of the controller's ANN can be depicted as follows:

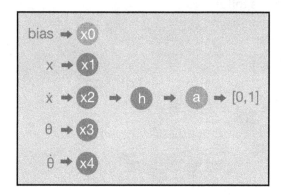

The initial ANN configuration of a single-pole balancing controller

The initial configuration of the single-pole balancing controller's ANN includes five input nodes for the horizontal position of the cart (**x1**) and its velocity (**x2**), for the vertical angle of the pole (**x3**) and its angular velocity (**x4**), and an additional input node for bias (**x0**) (*which can be optional depending on the particular NEAT library used*). The output node (**a**) is a binary node providing the control signal to the [0 or 1] application. The hidden node (**h**) is optional and can be skipped.

Objective function for a single-pole balancing experiment

Our goal is to create a pole balancing controller that's able to maintain a system in a stable state within defined constraints for as long as possible, but at least for the expected number of time steps specified in the experiment configuration (500,000). Thus, the objective function must optimize the duration of stable pole-balancing and can be defined as the logarithmic difference between the expected number of steps and the actual number of steps obtained during the evaluation of the phenotype ANN. The loss function is given as follows:

$$\mathcal{L} = \frac{\log t_{max} - \log t_{eval}}{\log t_{max}}$$

In this experiment, t_{max} is the expected number of time steps from the configuration of the experiment, and t_{eval} is the actual number of time steps during which the controller was able to maintain a stable pole balancer state within allowed bounds (refer to the reinforcement signal definition for details about permissible bounds).

Cart-pole apparatus simulation

The given definition of the objective function assumes that we can measure the number of time steps during which the single-pole balancer was in a stable state. To perform such measurements, we need to implement the simulator of the cart-pole apparatus, using the equations of motion and data constraints defined earlier.

The source code for this chapter is available at `https://github.com/PacktPublishing/Hands-on-Neuroevolution-with-Python/tree/master/Chapter4`.

First, we need to create a file called `cart_pole.py` in the `work` directory. This file contains the source code of the equations of motion and the function for evaluating the fitness of a single-pole balancer:

1. We start with a definition of the constants describing the physics of the cart-pole apparatus:

```
GRAVITY = 9.8 # m/s^2
MASSCART = 1.0 # kg
MASSPOLE = 0.5 # kg
TOTAL_MASS = (MASSPOLE + MASSCART)
# The distance from the center of mass of the pole to the pivot
# (actually half the pole's length)
LENGTH = 0.5 # m
POLEMASS_LENGTH = (MASSPOLE * LENGTH) # kg * m
FORCE_MAG = 10.0 # N
FOURTHIRDS = 4.0/3.0
# the number seconds between state updates
TAU = 0.02 # sec
```

2. After that, we are ready to implement the equations of motion using these constants:

```
force = -FORCE_MAG if action <= 0 else FORCE_MAG
cos_theta = math.cos(theta)
sin_theta = math.sin(theta)
temp = (force + POLEMASS_LENGTH * theta_dot * theta_dot * \
        sin_theta) / TOTAL_MASS
# The angular acceleration of the pole
theta_acc = (GRAVITY * sin_theta - cos_theta * temp) /\
            (LENGTH * (FOURTHIRDS - MASSPOLE * \
            cos_theta * cos_theta / TOTAL_MASS))
# The linear acceleration of the cart
x_acc = temp - POLEMASS_LENGTH * theta_acc * \
        cos_theta / TOTAL_MASS
# Update the four state variables, using Euler's method.
x_ret = x + TAU * x_dot
x_dot_ret = x_dot + TAU * x_acc
theta_ret = theta + TAU * theta_dot
theta_dot_ret = theta_dot + TAU * theta_acc
```

 Refer to the `do_step(action, x, x_dot, theta, theta_dot)` function implementation in the source code of this chapter for full details.

The preceding code snippet uses the current system state (`x, x_dot, theta, theta_dot`) along with a control action as input and applies the equations of motion described earlier to update the system state for the next time step. The updated system state then returns to update the simulator and to check for constraint violations. Thus, the simulation cycle is organized, as described in the next section.

The simulation cycle

Now we have fully implemented the equations of motion and the numerical approximation of the state variables for one step of the cart-pole apparatus simulation. With this, we are ready to start the implementation of a full simulation cycle, which uses the ANN of the controller to evaluate the current system state and to select the appropriate action (the force to be applied) for the next step. The ANN mentioned previously is created for each genome of the population for a particular generation of evolution, allowing us to evaluate the performance of all genomes.

Refer to the `run_cart_pole_simulation(net, max_bal_steps,`
`random_start=True)` function implementation for complete
implementation details.

We can refer to the following steps to perform the implementation of a full simulation
cycle:

1. First, we need to initialize the initial state variables, either with zeros or with
   random values within the constraints described previously and centered around
   zero. The random state values can be created as follows:

   ```
   # -1.4 < x < 1.4
   x = (random.random() * 4.8 - 2.4) / 2.0
   # -0.375 < x_dot < 0.375
   x_dot = (random.random() * 3 - 1.5) / 4.0
   # -0.105 < theta < 0.105
   theta = (random.random() * 0.42 - 0.21) / 2.0
   # -0.5 < theta_dot < 0.5
   theta_dot = (random.random() * 4 - 2) / 4.0
   ```

We intentionally reduced the range of all values compared to the
corresponding scaled constraints to make sure that the algorithm does not
start in the critical state, that is, when stabilization is no longer possible.

2. After that, we are ready to start the simulation cycle over the defined number of
   steps, which are specified by the `max_bal_steps` parameter. The
   following code is executed inside the *simulation loop*.
3. The state variables need to be scaled to fit into the `[0,1]` range before being
   loaded as inputs into the ANN of the controller. This procedure has a
   computational and evolutionary advantage, as previously described. The bias
   value is not explicitly provided because the NEAT-Python framework handles it
   internally, so the inputs of the ANN can be defined as follows in the source code:

   ```
   input[0] = (x + 2.4) / 4.8
   input[1] = (x_dot + 1.5) / 3
   input[2] = (theta + 0.21) / .42
   input[3] = (theta_dot + 2.0) / 4.0
   ```

4. Next, the scaled inputs can be used to activate the ANN of the phenotype, and its output is used to produce a discrete value of the action:

```
# Activate the NET
output = net.activate(input)
# Make action values discrete
action = 0 if output[0] < 0.5 else 1
```

5. With the produced value of the action and the current values of the state variables, you can run a single step of the cart-pole simulation. After the simulation step, the returned state variables are tested against the constraints to check whether the state of the system is still within the boundaries.

   In case of failure, the current number of simulation steps is returned, and its value will be used to evaluate the fitness of the phenotype:

```
# Apply action to the simulated cart-pole
x, x_dot, theta, theta_dot = do_step(action = action,
                x = x, x_dot = x_dot,
                theta = theta, theta_dot = theta_dot )

# Check for failure due constraints violation.
# If so, return number of steps.
if x < -2.4 or x > 2.4 or theta < -0.21 or theta > 0.21:
    return steps
```

If the controller's ANN was able to maintain a stable state of the cart-pole apparatus balancing for all simulation steps, the value with the maximum number of simulation steps is returned by the `run_cart_pole_simulation` function.

Genome fitness evaluation

Using the number of successful simulation steps returned by the `run_cart_pole_simulation` function described earlier, we are ready to implement the genome fitness evaluation function:

1. First, we run the cart-pole simulation loop, which returns the number of successful simulation steps:

```
steps = run_cart_pole_simulation(net, max_bal_steps)
```

2. After that, we are ready to evaluate the fitness score of the particular genome, as described previously:

```
log_steps = math.log(steps)
log_max_steps = math.log(max_bal_steps)
# The loss value is in range [0, 1]
error = (log_max_steps - log_steps) / log_max_steps
# The fitness value is a complement of the loss value
fitness = 1.0 - error
```

 Refer to the `eval_fitness(net, max_bal_steps=500000)` function for more details.

We use a logarithmic scale because most simulation runs fail in about 100 steps, but we test against `500000` balancing steps.

The single-pole balancing experiment

Now that we have an objective function defined and implemented along with a simulation of cart-pole apparatus dynamics, we are ready to start writing the source code to run the neuroevolutionary process with the NEAT algorithm. We will use the same NEAT-Python library as in the XOR experiment in the previous chapter, but with the NEAT hyperparameters adjusted appropriately. The hyperparameters are stored in the `single_pole_config.ini` file, which can be found in the source code repository related to this chapter. You need to copy this file into your local `Chapter4` directory, in which you already should have a Python script with the cart-pole simulator we created earlier.

Hyperparameter selection

In the NEAT section of the configuration file, we define the population of organisms set to 150 individuals, and the fitness threshold with a value of `1.0` as a termination criterion.

The `fitness_criterion` is set to max, which means that the evolutionary process terminates when any individual reaches a fitness score equal to the `fitness_threshold` value:

```
[NEAT]
fitness_criterion   = max
fitness_threshold   = 1.0
pop_size            = 150
reset_on_extinction = False
```

Also, we significantly decreased the probability of adding the new node to bias the evolutionary process into elaborating more on the connectivity patterns with a minimal number of ANN nodes in the controller. Thus, we aim to reduce the energy consumption of the evolved controller's ANN and to reduce the computational costs of training.

The corresponding parameters in the configuration file are as follows:

```
# node add/remove rates
node_add_prob    = 0.02
node_delete_prob = 0.02
```

The parameters describing our initial network configuration by a count of hidden, input, and output nodes are given as follows:

```
# network parameters
num_hidden = 0
num_inputs = 4
num_outputs = 1
```

We increased the species' compatibility threshold to bias the evolutionary process into producing fewer species. Also, we increased the minimum species' size to indicate that we are interested in much more highly populated species that have a bigger chance of preserving beneficial mutations. At the same time, we decreased the maximal stagnation age to intensify the evolutionary process by heightening the early extinction of stagnated species that do not show any fitness improvements.

The related parameters in the configuration file are as follows:

```
[DefaultSpeciesSet]
compatibility_threshold = 4.0

[DefaultStagnation]
species_fitness_func = max
max_stagnation = 15
species_elitism = 2

[DefaultReproduction]
```

```
elitism = 2
survival_threshold = 0.2
min_species_size = 8
```

 Refer to the `single_pole_config.ini` configuration file for full details.

As a result of the configuration parameters, more populated species will be used during the evolutionary process; however, the number of unique species will be kept low.

Working environment setup

Before you start writing the source code of the experiment runner, you must set up a virtual Python environment and install all the necessary dependencies. You can do this with Anaconda by executing the following commands in the command line:

```
$ conda create --name single_pole_neat python=3.5
$ conda activate single_pole_neat
$ pip install neat-python==0.92
$ conda install matplotlib
$ conda install graphviz
$ conda install python-graphviz
```

First, these commands create and activate a `single_pole_neat` virtual environment with Python 3.5. After that, the NEAT-Python library, version 0.92, is installed, along with the other dependencies used by our visualization utilities.

The experiment runner implementation

First, you need to create a `single_pole_experiment.py` file in the `Chapter4` directory. In that file, the source code of the single-pole balancing experiment will be written. Also, you need to copy the `visualize.py` file from the chapter's repository into this directory as well. We will use the visualization utilities from this file to render the results of the experiment.

The experiment runner script includes two essential functions.

Function to evaluate the fitness of all genomes in the population

The first function evaluates the list of all genomes in the population and assigns a fitness score to each of them. This function is passed by reference into the neuroevolution runner of the NEAT-Python library. The source code of this function is as follows:

```
def eval_genomes(genomes, config):
    for genome_id, genome in genomes:
        genome.fitness = 0.0
        net = neat.nn.FeedForwardNetwork.create(genome, config)
        fitness = cart.eval_fitness(net)
        if fitness >= config.fitness_threshold:
            # do additional steps of evaluation with random initial states
            # to make sure that we found stable control strategy rather
            # than special case for particular initial state
            success_runs = evaluate_best_net(net, config,
                                              additional_num_runs)
            # adjust fitness
            fitness = 1.0 - (additional_num_runs - success_runs) / \
                    additional_num_runs

        genome.fitness = fitness
```

 Note that we are introducing additional simulation runs for the winning genome to make sure that its control strategy is stable when starting from a variety of random initial states. This additional check guarantees that we have found the real winner rather than a special case that's specific to a particular initial state.

The preceding function receives the list of all genomes in the population and the NEAT configuration parameters. For each specific genome, it creates the phenotype ANN and uses it as a controller to run the cart-pole apparatus simulation, as defined in the following snippet from the preceding code:

```
fitness = cart.eval_fitness(net)
```

The returned fitness score is then compared with the fitness threshold value we defined in the configuration parameters. If it exceeds the threshold, we can assume that a successful controller was found. To further verify the validity of the found controller, it will be tested for additional simulation runs and a final fitness score will be calculated (as in the following snippet taken from the preceding code):

```
success_runs = evaluate_best_net(net, config, additional_num_runs)
fitness = 1.0 - (additional_num_runs - success_runs) / additional_num_runs
```

The additional simulation steps will use different seeds for a random number generator to cover the majority of possible initial configurations of the cart-pole apparatus.

The experiment runner function

The second function configures, executes, and outputs the results of the neuroevolution process. Here, we outline some critical places in the implementation of the experiment runner function:

1. The function begins with the loading of the hyperparameters from the configuration file and spawns the initial population using the loaded configuration:

   ```
   # Load configuration.
   config = neat.Config(neat.DefaultGenome,
                        neat.DefaultReproduction,
                        neat.DefaultSpeciesSet,
                        neat.DefaultStagnation,
                        config_file)

   # Create the population, which is the top-level object
   # for a NEAT run.
   p = neat.Population(config)
   ```

2. After that, it configures statistics' reporters to collect the statistics regarding execution of the evolutionary process. The output reporters are added as well in order to output the execution results to the console in real time. The checkpoints collector is also configured to save intermediary stages of execution, which can be useful if you need to restore the training process later:

   ```
   # Add a stdout reporter to show progress in the terminal.
   p.add_reporter(neat.StdOutReporter(True))
   stats = neat.StatisticsReporter()
   p.add_reporter(stats)
   p.add_reporter(neat.Checkpointer(5,
               filename_prefix='out/spb-neat—checkpoint-'))
   ```

3. Finally, the evolution process is executed over the specified number of generations, and the results are saved in the output directory:

   ```
   # Run for up to N generations.
   best_genome = p.run(eval_genomes, n=n_generations)

   # Display the best genome among generations.
   print('\nBest genome:\n{!s}'.format(best_genome))
   ```

```
# Check if the best genome is a winning Single-Pole
# balancing controller
net = neat.nn.FeedForwardNetwork.create(best_genome, config)
best_genome_fitness = cart.eval_fitness(net)
if best_genome_fitness >= config.fitness_threshold:
    print("\n\nSUCCESS: The Single-Pole balancing controller
has been found!!!")
    else:
        print("\n\nFAILURE: Failed to find Single-Pole balancing
controller!!!")
```

 Refer to the `run_experiment(config_file, n_generations=100)` function for full implementation details.

After the best genome has been found during the evolutionary process, it is verified whether it actually meets the fitness threshold criteria that we set in the configuration file. There may be no working solution found during the process, but nevertheless, the NEAT-Python library will return the best fit genome. That is why we need this additional check to ensure that the resulting best fit genome can actually solve the problem in practice.

Running the single-pole balancing experiment

You need to enter the directory containing the `single_pole_experiment.py` file and execute the following command:

```
$ python single_pole_experiment.py
```

 Do not forget to activate the appropriate virtual environment with the following command:

`conda activate single_pole_neat`

During the execution of the Python script, the console will print the following output for each generation of the evolution:

```
****** Running generation 13 ******

Population's average fitness: 0.26673 stdev: 0.12027
Best fitness: 0.70923 - size: (1, 2) - species 1 - id 2003
Average adjusted fitness: 0.161
Mean genetic distance 1.233, standard deviation 0.518
Population of 150 members in 1 species:
   ID age size fitness adj fit stag
```

```
==== === ==== ======= ======= ====
    1 13 150 0.7 0.161 7
Total extinctions: 0
Generation time: 4.635 sec (0.589 average)
```

In the output, you can see that the average fitness of the population in generation 14 is low, but the fitness of the best performing organism (0.70923) is already close to our completion threshold value (fitness_threshold = 1.0), which was set in the configuration file. The organism champion encodes the phenotype ANN that consists of one non-linear node (output) and only two connections (size: (1, 2)). Also, it is interesting to note that only one species exists in the population.

After the winner is found, the console output has the following lines:

```
****** Running generation 14 ******

Population's average fitness: 0.26776 stdev: 0.13359
Best fitness: 1.00000 - size: (1, 3) - species 1 - id 2110

Best individual in generation 14 meets fitness threshold - complexity: (1,
3)

Best genome:
Key: 2110
Fitness: 1.0
Nodes:
  0 DefaultNodeGene(key=0, bias=-3.328545880116371, response=1.0,
activation=sigmoid, aggregation=sum)
Connections:
  DefaultConnectionGene(key=(-4, 0), weight=2.7587300138861037,
enabled=True)
  DefaultConnectionGene(key=(-3, 0), weight=2.951449584136504,
enabled=True)
  DefaultConnectionGene(key=(-1, 0), weight=0.9448711043565166,
enabled=True)


Evaluating the best genome in random runs
Runs successful/expected: 100/100
SUCCESS: The stable Single-Pole balancing controller has been found!!!
```

The best genome that is an evolution winner encodes a phenotype ANN that consists of only one non-linear node (output) and three connections from input nodes (`size: (1, 3)`). It is interesting to note that evolution was able to produce a solid control strategy that completely ignores the linear velocity of the cart and only uses the other three inputs: x, θ, and θ. This fact is another sign of the correctness of the evolutionary selection because we decided to ignore friction of the cart, which effectively excluded the linear velocity of the cart from the equations of motion.

The graph with ANN of winning single-pole balancing controller is shown here:

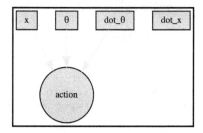

The ANN of the single-pole balancing controller found by the NEAT algorithm

The plot with the changes in fitness value over generations of evolution is as follows:

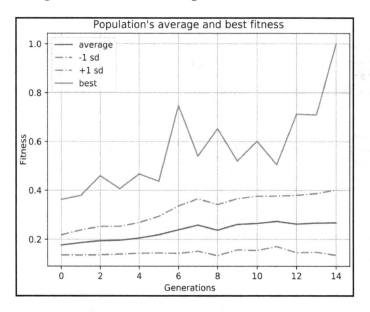

The population's average and best fitness in the single-pole experiment

The average fitness of the population in all generations was low, but from the very beginning, there was a beneficial mutation that spawned a particular lineage of organisms. From generation to generation, gifted individuals from that lineage were able not only to preserve their beneficial traits but also to improve them, which ultimately led to finding an evolution winner.

Exercises

1. Try to increase the value of the `node_add_prob` parameter and see what happens. Does the algorithm produce any number of hidden nodes, and if so, how many?
2. Try to decrease/increase the `compatibility_threshold` value. What happens if you set it to `2.0` or `6.0`? Can the algorithm find the solution in each case?
3. Try to set the `elitism` value to zero in the `DefaultReproduction` section. See what happens. How long did the evolutionary process take to find an acceptable solution in this case?
4. Set the `survival_threshold` value to `0.5` in the `DefaultReproduction` section. See how this affects speciation during evolution. Why does it?
5. Increase the `additional_num_runs` and `additional_steps` values in order of magnitude to examine further how well the found control strategy is generalized. Is the algorithm still able to find a winning solution?

 The last exercise will lead to an increase in the execution time of the algorithm.

The double-pole balancing problem

The single-pole balancing problem is easy enough for the NEAT algorithm, which can quickly find the optimal control strategy to maintain a stable system state. To make the experiment more challenging, we present a more advanced version of the cart-pole balancing problem. In this version, the two poles are connected to the moving cart by a hinge.

A schema of the new cart-poles apparatus is as follows:

The cart-poles apparatus with two poles

Before we move to the implementation details of the experiment, we need to define the state variables and equations of motion for the simulation of the double-pole balancing system.

The system state and equations of motion

The goal of the controller is to apply the force to the cart in order to keep two poles balanced for as long as possible. At the same time, the cart should stay within the defined boundaries. As with the single-pole balancing problem discussed previously, the control strategy can be defined as an avoidance control problem, which means that the controller must maintain a stable system state, avoiding the danger zones when the cart moves outside the track boundaries or either of the poles fall beyond the allowed vertical angle. There is no unique solution for this problem, but an appropriate control strategy can be found because the poles have different lengths and masses. Therefore, they respond differently to the control inputs.

The current state of the double-pole balancing apparatus can be defined by the following variables:

- Cart position on the track (x)
- Cart velocity ($\dot{x}$)
- First pole's angle from the vertical (θ_1)
- First pole's angular velocity ($\dot{\theta}_1$)
- Second pole's angle from the vertical (θ_2)
- Second pole's angular velocity ($\dot{\theta}_2$)

The equations of motion for two unjoined poles balanced on a single cart that ignores friction between cart wheels and the track are as follows:

$$\ddot{x} = \frac{F_x - \sum_{i=1}^{2} \tilde{F}_i}{M + \sum_{i=1}^{2} \tilde{m}_i}$$

$$\ddot{\theta}_i = -\frac{3}{4L_i}\left(\ddot{x}\cos\theta_i + g\sin\theta_i + \frac{\mu_{pi}\dot{\theta}_i}{m_i L_i}\right)$$

In this equation, $\tilde{F}_i$ is the reaction force from the ith pole on the cart:

$$\tilde{F}_i = m_i L_i \dot{\theta}_i^2 \sin\theta_i + \frac{3}{4}m_i \cos\theta_i \left(\frac{\mu_{pi}\dot{\theta}_i}{m_i L_i} + g\sin\theta_i\right)$$

In this equation, $\tilde{m}_i$ is the effective mass of the ith pole:

$$\tilde{m}_i = m_i\left(1 - \frac{3}{4}\cos^2\theta_i\right)$$

The following parameters are used for double-pole simulation:

Symbol	Description	Values
x	The position of the cart on a track	$\in [-2.4, 2.4]m$
θ	The angle of a pole from the vertical	$\in [-36, 36]degrees$
F_x	The control force applied to the cart	$\pm 10N$
L_i	The distance from the center of mass of the pole to the pivot	$L_1 = 0.5m$ $L_2 = 0.05m$
M	The mass of the cart	$1.0kg$

m_i	The mass of the ith pole	$m_1 = 0.1kg$ $m_2 = 0.01kg$
μ_p	The coefficient of friction of the **pivot** of the ith pole	0.000002
g	Acceleration of free fall due to gravity	$-9.8m/s^2$

The corresponding Python code defines these system parameters as constants:

```
GRAVITY = -9.8 # m/s^2 - here negative as equations of motion for 2-pole
system assume it to be negative
MASS_CART = 1.0 # kg
FORCE_MAG = 10.0 # N
# The first pole
MASS_POLE_1 = 1.0 # kg
LENGTH_1 = 0.5 # m - actually half the first pole's length
# The second pole
MASS_POLE_2 = 0.1 # kg
LENGTH_2 = 0.05 # m - actually half the second pole's length
# The coefficient of friction of pivot of the pole
MUP = 0.000002
```

The implementation of the equations of motion in Python is as follows:

```
# Find the input force direction
force = (action - 0.5) * FORCE_MAG * 2.0 # action has binary values
# Calculate projections of forces for the poles
cos_theta_1 = math.cos(theta1)
sin_theta_1 = math.sin(theta1)
g_sin_theta_1 = GRAVITY * sin_theta_1
cos_theta_2 = math.cos(theta2)
sin_theta_2 = math.sin(theta2)
g_sin_theta_2 = GRAVITY * sin_theta_2
# Calculate intermediate values
ml_1 = LENGTH_1 * MASS_POLE_1
ml_2 = LENGTH_2 * MASS_POLE_2
temp_1 = MUP * theta1_dot / ml_1
temp_2 = MUP * theta2_dot / ml_2
fi_1 = (ml_1 * theta1_dot * theta1_dot * sin_theta_1) + \
       (0.75 * MASS_POLE_1 * cos_theta_1 * (temp_1 + g_sin_theta_1))
fi_2 = (ml_2 * theta2_dot * theta2_dot * sin_theta_2) + \
       (0.75 * MASS_POLE_2 * cos_theta_2 * (temp_2 + g_sin_theta_2))
mi_1 = MASS_POLE_1 * (1 - (0.75 * cos_theta_1 * cos_theta_1))
mi_2 = MASS_POLE_2 * (1 - (0.75 * cos_theta_2 * cos_theta_2))
# Calculate the results: cart acceleration and poles angular accelerations
x_ddot = (force + fi_1 + fi_2) / (mi_1 + mi_2 + MASS_CART)
theta_1_ddot = -0.75 * (x_ddot * cos_theta_1 + \
                        g_sin_theta_1 + temp_1) / LENGTH_1
theta_2_ddot = -0.75 * (x_ddot * cos_theta_2 + \
```

```
g_sin_theta_2 + temp_2) / LENGTH_2
```

 More implementation details are available in the `cart_two_pole.py` file in the repository associated with `Chapter4` source code files. Refer to the `calc_step(action, x, x_dot, theta1, theta1_dot, theta2, theta2_dot)` function.

The preceding code receives the current system state (`x`, `x_dot`, `theta1`, `theta1_dot`, `theta2`, `theta2_dot`) along with the control action and calculates the derivatives (cart acceleration and angular acceleration of both poles).

Reinforcement signal

The simulation environment must provide minimal information about the system state after performing actions in the form of a reinforcement signal (r_t). The reinforcement signal indicates whether a double-pole balancing system violates the bounding constraints after applying an action. It can be defined as follows:

$$r_t = \begin{cases} 0 & \text{if} -0.63 \text{ radians} < \theta_i^t < 0.63 \text{ radians and} -2.4 \text{ m} < x_t < 2.4 \text{ m} \\ 1 & \text{otherwise} \end{cases}$$

The implementation of the reinforcement signal generation in Python is as follows:

```
res = x < -2.4 or x > 2.4 or \
    theta1 < -THIRTY_SIX_DEG_IN_RAD or theta1 > THIRTY_SIX_DEG_IN_RAD or \
    theta2 < -THIRTY_SIX_DEG_IN_RAD or theta2 > THIRTY_SIX_DEG_IN_RAD
```

The condition checks that the angle of each pole is $\pm 36 degrees$ ($0.63 radians$) from the vertical, and that the position of the cart is $\pm 2.4m$ from the center of the track.

Initial conditions and state update

In the single-pole balancing experiment, we used random initial state conditions, but with the two poles, the initial conditions are a bit more simplified. The system starts with all cart and pole velocities set to zero. The initial position of the long pole is one degree from the vertical, and the short pole is exactly upright.

The initial conditions are as follows:

- $x = 0$
- $\dot{x} = 0$
- $\theta_1 = \dfrac{\pi}{180}$
- $\dot{\theta}_1 = 0$
- $\theta_2 = 0$
- $\dot{\theta}_2 = 0$

The state of the cart-pole system is updated at each simulation step by numerical approximation of the equations of motion using the Runge-Kutta fourth-order method with a time step size of *0.01* seconds. The Runge-Kutta fourth-order approximation method allows calculation of the system response given the state variables of the current time step. The new control inputs are generated every $\tau = 0.02$ seconds. Thus, the control frequency is **50 Hz**, and the update frequency of the system state is **100 Hz**.

The Runge-Kutta fourth-order method implementation in Python is as follows:

1. Use the current cart-pole apparatus state variables to update the intermediate state for the next half-time step and do the first simulation step:

```
hh = tau / 2.0
yt = [None] * 6

# update intermediate state
for i in range(6):
    yt[i] = y[i] + hh * dydx[i]

# do simulation step
x_ddot, theta_1_ddot, theta_2_ddot = calc_step(action = f, yt[0],
yt[1], yt[2], yt[3], yt[4], yt[5])

# store derivatives
dyt = [yt[1], x_ddot, yt[3], theta_1_ddot, yt[5], theta_2_ddot]
```

2. Update the intermediate state using the derivatives obtained from the first simulation step and perform the second simulation step:

```
# update intermediate state
for i in range(6):
    yt[i] = y[i] + hh * dyt[i]

# do one simulation step
x_ddot, theta_1_ddot, theta_2_ddot = calc_step(action = f, yt[0],
```

```
    yt[1], yt[2], yt[3], yt[4], yt[5])

    # store derivatives
    dym = [yt[1], x_ddot, yt[3], theta_1_ddot, yt[5], theta_2_ddot]
```

3. Update the intermediate state using the derivatives from the first and second simulation steps and execute the third pole-balancing simulation step using the updated state:

```
    # update intermediate state
    for i in range(6):
        yt[i] = y[i] + tau * dym[i]
        dym[i] += dyt[i]

    # do one simulation step
    x_ddot, theta_1_ddot, theta_2_ddot = calc_step(action = f, yt[0],
    yt[1], yt[2], yt[3], yt[4], yt[5])

    # store derivatives
    dyt = [yt[1], x_ddot, yt[3], theta_1_ddot, yt[5], theta_2_ddot]
```

4. Finally, use the derivatives from the first three simulation steps to approximate the final state of the cart-pole apparatus that will be used in further simulation:

```
    # find system state after approximation
    yout = [None] * 6 # the approximated system state
    h6 = tau / 6.0
    for i in range(6):
        yout[i] = y[i] + h6 * (dydx[i] + dyt[i] + 2.0 * dym[i])
```

Let's examine the elements of the preceding equation:

- f is a control action to apply during simulation (**0** or **1**).
- y is a list with the current values of the state variables $(x, \dot{x}, \theta_1, \dot{\theta}_1, \theta_2, \dot{\theta}_2)$.
- dydx is a list with the derivatives of the state variables $(\dot{x}, \ddot{x}, \dot{\theta}_1, \ddot{\theta}_1, \dot{\theta}_2, \ddot{\theta}_2)$.
- tau is the size of the time step for approximation.

> For more implementation details, refer to the rk4(f, y, dydx, tau) function in the cart_two_pole.py file.

This implementation of the Runge-Kutta fourth-order method receives the current system state (x, x_dot, theta1, theta1_dot, theta2, theta2_dot) along with derivatives and approximates the system state at the next time step.

Control actions

As with the single-pole balancing experiment discussed earlier in this chapter, the control system for the double-pole balancing experiment generates only two control signals: push left and push right with a constant force. Thus, the control force at time t can be defined as follows:

$$F_t = \begin{cases} 10 \text{ N}, & \text{if } a[t] = 1 \\ -10 \text{ N}, & \text{if } a[t] = 0 \end{cases}$$

In the preceding equation, $a[t]$ is an action signal received from the controller at time t.

Interactions between the solver and the simulator

The state variables are scaled down to fit the [0,1] range before they are applied as inputs to the controller ANN. Thus, the equations for preprocessing of the state input variables are as follows:

$$x_0[t] = \frac{1}{4.8} \left(x[t] + 2.4 \right)$$
$$x_1[t] = \frac{1}{3} \left(\dot{x}[t] + 1.5 \right)$$

$$x_2[t] = \frac{1}{1.256} \left(\theta_1[t] + 0.628 \right)$$

$$x_3[t] = \frac{1}{4} \left(\dot{\theta}_1[t] + 2 \right)$$

$$x_4[t] = \frac{1}{1.256} \left(\theta_2[t] + 0.628 \right)$$

$$x_5[t] = \frac{1}{4} \left(\dot{\theta}_2[t] + 2 \right)$$

In the preceding equations, $x_0 \cdots x_5$ correspond to the cart's horizontal position, its horizontal velocity, the first pole's angle from the vertical, its angular velocity, and the second pole's angle and angular velocity, respectively.

Taking into account the system constraints defined earlier (see r_t), the scaled values of x_0, x_2, and x_4 are guaranteed to be within the [0,1] range, while the scaled values of x_1, x_3, and x_5 mostly fall within the 0...1 range, but can fall outside these bounds eventually.

The corresponding source code for input scaling is as follows:

```
input[0] = (state[0] + 2.4) / 4.8
input[1] = (state[1] + 1.5) / 3.0
input[2] = (state[2] + THIRTY_SIX_DEG_IN_RAD) / (THIRTY_SIX_DEG_IN_RAD *
2.0)
input[3] = (state[3] + 2.0) / 4.0
input[4] = (state[4] + THIRTY_SIX_DEG_IN_RAD) / (THIRTY_SIX_DEG_IN_RAD *
2.0)
input[5] = (state[5] + 2.0) / 4.0
```

The state list holds the current state variables in the following order: $x, \dot{x}, \theta_1, \dot{\theta}_1, \theta_2,$ and $\dot{\theta}_2$.

Objective function for a double-pole balancing experiment

The objective function for this problem is similar to the objective function defined earlier for the single-pole balancing problem. It is given by the following equations:

$$\mathcal{L} = \frac{\log t_{max} - \log t_{eval}}{\log t_{max}}$$

$$\mathcal{F} = 1.0 - \mathcal{L}$$

In these equations, t_{max} is the expected number of time steps specified in the configuration of the experiment (100,000), and t_{eval} is the actual number of time steps during which the controller was able to maintain a stable state of the pole balancer within the specified limits.

We use logarithmic scales because most of the trials fail in the first several 100 steps, but we are testing against 100,000 steps. With a logarithmic scale, we have a better distribution of fitness scores, even compared with a small number of steps in failed trials.

The first of the preceding equations defines the loss, which is in the [0,1] range, and the second is a fitness score that is complementing the loss value. Thus, the fitness score values are in the [0,1] range, and the higher the value, the better the outcome.

The Python source code is similar to the objective function definition in the single-pole balancing experiment, but it uses different simulator calls to get a number of balanced steps:

```
# First we run simulation loop returning number of successful
# simulation steps
steps = cart.run_markov_simulation(net, max_bal_steps)

if steps == max_bal_steps:
    # the maximal fitness
    return 1.0
elif steps == 0: # needed to avoid math error when taking log(0)
    # the minimal fitness
    return 0.0
else:
    log_steps = math.log(steps)
    log_max_steps = math.log(max_bal_steps)
    # The loss value is in range [0, 1]
    error = (log_max_steps - log_steps) / log_max_steps
    # The fitness value is a complement of the loss value
    return 1.0 - error
```

We use the logarithmic scale here because most of the runs fail too early, within 100 steps or so, but we are testing against 100,000 steps.

Double-pole balancing experiment

This experiment uses a version of the double-pole balancing problem that assumes full knowledge of the current system state, including the angular velocities of the poles and the velocity of the cart. The criteria of success in this experiment are to keep both poles balanced for 100,000 steps, or approximately 33 minutes of simulated time. The pole is considered balanced when it stays within ± 36 degrees of vertical, while the cart remains within ± 2.4 meters of the track's center.

Hyperparameter selection

Compared to the previous experiment described in this chapter, double-pole balancing is much harder to solve due to its complex motion dynamics. Thus, the search space for a successful control strategy is broader and requires a more diverse population. To increase the diversity of the population, we increase its size to become 10 times bigger than with a single-pole balancing experiment.

The fitness termination threshold remains the same as shown here:

```
[NEAT]
fitness_criterion = max
fitness_threshold = 1.0
pop_size = 1000
reset_on_extinction = False
```

To intensify evolutionary diversity further, we increase the probabilities of adding new nodes and connections, as well as changing the configuration scheme of initial connections. Also, the value of the `initial_connection` parameter contains the probability of connection creation, which introduces additional non-determinism into the process of the production of the connections graph:

```
# connection add/remove rates
conn_add_prob = 0.5
conn_delete_prob = 0.2

initial_connection = partial_direct 0.5

# node add/remove rates
node_add_prob = 0.2
node_delete_prob = 0.2
```

Finally, taking into account the size of a population and the possible size of a species, we reduced the fraction of individuals who are allowed to reproduce (`survival_threshold`). This tweak limits the search space of the solution by enabling only the fittest organisms to participate in the recombination process:

```
[DefaultReproduction]
elitism = 2
survival_threshold = 0.1
min_species_size = 2
```

The last tweak is controversial and can reduce the performance of the evolutionary process in general. But with large populations, it often works well by decreasing the number of possible recombinations. Thus, as a rule of thumb, large survival thresholds are used for small populations, and small values are used for large populations.

Due to the increased complexity of this experiment, the additional hyperparameter type becomes extremely important for the final outcome. The neuroevolution process is built around the likelihood of mutations occurring, and the probability of mutation is tested against the values produced by a random number generator.

As you know, in conventional computers, there is no true source of randomness. Instead, the randomness is generated by a pseudo-random algorithm that heavily depends on the random seed to start the generation of a random number sequence. Actually, the random seed value exactly defines a sequence of all pseudo-random numbers that will be produced by a given generator.

Thus, we can consider the random seed number as an essential parameter defining the initial conditions. This parameter sets the properties of the random attractor, which will amplify the tiny changes in the numerical search space of the algorithm. The effect of amplification ultimately determines whether the algorithm will be able to find the winner and how long it will take.

The random seed value is defined in the `two_pole_markov_experiment.py` file around line 100:

```
# set random seed
seed = 1559231616
random.seed(seed)
```

 For the complete list of hyperparameters used in the double-pole balancing experiment, please refer to the `two_pole_markov_config.ini` file in the source code repository associated with this chapter.

The preceding code sets the seed value of the standard random number generator supplied with the Python environment.

Working environment setup

The working environment for the double-pole balancing experiment can be set up with the following commands entered into your Terminal application of choice:

```
$ conda create --name double_pole_neat python=3.5
$ conda activate double_pole_neat
$ pip install neat-python==0.92
$ conda install matplotlib
$ conda install graphviz
$ conda install python-graphviz
```

These commands create and activate a `double_pole_neat` virtual environment with Python 3.5. After that, the NEAT-Python library with version 0.92 is installed, along with the other dependencies used by our visualization utilities.

The experiment runner implementation

The source code implementing the evaluation of the genome fitness is similar to the one used for a single-pole balancing experiment. The main difference is that it will refer to another simulation environment to get the number of balanced steps. Thus, you can refer to the source code of the `eval_fitness(net, max_bal_steps=100000)` and `eval_genomes(genomes, config)` functions in the `two_pole_markov_experiment.py` file for implementation details.

In this experiment, we introduced adaptive learning, which will try to find the correct short pole length during the evolution process. The length of the short pole changes the motion dynamics of the system. Not all combinations of hyperparameters combined with a particular length of the short pole can produce a successful control strategy. Thus, we implement a sequential increase of the short pole length until the solution is found:

```
# Run the experiment
pole_length = [0.1, 0.2, 0.3, 0.4, 0.5, 0.6, 0.7, 0.8]
num_runs = len(pole_length)
for i in range(num_runs):
    cart.LENGTH_2 = pole_length[i] / 2.0
    solved = run_experiment(config_path, n_generations=100, silent=False)
    print("run: %d, solved: %s, length: %f" %
                                (i + 1, solved, cart.LENGTH_2))
    if solved:
        print("Solution found in: %d run, short pole length: %f" %
                                (i + 1, cart.LENGTH_2))
    break
```

 Refer to the `two_pole_markov_experiment.py` file for more implementation details.

The preceding code runs the simulation using different short pole length values until the solution is found.

Running the double-pole balancing experiment

Having implemented the two-pole balancing simulator, genome fitness function evaluator, and experiment runner code, we are ready to start experimenting. Enter the directory containing the `two_pole_markov_experiment.py` file and execute the following command:

```
$ python two_pole_markov_experiment.py
```

 Do not forget to activate the appropriate virtual environment with the following command:
`conda activate double_pole_neat`

The preceding command will launch the evolutionary process under the control of the NEAT algorithm, using the hyperparameters specified in the `two_pole_markov_config.ini` file, as well as the simulator of the cart-two-pole apparatus that we already implemented.

After 96 generations, the winning solution can be found in generation 97. The console output for the last generation looks similar to the following:

```
****** Running generation 97 ******

Population's average fitness: 0.27393 stdev: 0.10514
Best fitness: 1.00000 - size: (1, 6) - species 26 - id 95605

Best individual in generation 97 meets fitness threshold - complexity: (1,
6)

Best genome:
Key: 95605
Fitness: 1.0
Nodes:
  0 DefaultNodeGene(key=0, bias=7.879760594997953, response=1.0,
activation=sigmoid, aggregation=sum)
Connections:
  DefaultConnectionGene(key=(-6, 0), weight=1.9934757746640883,
enabled=True)
  DefaultConnectionGene(key=(-5, 0), weight=3.703109977745863,
enabled=True)
  DefaultConnectionGene(key=(-4, 0), weight=-11.923951805881497,
enabled=True)
  DefaultConnectionGene(key=(-3, 0), weight=-4.152166115226511,
enabled=True)
  DefaultConnectionGene(key=(-2, 0), weight=-3.101569479910728,
```

```
enabled=True)
  DefaultConnectionGene(key=(-1, 0), weight=-1.379602358542496,
enabled=True)


Evaluating the best genome in random runs
Runs successful/expected: 1/1
SUCCESS: The stable Double-Pole-Markov balancing controller found!!!
Random seed: 1559231616
run: 1, solved: True, half-length: 0.050000
Solution found in: 1 run, short pole length: 0.100000
```

In the console output, we can see that the winning genome has a size (1, 6), which means that it has only one non-linear node—the output—and a full set of connections from six inputs to the output nodes. Thus, we can assume that the minimal possible configuration of the controller ANN was found because it does not include any hidden nodes, but instead encodes control behavior with specifically explored connection weights. Also, it is interesting to note that the solution for the smallest length value among the list of all possible short pole length values was found.

The configuration of the controller's ANN that's capable of executing a reliable control strategy is shown in the following graph:

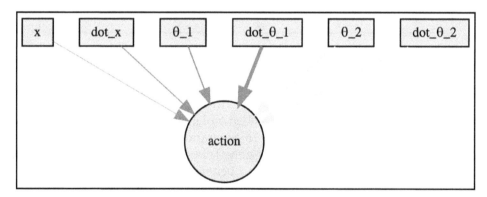

The ANN of the double-pole balancing controller

The fitness scores vary over generations, as shown in the following graph:

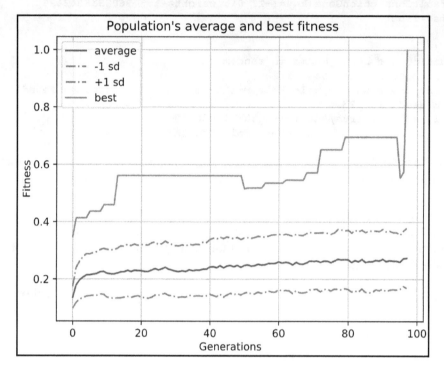

The fitness scores through generations for a double-pole balancing experiment

The preceding graph is interesting if we want to know how the evolution works. You can see that before finding a winner, the fitness score drops sharply. This is due to the extinction of stagnated species that have reached a plateau with medium-high fitness scores that showed no improvement over the past 15 generations. After that, the vacant place is occupied by fresh species endowed with the genetic knowledge accumulated by extinct species. This newborn species also introduces a beneficial mutation that combines its hereditary knowledge with new tricks and, ultimately, produces a winner.

In this experiment, we decided to intensify the species' diversity by significantly increasing the population size and making other tweaks to the hyperparameters. In the following graph, you can see that we have reached our goal, and that the neuroevolution process goes through a wide variety of species until a solution is found:

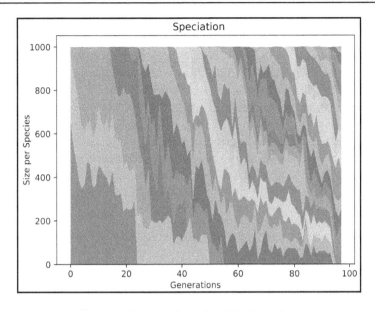

The speciation by generations for a double-pole balancing experiment

Next, we would like to learn how a change in the value of the random seed number impacts the NEAT algorithm. To begin with, we increased the value of the random seed number only by one (everything else has not changed). With this new condition, the NEAT algorithm could still find a stable control strategy but created a different, bizarre configuration of the controller's ANN instead of the optimal configuration shown earlier:

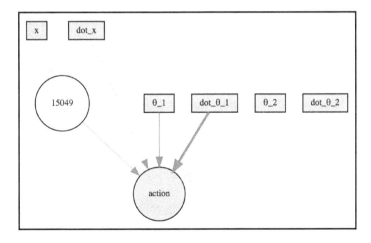

The ANN of a double-pole balancing controller with a random seed number increased by one (everything else is unchanged)

When the value of the random seed number increased, for example, by 10, the neuroevolution process could not find any solid control strategy at all.

 This experiment revealed another vital aspect of methods based on neuroevolution—the impact of the initial conditions determined by the value of the random seed number. The random seed defines the properties of a random attractor, which amplifies the effects of the evolution process, both good or bad. So, with this experiment, it is crucial to find a suitable value of the random seed number to bootstrap the process of neuroevolution. We will discuss methods for finding appropriate values of the random seed numbers at the end of this book.

Exercises

1. Try setting the `node_add` parameter value to `0.02` in the configuration file and see what happens.
2. Change the seed value of the random number generator and see what happens. Was a solution found with a new value? How is it different from what we have presented in this chapter?

Summary

In this chapter, we learned how to implement control strategies for controllers that can maintain a stable state of a cart-pole apparatus with one or two poles mounted on top. We improved our Python skills and expanded our knowledge of the NEAT-Python library by implementing accurate simulations of physical apparatuses, which was used to define the objective functions for the experiments. Besides this, we learned about two methods for numerical approximations of differential equations, Euler's and Runge-Kutta, and implemented them in Python.

We found that the initial conditions that determine the neuroevolutionary process, such as a random seed number, have a significant impact on the performance of the algorithm. These values determine the entire sequence of numbers that will be generated by a random number generator. They serve as a random attractor that can amplify or dampen the effects of evolution.

In the next chapter, we will discuss how to use neuroevolution to create navigator agents that can find their way through a maze. You will learn how to define a goal-oriented objective function to solve the maze problem and how to write an accurate simulation of a robotic agent that can navigate through the maze. We will take a look at two types of maze environments and examine how the goal-oriented fitness function can get stuck trying to find a solution in the deceptive environment of a hard maze configuration.

Autonomous Maze Navigation

5

The maze navigation is a classic computer science problem related to the autonomous navigation domain. In this chapter, you will learn how neuroevolution-based methods can be used to solve the challenge of maze navigation. Also, we will explain how to define a goal-oriented fitness function using the fitness scores of the navigator agent calculated as a derivative of the agent's distance from the final goal. By the end of this chapter, you will understand the basics of training an autonomous navigation agent using neuroevolution methods and will be able to create the more advanced maze solver that will be introduced in the next chapter. You will become familiar with advanced visualization techniques that will make it easier to understand the results of algorithm execution. Also, you will obtain hands-on experience of writing simulators of maze-navigating robots and related maze environments using the Python programming language.

In this chapter, you will become familiar with the following topics:

- The deceptive nature of the maze navigation problem
- Writing a simulator of a maze-navigating robot equipped with an array of sensors and actuators
- Defining a goal-oriented fitness function to guide the process of creating an appropriate maze solver using the neuroevolution algorithm
- Running the experiments with a simple and hard-to-solve maze configurations

Technical requirements

The following technical requirements should be met to complete the experiments described in this chapter:

- Windows 8/10, macOS 10.13 or newer, or modern Linux
- Anaconda Distribution version 2019.03 or newer

The code for this chapter can be found at `https://github.com/PacktPublishing/Hands-on-Neuroevolution-with-Python/tree/master/Chapter5`

Maze navigation problem

The maze navigation problem is a classic computer science problem that is closely related to creating autonomous navigation agents that can find a path through ambiguous environments. The maze environment is an illustrative domain for the class of problems that have a deceptive fitness landscape. This means that the goal-oriented fitness function can have steep gradients of fitness scores in dead ends in the maze that are close to the final goal point. Such areas of the maze become the local optima for objective-based search algorithms that may converge in these areas. When the search algorithm converges in such deceptive local optima, it cannot find an adequate maze-solver agent.

In the following example, you can see a two-dimensional maze with local optima dead ends, which are shaded in:

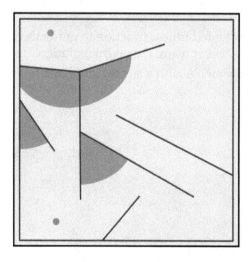

The two-dimensional maze configuration

The maze configuration in the diagram visualizes the landscape of the deceptive fitness scores concentrated in the local optima dead ends (marked as filled segments). The maze-solver agent navigating from the starting point (bottom circle) to the exit point (top circle) using the objective-based search algorithm will be prone to getting stuck in the local optima dead ends. Also, a deceptive fitness score landscape such as this can prevent the objective-based search algorithm from finding a successful maze solver.

The agent navigating through the maze is a robot equipped with a set of sensors, allowing it to detect nearby obstacles and get the direction to the maze exit. The motion of the robot is controlled by two actuators, which affect the linear and angular movement of the robot body. The actuators of the robot are controlled by an ANN, which receives input from the sensors and produces the two control signals for the actuators.

Maze simulation environment

The environment for the maze simulation consists of three major components that are implemented as separate Python classes:

- `Agent`: The class that holds information related to the maze navigator agent that is used by simulation (see the `agent.py` file for the implementation details).
- `AgentRecordStore`: The class that manages the storage of records relating to evaluations of all the solver agents during the evolutionary process. The collected records can be used to analyze the evolutionary process after its completion (see the `agent.py` file for the implementation details).
- `MazeEnvironment`: The class that contains information about the maze simulation environment. This class also provides methods that manage the simulation environment, control the position of a solver agent, perform collision detection, and generate the input data for sensors of the agent (see the `maze_environment.py` file for the implementation details).

In the following sections, we will look at each part of the maze simulation environment in more detail.

Maze-navigating agent

In this chapter, we consider a two-dimensional maze navigation task. This task is easy to visualize, and it is relatively easy to write the simulator of the maze-navigating robot for a two-dimensional maze. The main goal of the robot is to navigate through a maze to the defined goal point in a specified number of time steps. The ANN that controls the robot is a product of the neuroevolution process.

The neuroevolution algorithm starts with a very basic initial ANN configuration that only has input nodes for sensors and output nodes for actuators, which gradually becomes more complex until a successful maze solver is found. This task is complicated by a peculiar configuration of the maze that has several *cul-de-sacs*, which prevent finding the route to the goal by creating local optima in the fitness landscape, as discussed previously.

The following diagram shows the schematic drawing of the maze agent used in the maze-solving simulation:

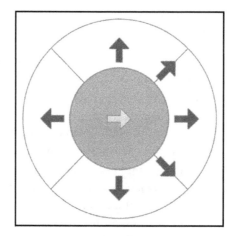

The maze agent (robot) schema

In the preceding diagram, the filled circle defines the rigid body of the robot. The arrow within the filled circle shows the heading of the robot. The six arrows around the filled circle represent **six rangefinder sensors** that indicate the distance to the nearest obstacle in a given direction. The four outer circle segments denote the **four pie-slice radar sensors** that act as a compass toward the goal point (maze exit).

The specific radar sensor becomes activated when the line from the goal point to the center of the robot falls within its **field of view** (**FOV**). The detection range of the radar sensor is limited by the area of the maze that falls into its FOV. Thus, at any given time, one of the four radar sensors is activated, indicating the maze exit direction.

The radar sensors have the following FOV zones relative to the robot's heading:

Sensor	FOV, degrees
Front	315.0 ~ 405.0
Left	45.0 ~ 135.0
Back	135.0 ~ 225.0
Right	225.0 ~ 315.0

The rangefinder sensor is a trace ray drawn from the center of the robot in a specific direction. It becomes activated when intersecting with any obstacle and returns a distance to the detected obstacle. The detection range of this sensor is defined by a particular configuration parameter.

The rangefinder sensors of the robot monitor the following directions relative to the agent heading:

Sensor	Direction, degrees
Right	-90.0
Front-right	-45.0
Front	0.0
Front-left	45.0
Left	90.0
Back	-180.0

The movement of the robot is controlled by two actuators that apply forces that turn and/or propel the agent frame, that is, change its linear and/or angular velocity.

The Python implementation of the maze-solver agent has multiple fields to hold its current state and to maintain the activation states of its sensors:

```python
def __init__(self, location, heading=0, speed=0,
             angular_vel=0, radius=8.0, range_finder_range=100.0):
    self.heading = heading
    self.speed = speed
    self.angular_vel = angular_vel
    self.radius = radius
    self.range_finder_range = range_finder_range
    self.location = location
    # defining the range finder sensors
```

```
self.range_finder_angles = [-90.0, -45.0, 0.0, 45.0, 90.0, -180.0]
# defining the radar sensors
self.radar_angles = [(315.0, 405.0), (45.0, 135.0),
                     (135.0, 225.0), (225.0, 315.0)]
# the list to hold range finders activations
self.range_finders = [None] * len(self.range_finder_angles)
# the list to hold pie-slice radar activations
self.radar = [None] * len(self.radar_angles)
```

For more implementation details, refer to the agent.py file at https://github.com/PacktPublishing/Hands-on-Neuroevolution-with-Python/blob/master/Chapter5/agent.py.

The preceding code shows a default constructor of the Agent class, where all fields of the agent are initialized. The maze environment simulation will use those fields to store the current state of the agent at each simulation step.

Maze simulation environment implementation

To simulate the solver agent navigating the maze, we need to define an environment that manages the configuration of the maze, tracks the position of the maze-solving agent, and provides inputs to the sensor data arrays of the navigating robot.

All of these features fit into one logical block that is encapsulated into the MazeEnvironment Python class, which has the following fields (as can be seen from the class constructor):

```
def __init__(self, agent, walls, exit_point, exit_range=5.0):
    self.walls = walls
    self.exit_point = exit_point
    self.exit_range = exit_range
    # The maze navigating agent
    self.agent = agent
    # The flag to indicate if exit was found
    self.exit_found = False
    # The initial distance of agent from exit
    self.initial_distance = self.agent_distance_to_exit()
```

The preceding code shows the default constructor of the `MazeEnvironment` class with initialization of all its fields:

- The maze configuration is determined by a list of walls and `exit_point`. Walls are lists of line segments; each line segment represents a specific wall in the maze, and `exit_point` is the location of maze's exit.
- The `exit_range` field stores value of the range distance around the `exit_point` that defines the exit area. We consider that the agent has successfully solved a maze when its position is in the exit area.
- The `agent` field holds a reference to the initialized `Agent` class described in the previous section, which defines the starting location of the solver agent in the maze among other agent-related data fields.
- The `initial_distance` field stores the distance from the agent's starting position to the maze exit point. This value will be later used for the agent's fitness score calculation.

Sensor data generation

The maze-solver agent is controlled by an ANN that needs to receive sensor data as input to produce the corresponding control signals as output. As we have already mentioned, the navigator agent is equipped with an array of two types of sensors:

- Six *rangefinder sensors* for the detection of collisions with the maze walls, which indicate the distance to the closest obstacle in a particular direction.
- Four *pie-slice radar sensors*, which indicate the direction to the maze's exit point from any place in the maze.

The sensor values need to be updated at each simulation step, and the `MazeEnvironment` class provides two designated methods that update both types of sensor.

The array of rangefinder sensors is updated as follows (see the `update_rangefinder_sensors` function):

```
for i, angle in enumerate(self.agent.range_finder_angles):
    rad = geometry.deg_to_rad(angle)
    projection_point = geometry.Point(
        x = self.agent.location.x + math.cos(rad) * \
            self.agent.range_finder_range,
        y = self.agent.location.y + math.sin(rad) * \
            self.agent.range_finder_range
    )
    projection_point.rotate(self.agent.heading,
```

```
                                    self.agent.location)
        projection_line = geometry.Line(a = self.agent.location,
                                        b = projection_point)
        min_range = self.agent.range_finder_range
        for wall in self.walls:
            found, intersection = wall.intersection(projection_line)
            if found:
                found_range = intersection.distance(
                                            self.agent.location)
                if found_range < min_range:
                    min_range = found_range
        # Store the distance to the closest obstacle
        self.agent.range_finders[i] = min_range
```

This code enumerates all detection directions of the rangefinder sensors, which are determined by the direction angles (see the `range_finder_angles` field initialization in the `Agent` constructor). For each direction, a projection line is then created, starting from the current position of the agent and with a length equal to the rangefinder's detection range. After that, the projection line is tested to see if it intersects any of the maze walls. If multiple intersections are detected, the distance to the closest wall is stored as a value to a specific rangefinder sensor. Otherwise, the maximal detection range will be saved as a value for a rangefinder sensor.

The array of pie-slice radar sensors needs to be updated with the following code in the `MazeEnvironment` class:

```
def update_radars(self):
    target = geometry.Point(self.exit_point.x, self.exit_point.y)
    target.rotate(self.agent.heading, self.agent.location)
    target.x -= self.agent.location.x
    target.y -= self.agent.location.y
    angle = target.angle()
    for i, r_angles in enumerate(self.agent.radar_angles):
        self.agent.radar[i] = 0.0 # reset specific radar
        if (angle >= r_angles[0] and angle < r_angles[1]) or
            (angle + 360 >= r_angles[0] and angle + 360 < r_angles[1]):
            # fire the radar
            self.agent.radar[i] = 1.0
```

The preceding code creates a copy of the maze exit point and rotates it with respect to the agent's heading and position within the global coordinate system. The target point is then translated to align it with the local coordinate system of the maze-solver agent; the agent is placed at the origin of the coordinates. After that, we calculate the angle of the vector drawn from the origin of the coordinates to the target point within the local coordinate system of the agent. This angle is an azimuth to the maze exit point from the current agent position. When the azimuth angle is found, we enumerate over the registered pie-sliced radar sensors to find the one that includes the azimuth angle in its FOV. The corresponding radar sensor is activated by setting its value to 1, while other radar sensors are deactivated by zeroing their values.

Agent position update

The position of the maze-solver agent within a maze needs to be updated in each simulation step after receiving the corresponding control signals from the controller ANN. The following code is executed to update the position of the maze-solver agent:

```
def update(self, control_signals):
    if self.exit_found:
        return True # Maze exit already found
    self.apply_control_signals(control_signals)
    vx = math.cos(geometry.deg_to_rad(self.agent.heading)) * \
                self.agent.speed
    vy = math.sin(geometry.deg_to_rad(self.agent.heading)) * \
                self.agent.speed
    self.agent.heading += self.agent.angular_vel
    if self.agent.heading > 360:
        self.agent.heading -= 360
    elif self.agent.heading < 0:
        self.agent.heading += 360
    new_loc = geometry.Point(
        x = self.agent.location.x + vx,
        y = self.agent.location.y + vy
    )
    if not self.test_wall_collision(new_loc):
        self.agent.location = new_loc
    self.update_rangefinder_sensors()
    self.update_radars()
    distance = self.agent_distance_to_exit()
    self.exit_found = (distance < self.exit_range)
    return self.exit_found
```

The update(self, control_signals) function is defined in the MazeEnvironment class and is invoked in each simulation time step. It receives a list with control signals as input and returns a Boolean value indicating whether the maze-solver agent has reached the exit area after its position update.

The code at the beginning of this function applies received control signals to the current values of the agent's angular and linear velocities as follows (see the apply_control_signals(self, control_signals) function):

```
self.agent.angular_vel += (control_signals[0] - 0.5)
self.agent.speed += (control_signals[1] - 0.5)
```

After that, the x and y velocity components, along with the agents heading, are calculated and used to estimate its new position within the maze. If this new position doesn't collide with any of the maze walls, then it is assigned to the agent and becomes its current position:

```
vx = math.cos(geometry.deg_to_rad(self.agent.heading)) * \
            self.agent.speed
vy = math.sin(geometry.deg_to_rad(self.agent.heading)) * \
            self.agent.speed
self.agent.heading += self.agent.angular_vel
if self.agent.heading > 360:
    self.agent.heading -= 360
elif self.agent.heading < 0:
    self.agent.heading += 360
new_loc = geometry.Point(
    x = self.agent.location.x + vx,
    y = self.agent.location.y + vy
)
if not self.test_wall_collision(new_loc):
    self.agent.location = new_loc
```

After this, the new agent position is used in the following functions, which update the rangefinder and radar sensors to estimate new sensor inputs for the next time step:

```
self.update_rangefinder_sensors()
self.update_radars()
```

Finally, the following function tests whether the agent has reached the maze exit, which is defined by the circular area around the exit point with a radius equal to the value of the exit_range field:

```
distance = self.agent_distance_to_exit()
self.exit_found = (distance < self.exit_range)
return self.exit_found
```

If the maze exit has been reached, the value of the `exit_found` field is set to `True` to indicate the successful completion of the task, and its value is returned from the function call.

 For more implementation details, refer to the `maze_environment.py` file at `https://github.com/PacktPublishing/Hands-on-Neuroevolution-with-Python/blob/master/Chapter5/maze_environment.py`.

Agents records store

After completing the experiment, we are interested in evaluating and visualizing how each individual solver agent performed during the evolutionary process through all generations. This is accomplished by collecting additional statistical data about each agent after running the maze-solving simulation for a specified number of time steps. The collection of agent records is mediated by two Python classes: `AgentRecord` and `AgentRecordStore`.

The `AgentRecord` class consists of several data fields, as can be seen in the class constructor:

```
def __init__(self, generation, agent_id):
    self.generation = generation
    self.agent_id = agent_id
    self.x = -1
    self.y = -1
    self.fitness = -1
    self.hit_exit = False
    self.species_id = -1
    self.species_age = -1
```

The fields are defined as follows:

- `generation` holds the ID of the generation when the agent record was created.
- `agent_id` is a unique agent identifier.
- `x` and `y` is the agent's position within the maze after a simulation has been completed.
- `fitness` is the resulting fitness score of the agent.
- `hit_exit` is a flag that indicates whether the agent has reached the maze exit area or not.
- `species_id` and `species_age` are the ID and age of the species the agent belongs to.

The `AgentRecordStore` class holds a list of agent records and provides functions to load/dump the collected records from/to the specific file.

 See the `agent.py` file in the directory associated with this chapter in the source code repository for the complete implementation details.

New `AgentRecord` instances are added to the store after evaluation of the genome fitness, as defined in the `eval_fitness(genome_id, genome, config, time_steps=400)` function implemented in the `maze_experiment.py` file. This is done with the following code:

```
def eval_fitness(genome_id, genome, config, time_steps=400):
    maze_env = copy.deepcopy(trialSim.orig_maze_environment)
    control_net = neat.nn.FeedForwardNetwork.create(genome, config)
    fitness = maze.maze_simulation_evaluate(
            env=maze_env, net=control_net, time_steps=time_steps)
    record = agent.AgentRecord(
        generation=trialSim.population.generation,
        agent_id=genome_id)
    record.fitness = fitness
    record.x = maze_env.agent.location.x
    record.y = maze_env.agent.location.y
    record.hit_exit = maze_env.exit_found
    record.species_id = trialSim.population.species.\
                                    get_species_id(genome_id)
    record.species_age = record.generation - \
       trialSim.population.species.get_species(genome_id).created
    trialSim.record_store.add_record(record)
    return fitness
```

This code first creates a deep copy of the original maze environment to avoid interference between evaluation runs. After that, it creates the control ANN from the specified genome using the provided NEAT configuration and starts the evaluation of the maze simulation for a given number of time steps. The returned fitness score of the agent along with other statistics are then stored into a particular `AgentRecord` instance and are added to the record store.

The records collected during one trial of the experiment will be saved to the `data.pickle` file in the `output` directory and used to visualize the performance of all the evaluated agents.

See the `maze_experiment.py` file for the complete implementation details: `https://github.com/PacktPublishing/Hands-on-Neuroevolution-with-Python/blob/master/Chapter5/maze_experiment.py`.

The agent record visualization

After all agents' evaluation records are collected during the neuroevolutionary process, we are interested in visualizing the recorded data to get insights into performance. The visualization should include the final positions of all solver agents and allow to set the threshold value for the fitness of the species to control what species will be added to the corresponding plot. We decided to present the collected agent records in two plots drawn one above the other. The top plot is for the agent records that belong to the species with a fitness score greater than or equal to the specified fitness threshold, and the bottom plot is for the rest of the records.

The visualization of the agent records is implemented in the new methods in the `visualize.py` script. You should already be familiar with this script from the previous experiments described in this book.

See the `draw_maze_records(maze_env, records, best_threshold=0.8, filename=None, view=False, show_axes=False, width=400, height=400)` function definition in the `visualize.py` file at `https://github.com/PacktPublishing/Hands-on-Neuroevolution-with-Python/blob/master/Chapter5/visualize.py`.

Objective function definition using the fitness score

In this section, you will learn about the creation of successful maze-solver agents using a goal-oriented objective function to guide the evolutionary process. This objective function is based on the estimation of the fitness score of the maze solver by measuring the distance between its final position and the maze exit after executing the 400 simulation steps. Thus, the objective function is goal-oriented and solely depends on the ultimate goal of the experiment: reaching the maze exit area.

In the next chapter, we will consider a different approach for solution search optimization, which is based on the **Novelty Search** (**NS**) optimization method. The NS optimization method is built around exploring new configurations of the solver agent during evolution and doesn't include proximity to the final goal (in this case, the maze exit) in the objective function definition. We will demonstrate that the NS approach can outperform the conventional goal-oriented objective function definition that we consider in this chapter.

The goal-oriented objective function used in this experiment is determined as follows. First, we need to define the loss function as the *Euclidean distance* between the final position of the agent at the end of the simulation and the position of the maze exit:

$$\mathcal{L} = \sqrt{\sum_{i=1}^{2}(a_i - b_i)^2}$$

$\mathcal{L}$ is a loss function, a is the coordinates of the final position of the agent, and b is the coordinates of the maze exit. In this experiment, we considered a two-dimensional maze configuration, so the coordinates have two values, one for each dimension.

With the loss function defined previously, we now can specify the fitness function:

$$\mathcal{F} = \begin{cases} 1.0 & \mathcal{L} <= R_{exit} \\ \mathcal{F}_n & \text{otherwise} \end{cases}$$

R_{exit} is the radius of the exit area around the maze exit point and $\mathcal{F}_n$ is the normalized fitness score. The normalized fitness score is given as follows:

$$\mathcal{F}_n = \frac{\mathcal{L} - D_{init}}{D_{init}}$$

D_{init} is the initial distance from the solver agent to the maze exit at the start of the navigation simulation.

The equation normalizes the fitness score to be in the range $(0, 1]$, but can result in negative values in rare cases when the final position of the agent is far away from its initial position and the maze exit. The following amendments to the normalized fitness score will be applied to avoid negative values:

$$\mathcal{F}_n = \begin{cases} 0.01 & \mathcal{F}_n <= 0 \\ \mathcal{F}_n & \text{otherwise} \end{cases}$$

When the fitness score is less than or equal to `0.01`, it will be assigned the minimal fitness score value (`0.01`) supported; otherwise, it will be used as is. We selected the minimal fitness score to be higher than zero to give every genome the chance to reproduce.

The following code in Python implements the goal-oriented objective function:

```python
# Calculate the fitness score based on distance from exit
fitness = env.agent_distance_to_exit()
if fitness <= self.exit_range:
    fitness = 1.0
else:
    # Normalize fitness score to range (0,1]
    fitness = (env.initial_distance - fitness) / \
            env.initial_distance
    if fitness <= 0.01:
        fitness = 0.01
```

The code first invokes the `agent_distance_to_exit()` function, which calculates the Euclidean distance from the current agent position to the maze exit and uses the returned value as a first approximation of the fitness score. After that, the fitness score (distance to the maze exit) is compared with the exit range value. If the fitness score is less or equal to the exit range value, we assign it the final value of `1.0`. Otherwise, the normalized fitness score is calculated as a division of the difference between the final and initial distances from the agent to the maze exit by the initial distance. Sometimes, this can lead to a negative value of the normalized fitness value, which is corrected by comparing the fitness value with `0.01` and making the necessary amendments.

 See the `maze_environment.py` script for complete implementation details.

Running the experiment with a simple maze configuration

We start our experiments related to the creation of the successful maze navigation agent with a simple maze configuration. The simple maze configuration, while having the deceptive *local optima cul-de-sacs* discussed earlier, has a relatively straightforward path from the start point to the exit point.

The following diagram represents the maze configuration used for this experiment:

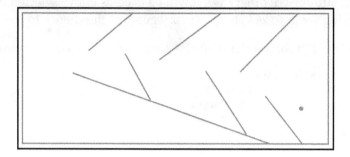

The simple maze configuration

The maze in the diagram has two specific positions marked with filled circles. The top-left circle denotes the starting position of the maze navigator agent. The bottom-right circle marks the exact location of the maze exit that needs to be found by the maze solver. The maze solver is required to reach the vicinity of the maze exit point denoted by the specific exit range area around it in order to complete the task.

Hyperparameter selection

According to the objective function definition, the maximum value of the navigator agent fitness score that can be obtained by reaching the maze exit area is 1.0. We are also expecting that the initial configuration of the controller ANN is more complicated than in the previous experiments described earlier in the book, and this will impact the speed of the algorithm's execution. Due to this, it would take too long on a moderate PC to complete the neuroevolution algorithm with a significantly large genome population. But at the same time, the task at hand is much more complicated than in previous experiments and requires using a wider search area for successful solution exploration. Thus, through trial and error, we found that the population size can be set to 250.

The following section from the configuration file contains the definition of the parameters we've just discussed:

```
[NEAT]
fitness_criterion = max
fitness_threshold = 1.0
pop_size = 250
reset_on_extinction = False
```

The initial configuration of the phenotype ANN includes 10 input nodes, 2 output nodes, and 1 hidden node. The input and output nodes correspond to the input sensors and the control signal outputs. The hidden node is provided to introduce non-linearity from the start of the neuroevolutionary process and to save time for the evolution process to discover it. The ANN configuration is as follows:

```
num_hidden = 1
num_inputs = 10
num_outputs = 2
```

To extend the solution search area, we need to boost the speciation of the population to try different genome configurations within a limited number of generations. This can be done either by reducing the compatibility threshold or by increasing the values of the coefficients that are used to perform the calculation of genome compatibility scores.

In this experiment, we used both amendments because the fitness function landscape is deceptive, and we need to emphasize even tiny changes in the genome configurations to create a new species. The following configuration parameters are affected:

```
[NEAT]
compatibility_disjoint_coefficient = 1.1
[DefaultSpeciesSet]
compatibility_threshold = 3.0
```

We are particularly interested in creating the optimal configuration of a maze solver control ANN that has a minimum number of hidden nodes and connections. The optimal ANN configuration is less computationally expensive during training by the neuroevolutionary process, as well as during the inference phase in a maze-solving simulator. The optimal ANN configuration can be produced by reducing the likelihood of adding new nodes, as shown in the following snippet from the NEAT configuration file:

```
node_add_prob            = 0.1
node_delete_prob         = 0.1
```

Finally, we allow the neuroevolutionary process to exploit not only the ANN configurations with feed-forward connections, but also recurrent ones. By having the recurrent connections, we enable the possibility for the ANN to have a memory and become a state machine. This happens to be beneficial for the evolutionary process. The following configuration hyperparameter controls this behavior:

```
feed_forward             = False
```

The hyperparameters described in this section were found to be beneficial to the NEAT algorithm that is used in the experiment to create a successful maze-solving agent within a limited number of generations.

 For the complete list of the hyperparameters used in the simple maze-solving experiment, please refer to the `maze_config.ini` file at `https://github.com/PacktPublishing/Hands-on-Neuroevolution-with-Python/blob/master/Chapter5/maze_config.ini`.

Maze configuration file

The maze configuration for our experiment is provided in plain text. This file is loaded into the simulation environment, and the corresponding maze configuration becomes instantiated. The configuration file has content similar to the following:

```
11
30 22
0
270 100
5 5 295 5
295 5 295 135
295 135 5 135
...
```

The format of the maze configuration file is as follows:

- The first line holds the number of walls in the maze.
- The second line determines the agent's starting position (x, y).
- The third line denotes the initial heading of the agent in degrees.
- The fourth line holds the maze exit position (x, y).
- The following lines define the walls of the maze. The number of maze walls is given by the first number in the file.

The maze wall is presented as a line segment with the first two numbers defining the coordinates of the starting point and the last two numbers determining the coordinates of the endpoint. The starting position of the agent and the maze exit are presented in the form of two numbers indicating the x and y coordinates of a point in a two-dimensional space.

Working environment setup

The working environment for the simple maze-solving experiment can be set up with the following commands entered in your terminal application of choice:

```
$ conda create --name maze_objective_neat python=3.5
$ conda activate maze_objective_neat
$ pip install neat-python==0.92
$ conda install matplotlib
$ conda install graphviz
$ conda install python-graphviz
```

These commands create and activate a `maze_objective_neat` virtual environment with Python 3.5. After that, the NEAT-Python library with version 0.92 was installed, along with other dependencies used by our visualization utilities.

After that, we are ready to start with the implementation of the experiment runner.

The experiment runner implementation

The experiment runner is implemented in the `maze_experiment.py` file, which you should refer to for the complete implementation details. This Python script provides functions to read command-line arguments, to configure and start the neuroevolution process, and to render the experiment's results after completion. Also, it includes the implementation of callback functions to evaluate the fitness of genomes belonging to the particular population. These callback functions will be provided to the NEAT-Python library environment during the initialization.

Further, we discuss the essential parts of the experiment runner's implementation that were not addressed previously in this chapter:

1. We begin by initializing the maze simulation environment with the following lines:

```
maze_env_config = os.path.join(local_dir, '%s_maze.txt' %
                               args.maze)
maze_env = maze.read_environment(maze_env_config)
```

`args.maze` refers to the command-line argument supplied by the user when starting the Python script and refers to the type of maze environment with which we would like to experiment. It can have two values: *medium* and *hard*. The former refers to the simple maze configuration that we use in this experiment.

2. After that, we set the specific seed number for the random number generator, create the NEAT configuration object, and create the `neat.Population` object using the created configuration object:

```
seed = 1559231616
random.seed(seed)
config = neat.Config(neat.DefaultGenome,
                     neat.DefaultReproduction,
                     neat.DefaultSpeciesSet,
                     neat.DefaultStagnation,
                     config_file)
p = neat.Population(config)
```

 It happens that the random seed value found in the double-pole balancing experiment is suitable for this experiment too. We can assume that we found a random attractor that is specific to the stochastic process implemented by the NEAT-Python library. Later in the book, we will check whether this is true for other experiments as well.

3. Now we are ready to create the appropriate maze simulation environment and store it as a global variable to simplify access to it from the fitness evaluation callback functions:

```
global trialSim
trialSim = MazeSimulationTrial(maze_env=maze_env,
                               population=p)
```

The `MazeSimulationTrial` object holds fields that provide access to the original maze simulation environment and to the record store used to save the evaluation results of the maze-solver agents. At each call to the fitness evaluation callback function, `eval_fitness(genome_id, genome, config, time_steps=400)`, the original maze simulation environment will be duplicated and will be used for the maze-solving simulation by a specific solver agent for 400 time steps. After that, the full statistics about the maze-solver agent, including its final position within the maze, will be collected from the environment and added to the record store.

4. The following code has become standard for our experiments, and it is related to adding various statistics reporters:

```
p.add_reporter(neat.StdOutReporter(True))
stats = neat.StatisticsReporter()
p.add_reporter(stats)
p.add_reporter(neat.Checkpointer(5,
            filename_prefix='%s/maze-neat-checkpoint-' %
            trial_out_dir))
```

The reporters are used to display the intermediate results of the neuroevolution process to the console, as well as to collect more detailed statistics that will be rendered after the process is completed.

5. Finally, we run the neuroevolution process for the specified number of generations and check whether the solution has been found:

```
start_time = time.time()
best_genome = p.run(eval_genomes, n=n_generations)
elapsed_time = time.time() - start_time
solution_found = (best_genome.fitness >= \
            config.fitness_threshold)
if solution_found:
    print("SUCCESS: The stable maze solver controller was
found!!!")
    else:
        print("FAILURE: Failed to find the stable maze solver
controller!!!")
```

We assume that a solution has been found if the best genome returned by the NEAT-Python library has a fitness score that is greater than or equal to the fitness threshold value set in the configuration file (1.0). The elapsed time is calculated to print how long it took to complete the process.

Genome fitness evaluation

The callback function to evaluate the fitness scores of all genomes belonging to a particular population of organisms is implemented as follows:

```
def eval_genomes(genomes, config):
    for genome_id, genome in genomes:
        genome.fitness = eval_fitness(genome_id, genome, config)
```

The `eval_fitness(genome_id, genome, config)` function evaluates the fitness of a specific genome by running the maze-solving simulation against the solver agent controlled by the ANN encoded with this genome. The implementation of this function is not provided here as it has already been discussed in this chapter.

Running the simple maze navigation experiment

Having implemented the maze-solver simulator, as well as the experiment runner and fitness evaluation callbacks, we are ready to start a maze-solving experiment. Make sure you copy all the related Python scripts and configuration files (`maze_config.ini` and `medium_maze.txt`) into the working directory.

After that, enter this directory and execute the following command from your terminal application of choice:

```
$ python maze_experiment.py -m medium -g 150
```

 Do not forget to activate the appropriate virtual environment with the following command:

```
conda activate maze_objective_neat
```

The preceding command loads the simple maze configuration from the `medium_maze.txt` file and creates the appropriate maze simulation environment. After that, it launches the neuroevolutionary process under the control of the NEAT algorithm, using the hyperparameters specified in the `maze_config.ini` file. The NEAT algorithm uses a maze-solver simulation environment to evaluate the fitness of every genome produced during the neuroevolution over 150 generations (`-g` in the command-line arguments).

After 144 generations of evolution, the successful maze-solver agent is found at generation 145. The console output for the last generation is as follows:

1. First, general statistics about the genome population:

```
****** Running generation 145 ******

Maze solved in 388 steps
Population's average fitness: 0.24758 stdev: 0.25627
Best fitness: 1.00000 - size: (3, 11) - species 7 - id 35400

Best individual in generation 145 meets fitness threshold -
complexity: (3, 11)
```

2. Second, the configuration of the genome encoding the successful maze-solver controller ANN:

```
Best genome:
Key: 35400
Fitness: 1.0
Nodes:
  0 DefaultNodeGene(key=0, bias=5.534849614521037, response=1.0,
activation=sigmoid, aggregation=sum)
  1 DefaultNodeGene(key=1, bias=1.8031133229851957, response=1.0,
activation=sigmoid, aggregation=sum)
  158 DefaultNodeGene(key=158, bias=-1.3550878188609456,
response=1.0, activation=sigmoid, aggregation=sum)
Connections:
  DefaultConnectionGene(key=(-10, 158), weight=-1.6144052085440168,
enabled=True)
  DefaultConnectionGene(key=(-8, 158), weight=-1.1842193888036392,
enabled=True)
  DefaultConnectionGene(key=(-7, 0), weight=-0.3263706518456319,
enabled=True)
  DefaultConnectionGene(key=(-7, 1), weight=1.3186165993348418,
enabled=True)
  DefaultConnectionGene(key=(-6, 0), weight=2.0778575294986945,
enabled=True)
  DefaultConnectionGene(key=(-6, 1), weight=-2.9478037554862824,
enabled=True)
  DefaultConnectionGene(key=(-6, 158), weight=0.6930281879212032,
enabled=True)
  DefaultConnectionGene(key=(-4, 1), weight=-1.9583885391583729,
enabled=True)
  DefaultConnectionGene(key=(-3, 1), weight=5.5239054588484775,
enabled=True)
  DefaultConnectionGene(key=(-1, 0), weight=0.04865917999517305,
enabled=True)
  DefaultConnectionGene(key=(158, 0), weight=0.6973191076874032,
enabled=True)
SUCCESS: The stable maze solver controller was found!!!
Record store file: out/maze_objective/medium/data.pickle
```

In the console output, you can see that the successful maze solver controller was found during evolution and was able to reach the maze exit area in 388 steps from the allotted 400. The configuration of the control ANN of the successful maze solver consists of 2 output nodes and 1 hidden node, with 11 connections in between these nodes and from the inputs. The final configuration of the controller ANN is shown in the following diagram:

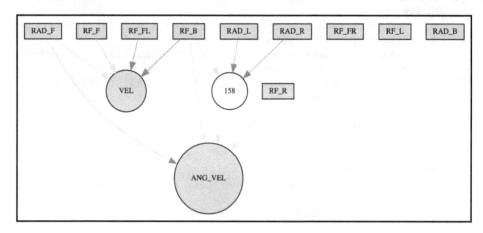

The ANN configuration controlling a successful solver of a simple maze

It is interesting to look at the graph to study how different sensor inputs influence the output control signals. We can see that the ANN configuration completely ignores the inputs from the front and left rangefinder sensors (**RF_FR** and **RF_L**) and from the backward pie-slice radar sensor (**RAD_B**) of the robot. At the same time, the linear and angular velocities of the robot are controlled by unique combinations of other sensors.

Furthermore, we can see the aggregation of the left and right pie-slice radar sensors (**RAD_L** and **RAD_R**) with the backward rangefinder (**RF_B**) through the hidden node, which then relayed an aggregated signal to a node controlling the angular velocity. If we take a look at the simple maze configuration image shown in this chapter (see the simple maze configuration image), the aggregation seems pretty natural. This allows the robot to turn around and continue to explore the maze when it is trapped in dead ends, where the local fitness optima are located.

The fitness scores of the solver agents over generations is shown here:

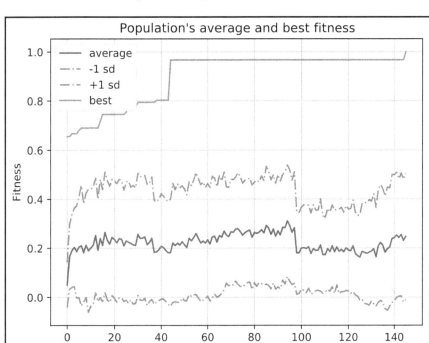

The average fitness scores over generations

In this plot, we can see that the evolutionary process was able to produce pretty successful maze-solver agents at generation 44 with a fitness score of **0.96738**. But it took an additional 100 generations to evolve the genome that encodes the ANN of the successful maze-solver agent.

Also, it is interesting to note that the boost in performance at generation 44 is generated by the species with ID 1, but the genome of the successful maze solver belongs to a species with ID 7, which was not even known at the time of the first spike. The species producing the champion appeared after 12 generations and remained in the population until the end, preserving the beneficial mutation and elaborating over it.

The speciation over generations is shown in the following plot:

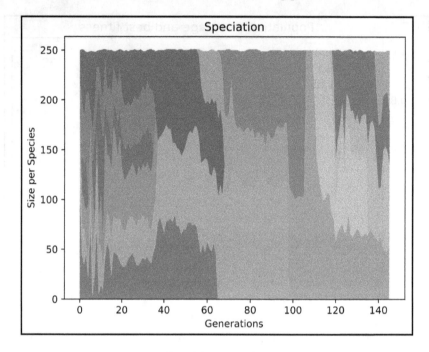

The speciation over generations

On the speciation plot, we can see the species with ID 7 marked in pink. This species ultimately produced the genome of the successful maze solver during the evolutionary process. The size of species 7 varies considerably throughout its life, and at one time it was the only species in the entire population for several generations (from 105 until 108).

Agent record visualization

In this experiment, we presented a new visualization method that allows us to visually discern the performance of various species in the evolutionary process. The visualization can be performed using the following command, executed from the working directory of the experiment:

```
$ python visualize.py -m medium -r out/maze_objective/medium/data.pickle --
width 300 --height 150
```

The command loads records about the fitness evaluation of each maze-solving agent during the evolution, which is stored in the `data.pickle` file. After that, it draws the final positions of the agents on the maze map at the end of the maze-solving simulation. Each agent's final position is presented as a color-coded circle. The color of the circle encodes the species to which the particular agent belongs. Each species produced during the evolution has a unique color code. The results of this visualization can be seen in the following plot:

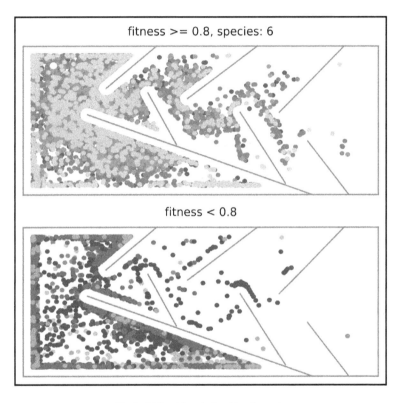

The visualization of the evaluation of the solver agents

To make the visualization more informative, we have introduced the fitness threshold to filter out the most performant species. The top subplot shows the final positions of the solver agents belonging to the champion species (the fitness score is above **0.8**). As you can see, the organisms belonging to these six species are active explorers, who have genes inciting search through unknown places in the maze. Their final locations are distributed almost uniformly through the maze area around the starting point and have a low density at the local optima *cul-de-sacs*.

At the same time, you can see in the bottom subplot that the evolutionary losers demonstrate more conservative behavior, concentrating mainly near the walls in the starting area and in the strongest local optima region—the biggest *cul-de-sac*, which is at the bottom of the maze.

Exercises

1. Try to increase the `compatibility_disjoint_coefficient` parameter in the `maze_config.ini` file and run the experiment with new settings. What impact does this modification have on the number of species produced during the evolution? Is the neuroevolution process able to find a successful maze solver?
2. Increase the population size by 200% (the `pop_size` parameter). Was the neuroevolution process able to find a solution in this case, and if so, how many generations did it take?
3. Change the seed value of the random number generator (see line 118 of the `maze_experiment.py` file). Does the neuroevolution process succeed with this new value?

Running the experiment with a hard-to-solve maze configuration

The next experiment in this chapter is to run the neuroevolution process to find an agent that can solve a maze with a more complex configuration of walls. This hard-to-solve maze configuration introduces powerful local fitness optima traps and does not have a straightforward route from the start position of the agent to the exit area of the maze. You can see the maze configuration in the following diagram:

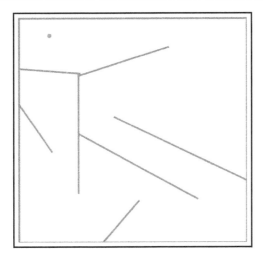

The hard-to-solve maze configuration

The maze configuration has its start position in the bottom-left corner, marked with a green circle, and the position of the maze exit point is in the top-left corner, marked with a red circle. You can see that, to solve the maze, the navigator agent must develop a complex control strategy that allows it to avoid the local fitness optima traps around the starting point. The control strategy needs to be able to follow an elaborate trajectory from the starting point to the exit, which has several turns and more local optima traps.

Hyperparameter selection

For this experiment, we will use the same hyperparameters that we used in the simple maze solving experiment. Our idea is to have the same initial conditions for the neuroevolutionary algorithm and to see whether it can evolve a successful solver agent for a different, more complex maze configuration. This will indicate how well the algorithm generalizes using the hyperparameter settings used for a different maze configuration.

Working environment setup and experiment runner implementation

The setup of the working environment remains the same as for a simple maze navigation experiment. The experiment runner implementation also remains the same. We only change the file describing the maze environment configuration.

Running the hard-to-solve maze navigation experiment

As we mentioned, we will use the same experiment runner implementation and the same NEAT hyperparameters settings as in the previous experiment. But we will configure the different maze environment as follows:

```
$ python maze_experiment.py -m hard -g 500
```

After a while, when the experiment is over, we see that even after 500 generations of evolution, a successful maze solver has not been found. The best genome obtained using the neuroevolution algorithm encodes a bizarre and non-functional controller ANN configuration, which is shown in the following diagram:

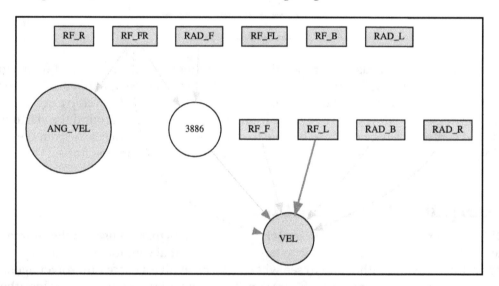

ANN configuration controlling the solver of the hard-to-solve maze

It can be seen in the graph that the rotation of the robot depends only on the frontal rangefinder sensor (**RF_FR**), and the linear movement is controlled by a combination of several rangefinders and radar sensors. Such control configuration leads to simplified linear movements of the robot until a wall is detected in front of the robot. Our assumption about motion patterns is confirmed when we look at the visualization of the agent evaluation records:

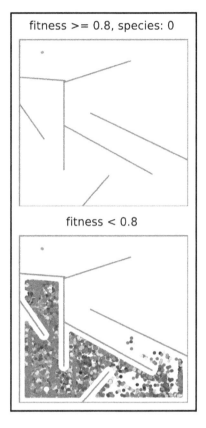

The visualization of solver agents' evaluation records

The visualization of the final positions of the solver agents demonstrates that most species are trapped around the start position, where some areas of local fitness score optima are located. None of the species could even show a fitness score above our threshold (**0.8**). Also, as we mentioned earlier, there are clearly distinguishable vertical lines formed by the final positions of the solver agents (gray dots creating vertical columns). This confirms our assumption about the incorrect configuration of the controller ANN that was encoded by the best genome found during the evolutionary process.

The average fitness scores over generations are shown in the following plot:

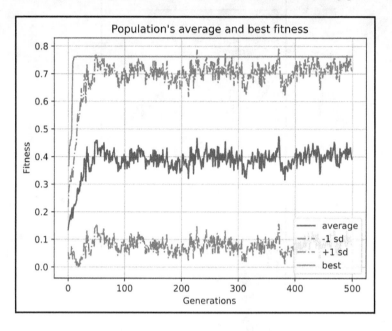

The average fitness score over generations

In the plot of the average fitness scores, we can see that the neuroevolutionary process was able to significantly increase the fitness scores of solver agents in the very first generations, but after that it reached a plateau, showing no improvements. This means that a further increase in the number of evolutionary generations does not make any sense, and other measures need to be taken to improve the performance of the neuroevolutionary process.

Exercises

1. Try to increase the population size by tweaking the `pop_size` parameter in the `maze_config.ini` file. Did this help the neuroevolutionary process to evolve a successful maze solver?

 This may take a long time to execute.

Summary

In this chapter, you have learned about a class of planning and control problems that use goal-oriented fitness functions that have a deceptive definition landscape. In this landscape, there are multiple traps created by the local optima areas of the fitness function that mislead the solution search process, which is based only on the fitness score calculated as a derivative of the distance from the agent to the goal. You have learned that the conventional goal-oriented fitness function can help the search process to create a successful maze navigator agent for a simple maze configuration, but failed with a more complex maze due to the local optima traps.

We presented a useful visualization method that allowed us to visualize the final positions of all evaluated agents on the maze map. With this visualization, you can make assumptions about the performance of the evolutionary process. You can then make decisions about changes to the configuration settings that may lead to further performance improvements.

Also, you have learned that when there is a higher chance of fitness function convergence in the local optima, the neuroevolution process tends to produce fewer species. In extreme cases, it creates only one species, which impedes innovation and hinders the evolutionary process. To avoid this, you learned how speciation can be boosted by changing the value of the compatibility disjoint coefficient, which is used in the calculation of the genome compatibility factor. This coefficient controls the weight that will be assigned to the excess or disjoint parts of genomes being compared. Higher coefficient values increase the importance of topological differences in the compared genomes and allow more diverse genomes to belong to the same species.

In the next chapter, we will present the NS optimization method, which is better at solving deceptive tasks such as maze navigation.

6
Novelty Search Optimization Method

In this chapter, you will learn about an advanced solution search optimization method that can be used to create autonomous navigator agents. This method is called **Novelty Search (NS)**. The main idea of this method is that an objective function can be defined using the novelty of the behavior exposed by the solver agent, rather than the distance to a goal in the solution search space.

In this chapter, you will learn how to use NS-based search optimization methods with the neuroevolution algorithm to train successful maze navigation agents. By conducting the experiments presented in this chapter, you will also see that the NS method is superior to the conventional goal-oriented search optimization method for specific tasks. By the end of this chapter, you will have learned the basics of the NS optimization method. You will be able to define the fitness function using the novelty score and apply it to solve practical tasks related to your work or experiments.

The following topics will be covered in this chapter:

- The NS optimization method
- NS implementation basics
- The fitness function with the novelty score
- Experimenting with a simple maze configuration
- Experimenting with a hard-to-solve maze configuration

Technical requirements

The following technical requirements should be met in order to carry out the experiments described in this chapter:

- Windows 8/10, macOS 10.13 or newer, or modern Linux
- Anaconda Distribution version 2019.03 or newer

The code for this chapter can be found at `https://github.com/PacktPublishing/Hands-on-Neuroevolution-with-Python/tree/master/Chapter6`

The NS optimization method

The main idea behind NS is to reward the novelty of the produced solution rather than its progress to the final goal. This idea is inspired by natural evolution. When looking for a successful solution, it is not always obvious the exact steps that should be taken. Natural evolution continuously produces novel forms, with different phenotypes trying to exploit the surrounding environment and adapt to the changes. This has allowed an explosion of life forms on Earth and ignited qualitative leaps forward in the evolution of life. The same process allowed life forms to leave the sea and conquer the land. The extraordinary genesis of eukaryotes became the source of all higher life forms on the planet. All these are examples of rewarding novelty during evolution. At the same time, there is no clear objective or final goal in natural evolution.

As you learned in the previous chapter, conventional goal-oriented fitness functions are susceptible to local optima traps. This pathology produces pressure on the evolutionary process to converge to a single solution that often gets stuck in dead ends in a search space, with no local steps available that can improve the performance of the fitness function any further. Thus, as a result, the successful solution is left unexplored.

On the other hand, NS drives evolution toward diversity. This drive helps the neuroevolution process to produce successful solver agents, even for tasks with a deceptive landscape of the fitness function values, such as maze navigation problems.

A real-life example of such a deceptive problem is the task of navigating around an unknown city. If you visit old cities with irregular road maps, you need to use a different strategy to get from point A to point B than in modern cities with regular grid patterns of roads. In modern cities, traveling along roads that point in the direction of your destination is sufficient, but navigation in old cities is much more tricky. Heading toward the destination often leads you to dead ends (deceptive local optima). You need to employ a more explorative approach, trying novel and often counterintuitive directions that seemingly lead you away from your destination. So, finally, after another twist in the road, you reach your destination. However, note that from the start it was not obvious which turns to take based only on the distance to the final destination (that is, the goal-oriented fitness score). The stepping stones leading to the ultimate solution are often placed in counterintuitive places that seem to lead you away, but ultimately help you to succeed.

Please refer to `Chapter 1`, *Overview of Neuroevolution Methods*, for more details about NS optimization.

NS implementation basics

NS implementation should include data structure to hold information about the explored novel item and the structure to maintain and manage a list of novel items. In our implementation, this functionality is encapsulated in three Python classes:

- `NoveltyItem`: The structure that holds all relevant information about the novelty score of the individual that was evaluated during the evolution.
- `NoveltyArchive`: The class that maintains a list of the relevant `NoveltyItem` instances. It provides methods to evaluate the novelty scores of individual genomes compared to the already collected `NoveltyItem` instances and the current population.
- `ItemsDistance`: The auxiliary structure that holds the distance (novelty) metric value between the two `NoveltyItem` instances. It is used in calculations of the average k-nearest neighbor distance, which is used as a novelty score value in our experiment.

For implementation details, refer to the `novelty_archive.py` file at `https://github.com/PacktPublishing/Hands-on-Neuroevolution-with-Python/blob/master/Chapter6/novelty_archive.py`.

NoveltyItem

This class is the main structure that holds information about the novelty score of each individual evaluated during the evolution. It has several fields that store relevant information, as we can see in the source code:

```
def __init__(self, generation=-1, genomeId=-1, fitness=-1, novelty=-1):
    self.generation = generation
    self.genomeId = genomeId
    self.fitness = fitness
    self.novelty = novelty
    self.in_archive = False
    self.data = []
```

The `generation` field holds the ID of the generation at which this item was created. Basically, `genomeId` is the ID of the genome that was evaluated, and `fitness` is a goal-oriented fitness score of the evaluated genome (the proximity to the maze exit). Furthermore, `novelty` is the novelty score given to the evaluated genome, as we discuss in the next section, and `data` is a list of data points representing the coordinates of specific maze positions that the maze solver agent visited during a simulation. This data list is used to estimate the distance between the current and other novelty items. The calculated distance after that can be used to estimate the novelty score associated with the specific novelty item.

NoveltyArchive

This class maintains a list of relevant novelty items and provides methods to evaluate the novelty scores of individual genomes as well as of the entire population of genomes as a whole. It has the following fields defined in the constructor:

```
def __init__(self, threshold, metric):
    self.novelty_metric = metric
    self.novelty_threshold = threshold
    self.novelty_floor = 0.25
    self.items_added_in_generation = 0
    self.time_out = 0
    self.neighbors = KNNNoveltyScore
    self.generation = 0
    self.novel_items = []
    self.fittest_items = []
```

Note that `novelty_metric` is a reference to the function that can be used to estimate the novelty metric or distance between two novelty items.

Furthermore, `novelty_threshold` defines the current minimal novelty score value of `NoveltyItem` to be eligible for adding to this archive. This value is dynamic and is changed during execution to maintain the size of the archive within particular limits; `novelty_floor` is the minimal possible value of `novelty_threshold`. The `items_added_in_generation` and `time_out` fields are used to schedule the dynamics of the change of the `novelty_threshold` values. The `neighbors` field is a default number of *k-nearest neighbors* to use for a novelty score estimation. The generation is the current evolutionary generation. Basically, `novel_items` is a list of all the relevant `NoveltyItem` instances collected so far, and `fittest_items` is the list of the novel items having the maximal goal-oriented fitness score among all.

The dynamics of the `novelty_threshold` field are determined by the following source code:

```python
def _adjust_archive_settings(self):
    if self.items_added_in_generation == 0:
        self.time_out += 1
    else:
        self.time_out = 0
    if self.time_out >= 10:
        self.novelty_threshold *= 0.95
        if self.novelty_threshold < self.novelty_floor:
            self.novelty_threshold = self.novelty_floor
        self.time_out = 0
    if self.items_added_in_generation >= 4:
        self.novelty_threshold *= 1.2
    self.items_added_in_generation = 0
```

The preceding function is invoked at the end of each evolutionary generation to adjust the `novelty_threshold` field value for the next generation. As already mentioned, this value determines how many novelty items should be added to the archive in the next generation. The dynamic adjustment of this property is necessary to match the difficulty of finding novel solutions using the NS method over time. At the beginning of the evolution, there were immense opportunities to find novel solutions with high novelty scores, since only a few paths were explored in the maze. However, toward the end of the evolution, it becomes harder because fewer unexplored paths remain. To compensate for this, if a novel path is not found in the last 2,500 evaluations (10 generations), the `novelty_threshold` value is lowered by 5%. On the other hand, to decrease the speed of adding a new `NoveltyItem` to the archive in the early stages of evolution, the `novelty_threshold` value is raised by 20%, if over four items were added in the last generation.

The following source code shows how the `novelty_threshold` value is used to determine which `NoveltyItem` to add:

```
def evaluate_individual_novelty(self, genome, genomes, n_items_map,
                                only_fitness=False):
    item = n_items_map[genome.key]
    result = 0.0
    if only_fitness:
        result = self._novelty_avg_knn(item=item, genomes=genomes,
                                       n_items_map=n_items_map)
    else:
        result = self._novelty_avg_knn(item=item, neighbors=1,
                                       n_items_map=n_items_map)
        if result > self.novelty_threshold or \
            len(self.novel_items) < ArchiveSeedAmount:
             self._add_novelty_item(item)
    item.novelty = result
    item.generation = self.generation
    return result
```

The preceding code uses a function to evaluate the novelty score, which we will describe in the next section to estimate the novelty of the provided genome. If this function is invoked in the update archive mode (`only_fitness = False`), then the obtained novelty score (`result`) is compared with the current value of the `novelty_threshold` field. Based on the results of the comparison, the `NoveltyItem` object is added to the `NoveltyArchive` object or not. Furthermore, the `ArchiveSeedAmount` constant is introduced to do initial seeding of the archive with the `NoveltyItem` instances at the beginnings of the evolution when the archive is still empty.

The fitness function with the novelty score

Now we have defined the basic principles behind the NS method, we need to find a way to integrate it into the definition of the fitness function that will be used to guide the neuroevolution process. In other words, we need to define the novelty metric that can capture the amount of novelty that is introduced by a particular solver agent during the evolutionary process. There are several characteristics that can be used as novelty metrics for a solver agent:

- The novelty of the solver genotype structure—the *structural* novelty
- The stepping stones found in the search space of the solution—the *behavioral* novelty

Our primary interest in this chapter is to create a successful maze navigator agent. To successfully navigate through the maze, the agent must pay equal attention to most places in the maze. Such behavior can be achieved by rewarding agents who choose a unique exploration path compared to already known paths from the previously tested agents. In terms of the types of the previously mentioned novelty metrics, this means that we need to define a fitness function using a metric built around *behavioral* novelty.

The novelty score

The behavioral space of the maze solver agent is defined by its trajectory through the maze while running the maze-solving simulation. An effective novelty score implementation needs to compute the sparseness at any point in such a behavioral space. Thus, any area with a denser cluster of visited points of behavior space is less novel, giving fewer rewards to the solver agent.

As mentioned in `Chapter 1`, *Overview of Neuroevolution Methods*, the most straightforward measure of sparseness at a point is the average distance from it to the *k-nearest neighbors*. The sparse areas have higher distance values, and the denser areas have lower distance values, correspondingly. The following formula gives the sparseness at point x of the behavioral space:

$$\rho(x) = \frac{1}{k} \sum_{i=0}^{k} dist(x, \mu_i)$$

Note μ_i is the $i - th$ nearest neighbor of x as calculated by the distance (novelty) metric, $dist(x, y)$.

The calculated by the above formula sparseness at the particular point in the behavioral space is a novelty score that can be used by the fitness function.

The Python code to find a novelty score is defined in the following function:

```
def _novelty_avg_knn(self, item, n_items_map, genomes=None,
                     neighbors=None):
    distances = None
    if genomes is not None:
        distances = self._map_novelty_in_population(item=item,
                       genomes=genomes, n_items_map=n_items_map)
    else:
        distances = self._map_novelty(item=item)
    distances.sort()
```

```
    if neighbors is None:
        neighbors = self.neighbors

    density, weight, distance_sum = 0.0, 0.0, 0.0
    length = len(distances)
    if length >= ArchiveSeedAmount:
        length = neighbors
        if len(distances) < length:
            length = len(distances)
        i = 0
        while weight < float(neighbors) and i < length:
            distance_sum += distances[i].distance
            weight += 1.0
            i += 1
        if weight > 0:
            sparsity = distance_sum / weight
    return sparsity
```

The preceding function has the following major implementation parts:

1. First, we check whether the `_novelty_avg_knn` function provided with the argument holds a list of all the genomes in the current population. In that case, we start by populating the list of distances between behavioral characteristics of all genomes in the population, including all the `NoveltyItem` objects from `NoveltyArchive`. Otherwise, we use the provided novelty item (`item`) to find distances between it and all `NoveltyItem` objects from `NoveltyArchive`.

   ```
   distances = None
   if genomes is not None:
       distances = self._map_novelty_in_population(item=item,
                       genomes=genomes, n_items_map=n_items_map)
   else:
       distances = self._map_novelty(item=item)
   ```

2. After that, we sort a list of distances in ascending order to have the smallest distances first because we are interested in the points that are closest to the provided novel item in the behavioral space:

   ```
   distances.sort()
   ```

3. Next, we initialize all the intermediate variables necessary for the k-nearest neighbors scores calculation, and test whether the number of distance values collected in the previous step is higher than the `ArchiveSeedAmount` constant value:

```
if neighbors is None:
    neighbors = self.neighbors

density, weight, distance_sum = 0.0, 0.0, 0.0
length = len(distances)
```

4. Now, we can check whether the length of the found distances list is less than the number of neighbors that we are asked to test against (`neighbors`). If so, we update the value of the related variable:

```
if length >= ArchiveSeedAmount:
    length = neighbors
    if len(distances) < length:
        length = len(distances)
```

5. After all the local variables are set to the correct values, we can start the cycle that collects the sum of all distances and weights for each connection:

```
i = 0
while weight < float(neighbors) and i < length:
    distance_sum += distances[i].distance
    weight += 1.0
    i += 1
```

6. When the preceding cycle exits because of the calculated weight value exceeding the specified number of neighbors, or if we already iterated over all distance values in the `distances` list, we are ready to calculate the novelty score for a given item as an average distance to the k-nearest neighbors:

```
if weight < 0:
    sparsity = distance_sum / weight
```

The function then returns the estimated novelty score value.

 For more implementation details, see the `novelty_archive.py` file at `https://github.com/PacktPublishing/Hands-on-Neuroevolution-with-Python/blob/master/Chapter6/novelty_archive.py`.

The novelty metric

The novelty metric is a measure of how different the current solution is from the already known ones. It is used to calculate the novelty score when estimating the distance from the current point in the behavioral space to its *k-nearest neighbors*.

In our experiment, the novelty metric measuring the difference in the behavior of the two agents is determined by the *item-wise distance* between the two trajectory vectors (one vector per agent). The trajectory vector contains the coordinates of the positions that were visited by the maze navigator agent during a simulation. The following formula gives the definition of the metric:

$$dist(x, \mu) = \frac{1}{n} \sum_{j=0}^{n} |x_j - \mu_j|$$

Note n is the size of the trajectory vector, and μ_j and x_j are the values at position j of the compared trajectory vectors, μ and x.

In a maze navigation experiment, we are mostly interested in the final position of the solver agent. Thus, the trajectory vector may only contain the final coordinates of the agent after completing all the necessary steps in the maze navigation simulation or when the maze exit is found.

The Python code for the novelty metric value estimation is as follows:

```python
def maze_novelty_metric(first_item, second_item):
    diff_accum = 0.0
    size = len(first_item.data)
    for i in range(size):
        diff = abs(first_item.data[i] - second_item.data[i])
        diff_accum += diff
    return diff_accum / float(size)
```

The preceding code takes two novelty items and finds the *item-wise* distance between the two trajectory vectors holding the positions of a corresponding solver agent during the simulation of a maze navigation.

Fitness function

The fitness function used in the experiments described in this chapter directly applies the novelty score defined previously as the fitness value of the genome. As a result, the neuroevolution process tries to maximize the novelty of the produced individuals by using such a fitness function.

For different tasks in this experiment, we use various fitness factors:

- The novelty score is used to guide the neuroevolution process (solution search optimization). It is assigned as a fitness value to each genome and used for genome evaluation during generations of evolution.
- The goal-oriented fitness score (the distance to the maze exit) obtained from the maze simulator is used to test if the ultimate goal has been achieved (that is, the maze exit has been found)—also, this value is recorded for performance evaluation of each solver agent.

The source code of the fitness values evaluation is presented in two functions:

- The callback function to evaluate the fitness scores of the entire population (`eval_genomes`)
- The function to evaluate individual genomes through the maze solving simulation (`eval_individual`)

The population fitness evaluation function

The fitness evaluation function is a callback function that is registered with the NEAT-Python library, allowing this library to run an evaluation of population genomes against specific conditions of a particular task that needs to be solved. We implement this function to evaluate each genome in the current population using the maze-solving task, and to use the obtained novelty score as a genome fitness value.

The NEAT-Python library doesn't allow us to send any signals about task completion from the callback function other than by specifying the specific fitness score value of the winner genome. This fitness value must be higher than the fitness threshold in the NEAT-Python hyperparameter configuration. However, with the NS algorithm, it is not possible to accurately estimate the upper limit of the novelty score that can be achieved by the winner genome. Furthermore, the winner genome can have the novelty score value that is below the values obtained by genomes earlier in the evolution process, when the solution search space was not so thoroughly explored.

Thus, given that the novelty score is assigned to genomes as their fitness values, we need to come up with a workaround that allows us to use the standard termination criteria defined by the NEAT-Python library. We do this by using a specific indicative novelty score value that is big enough to be encountered during normal algorithm execution. This value determines the termination criterion that is provided through the NEAT-Python hyperparameter configuration. We use `800000` as an indicative measure of the novelty score and its natural logarithm (about `13.59`) as the appropriate fitness threshold.

The full source code of the function is as follows:

```
def eval_genomes(genomes, config):
    n_items_map = {}
    solver_genome = None
    for genome_id, genome in genomes:
        found = eval_individual(genome_id=genome_id,
                                genome=genome,
                                genomes=genomes,
                                n_items_map=n_items_map,
                                config=config)
        if found:
            solver_genome = genome
    trial_sim.archive.end_of_generation()
    # Now evaluate fitness of each genome in population
    for genome_id, genome in genomes:
        fitness = trial_sim.archive.evaluate_individual_novelty(
                genome=genome,
                genomes=genomes,
                n_items_map=n_items_map,
                only_fitness=True)
        if fitness > 1:
            fitness = math.log(fitness)
        else:
            fitness = 0
        genome.fitness = fitness

    if solver_genome is not None:
        solver_genome.fitness = math.log(800000)  # ~=13.59
```

The significant parts of the implementation of the function are as follows:

1. First, we create the dictionary to store evaluated novelty items (`n_items_map`) for each genome in the population, and cycle through all genomes in the population, evaluating their maze-solving performance:

   ```
   n_items_map = {}
   solver_genome = None
   for genome_id, genome in genomes:
   ```

```
        found = eval_individual(genome_id=genome_id,
                                 genome=genome,
                                 genomes=genomes,
                                 n_items_map=n_items_map,
                                 config=config)
    if found:
        solver_genome = genome
trial_sim.archive.end_of_generation()
```

2. After that, we cycle through all genomes in the population one more time to assign fitness scores to the genomes using estimated novelty scores. The process of novelty score estimation uses the NoveltyItem objects collected in n_items_map in the first cycle (described earlier) during the maze-solving simulation:

```
for genome_id, genome in genomes:
    fitness = trial_sim.archive.evaluate_individual_novelty(
            genome=genome,
            genomes=genomes,
            n_items_map=n_items_map,
            only_fitness=True)
    if fitness > 1:
        fitness = math.log(fitness)
    else:
        fitness = 0
    genome.fitness = fitness
```

3. Finally, if a successful solver genome is found in the first cycle, we assign it with a fitness value equal to the indicative fitness score described earlier (~13.59):

```
if solver_genome is not None:
    solver_genome.fitness = math.log(800000) # ~13.59
```

Please note that we apply the natural logarithm to the obtained novelty score values and to the indicative novelty score to keep them in numerical proximity. As a result, we can properly render performance plots using statistics collected during the experiment.

The individual fitness evaluation function

This function is an essential part of the population fitness evaluation, and it is invoked from the eval_genomes function, discussed earlier, to evaluate the maze-solving performance of each genome in the population.

The evaluation of the individual genome as a maze-solving agent through the maze navigation simulation is as follows:

```python
def eval_individual(genome_id, genome, genomes, n_items_map, config):
    n_item = archive.NoveltyItem(
                         generation=trial_sim.population.generation,
                         genomeId=genome_id)
    n_items_map[genome_id] = n_item
    maze_env = copy.deepcopy(trial_sim.orig_maze_environment)
    control_net = neat.nn.FeedForwardNetwork.create(genome, config)
    goal_fitness = maze.maze_simulation_evaluate(
                                   env=maze_env,
                                   net=control_net,
                                   time_steps=SOLVER_TIME_STEPS,
                                   n_item=n_item,
                                   mcns=MCNS)

    if goal_fitness == -1:
        # The individual doesn't meet the min. fitness criterion
        print("Individ with ID %d marked for extinction, MCNS %f"
              % (genome_id, MCNS))
        return False

    record = agent.AgentRecord(
        generation=trial_sim.population.generation,
        agent_id=genome_id)
    record.fitness = goal_fitness
    record.x = maze_env.agent.location.x
    record.y = maze_env.agent.location.y
    record.hit_exit = maze_env.exit_found
    record.species_id = trial_sim.population.species \
        .get_species_id(genome_id)
    record.species_age = record.generation - \
        trial_sim.population.species.get_species(genome_id).created
    trial_sim.record_store.add_record(record)

    if not maze_env.exit_found:
        record.novelty = trial_sim.archive \
          .evaluate_individual_novelty(genome=genome,
                        genomes=genomes, n_items_map=n_items_map)

    trial_sim.archive.update_fittest_with_genome(genome=genome,
                                   n_items_map=n_items_map)
    return maze_env.exit_found
```

Let's delve into the meaning of all the central parts of the implementation of the `eval_individual` function:

1. First, we create the `NoveltyItem` object to hold information about the novelty score associated with a particular genome and save it under the `genome_id` key in the `n_items_map` dictionary:

```
n_item = archive.NoveltyItem(
                        generation=trial_sim.population.generation,
                        genomeId=genome_id)
n_items_map[genome_id] = n_item
```

2. After that, we create a deep copy of the original maze environment to avoid side effects during the simulation, and create the control ANN from the provided genome:

```
maze_env = copy.deepcopy(trial_sim.orig_maze_environment)
control_net = neat.nn.FeedForwardNetwork.create(genome, config)
```

3. Now, using a copy of the maze environment and the created control ANN, we execute the maze-solving simulation for a given number of simulation steps:

```
goal_fitness = maze.maze_simulation_evaluate(
                        env=maze_env,
                        net=control_net,
                        time_steps=SOLVER_TIME_STEPS,
                        n_item=n_item,
                        mcns=MCNS)
```

4. After the simulation is finished, the returned goal-based fitness score (proximity to the maze exit) and other simulation and genome parameters are stored in `AgentRecord`, which is then added to the record store:

```
record = agent.AgentRecord(
    generation=trial_sim.population.generation,
    agent_id=genome_id)
record.fitness = goal_fitness
record.x = maze_env.agent.location.x
record.y = maze_env.agent.location.y
record.hit_exit = maze_env.exit_found
record.species_id = trial_sim.population.species \
    .get_species_id(genome_id)
record.species_age = record.generation - \
    trial_sim.population.species.get_species(genome_id).created
trial_sim.record_store.add_record(record)
```

5. Finally, we estimate the novelty score of the given genome if it is not a winner, and update the list of the fittest genomes in `NoveltyArchive` with `NoveltyItem` of the current genome, if appropriate:

```
if not maze_env.exit_found:
    record.novelty = trial_sim.archive \
      .evaluate_individual_novelty(genome=genome,
          genomes=genomes, n_items_map=n_items_map)

trial_sim.archive.update_fittest_with_genome(genome=genome,
                              n_items_map=n_items_map)
```

In this experiment, the fitness score of the genome is defined as two separate values, each serving a different purpose. The goal-oriented fitness score helps to test whether a solution has been found and collects useful performance statistics. The novelty-based fitness score guides the neuroevolution process in the direction of the maximal diversity of solver behavior, which means that the gradient of the solution search is directed toward exploring different behaviors, without any explicit objective.

 For more details about the implementation, please refer to the `maze_experiment.py` file at https://github.com/PacktPublishing/Hands-on-Neuroevolution-with-Python/blob/master/Chapter6/maze_experiment.py.

Experimenting with a simple maze configuration

We start our experiments using a simple maze configuration similar to the one described in the previous chapter. However, instead of the goal-oriented objective function, we use the NS optimization method to guide the neuroevolution process. We hope that with Novelty Search method it will be possible to find a successful maze solver with fewer epochs of evolution.

You can see the schema of the simple maze in the following plot:

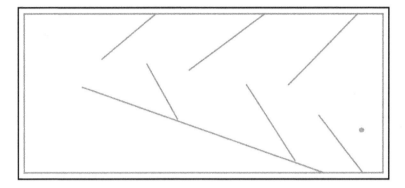

The simple maze configuration

The maze configuration is the same as in the previous chapter. However, we need to adjust the corresponding NEAT hyperparameters to meet the specifications of the NS optimization method.

Hyperparameter selection

The objective function used in the experiments described in this chapter is based on a novelty metric that has no clear upper-boundary value. As a result, the fitness threshold value cannot be estimated precisely. Thus, to signal that the winning solution was found, we use an indicative value that is big enough to not be encountered during the normal algorithm execution.

We selected `800000` as the indicative novelty score value. However, to maintain the visual presentation of the fitness scores when plotting the results of an experiment, we scaled down the obtained novelty scores of the solver agents using the natural logarithm. Thus, the fitness threshold value used in the configuration file becomes `13.5`, which is a bit less than the maximum possible fitness score (`13.59`) to avoid issues with rounding float numbers. Also, we increase the population size from the value described in the previous chapter (`250`) to make the solution search space deeper because we need to examine the maximum number of unique places in the maze:

```
[NEAT]
fitness_criterion = max
fitness_threshold = 13.5
pop_size = 500
reset_on_extinction = False
```

We run more generations in each trial than we did in the experiment in the previous chapter. Therefore, we have increased the stagnation value to keep species around for longer:

```
[DefaultStagnation]
max_stagnation = 100
```

All other NEAT hyperparameters have similar values to the ones presented in the previous chapter. Please refer to the previous chapter for the rationales for selecting the specific hyperparameter values.

> The complete list of hyperparameters used in the experiment can be found in the `maze_config.ini` file at
> `https://github.com/PacktPublishing/Hands-on-Neuroevolution-with-Python/blob/master/Chapter6/maze_config.ini`.

Working environment setup

The working environment for the experiment should include all dependencies and can be created using Anaconda with the following commands:

```
$ conda create --name maze_ns_neat python=3.5
$ conda activate maze_ns_neat
$ pip install neat-python==0.92
$ conda install matplotlib
$ conda install graphviz
$ conda install python-graphviz
```

These commands create and activate a `maze_ns_neat` virtual environment with Python 3.5. After that, the NEAT-Python library with version 0.92 is installed, along with other dependencies used by our visualization utilities.

The experiment runner implementation

The experiment runner implementation used in this chapter is similar for the most part to the one used in the previous chapter but has significant differences, which we will discuss in this section.

The trials cycle

In this chapter, we introduce an upgrade to the experiment runner implementation. We implement support to run multiple trials sequentially until the solution is found. Such an upgrade dramatically simplifies working with the multiple experiment trials sequentially, especially taking into account that each trial can take a long time to execute.

The main cycle of the experiment runner now looks like this (see `__main__` in the `maze_experiment.py` script):

```
print("Starting the %s maze experiment (Novelty Search), for %d trials"
    % (args.maze, args.trials))
for t in range(args.trials):
    print("\n\n----- Starting Trial: %d ------" % (t))
    # Create novelty archive
    novelty_archive = archive.NoveltyArchive(
                            threshold=args.ns_threshold,
                            metric=maze.maze_novelty_metric)
    trial_out_dir = os.path.join(out_dir, str(t))
    os.makedirs(trial_out_dir, exist_ok=True)
    solution_found = run_experiment( config_file=config_path,
                            maze_env=maze_env,
                            novelty_archive=novelty_archive,
                            trial_out_dir=trial_out_dir,
                            n_generations=args.generations,
                            args=args,
                            save_results=True,
                            silent=True)
    print("\n------ Trial %d complete, solution found: %s ------\n"
            % (t, solution_found))
```

The cycle runs the `args.trials` number of experiment trials, where `args.trials` is provided by the user from the command-line.

The first lines of the cycle create the `NoveltyArchive` object, which is a part of the Novelty Search algorithm. Later, during a specific trial, this object will be used to store all the relevant `NoveltyItems`:

```
novelty_archive = archive.NoveltyArchive(
                    threshold=args.ns_threshold,
                    metric=maze.maze_novelty_metric)
```

Note that `maze.maze_novelty_metric` is a reference to the function that is used to evaluate the novelty score of each solver agent.

With the source code for this chapter, we provide implementations of two novelty metric functions:

- The item-wise distance novelty metric (`maze.maze_novelty_metric`)
- The Euclidean distance novelty metric
  (`maze.maze_novelty_metric_euclidean`)

However, in our experiments, we use the first implementation. The second implementation is intended for you to run additional experiments.

The experiment runner function

The runner function has many similarities to the runner function introduced in the previous chapter, but, at the same time, it has unique features that are specific to the NS optimization algorithm.

Here, we consider the most significant parts of the implementation:

1. It starts with selecting a specific seed value for a random number generator, based on the current system time:

```
seed = int(time.time())
random.seed(seed)
```

2. After that, it loads the NEAT algorithm configuration and creates an initial population of genomes:

```
config = neat.Config(neat.DefaultGenome,
                     neat.DefaultReproduction,
                     neat.DefaultSpeciesSet,
                     neat.DefaultStagnation,
                     config_file)
p = neat.Population(config)
```

3. To hold the intermediate results after each generation evaluation, we initialize a `trial_sim` global variable with the `MazeSimulationTrial` object.

   We use a global variable so it can be accessed by the fitness evaluation callback function (`eval_genomes(genomes, config)`) that is passed to the NEAT-Python framework:

```
global trial_sim
trial_sim = MazeSimulationTrial(maze_env=maze_env,
                                population=p,
                                archive=novelty_archive)
```

4. Also, traditionally, we register with the `Population` object the number of reporters to output algorithm results and to collect statistics:

```
p.add_reporter(neat.StdOutReporter(True))
stats = neat.StatisticsReporter()
p.add_reporter(stats)
```

5. Now we are ready to run the NEAT algorithm over a specified number of generations and evaluate the results:

```
start_time = time.time()
best_genome = p.run(eval_genomes, n=n_generations)
elapsed_time = time.time() - start_time
# Display the best genome among generations.
print('\nBest genome:\n%s' % (best_genome))
solution_found = \
    (best_genome.fitness >= config.fitness_threshold)
if solution_found:
    print("SUCCESS: The stable maze solver controller was
found!!!")
    else:
        print("FAILURE: Failed to find the stable maze solver
controller!!!")
```

6. After that, the collected statistics and novelty archive records can be visualized and saved to the filesystem:

```
node_names = {-1:'RF_R', -2:'RF_FR', -3:'RF_F', -4:'RF_FL',
              -5:'RF_L', -6: 'RF_B', -7:'RAD_F', -8:'RAD_L',
              -9:'RAD_B', -10:'RAD_R', 0:'ANG_VEL', 1:'VEL'}
visualize.draw_net(config, best_genome, view=show_results,
                   node_names=node_names,
                   directory=trial_out_dir, fmt='svg')
if args is None:
    visualize.draw_maze_records(maze_env,
                                trial_sim.record_store.records,
                                view=show_results)
else:
    visualize.draw_maze_records(maze_env,
                                trial_sim.record_store.records,
                                view=show_results, width=args.width,
                                height=args.height,
                                filename=os.path.join(trial_out_dir,
                                    'maze_records.svg'))
visualize.plot_stats(stats, ylog=False,
                     view=show_results,
                     filename=os.path.join(trial_out_dir,
                         'avg_fitness.svg'))
```

```
visualize.plot_species(stats, view=show_results,
                    filename=os.path.join(trial_out_dir,
                                    'speciation.svg'))
# store NoveltyItems archive data
trial_sim.archive.write_fittest_to_file(
                        path=os.path.join(trial_out_dir,
                                'ns_items_fittest.txt'))
trial_sim.archive.write_to_file(
                        path=os.path.join(trial_out_dir,
                                'ns_items_all.txt'))
```

7. Finally, we perform additional visualization routines introduced in this chapter that visualize the path of the maze-solver agents through the maze.

   We do this by running a simulation of maze navigation against the controller ANN of the best solver agent found during the evolution. During this simulation run, all the path points visited by a solver agent are collected to be rendered later by the draw_agent_path function:

```
maze_env = copy.deepcopy(trial_sim.orig_maze_environment)
control_net = neat.nn.FeedForwardNetwork.create(
                                    best_genome, config)
path_points = []
evaluate_fitness = maze.maze_simulation_evaluate(
                        env=maze_env,
                        net=control_net,
                        time_steps=SOLVER_TIME_STEPS,
                        path_points=path_points)
print("Evaluated fitness of best agent: %f"
        % evaluate_fitness)
visualize.draw_agent_path(trial_sim.orig_maze_environment,
                    path_points, best_genome,
                    view=show_results,
                    width=args.width,
                    height=args.height,
                    filename=os.path.join(trial_out_dir,
                            'best_solver_path.svg'))
```

In the end, the run_experiment function returns a Boolean value indicating whether a successful maze solver agent was found during the trial or not.

Please refer to the `run_experiment(config_file, maze_env, novelty_archive, trial_out_dir, args=None, n_generations=100, save_results=False, silent=False)` function in the `maze_experiment.py` file at `https://github.com/PacktPublishing/Hands-on-Neuroevolution-with-Python/blob/master/Chapter6/maze_experiment.py`.

Running the simple maze navigation experiment with NS optimization

Make sure you copy all related Python scripts and configuration files (`maze_config.ini` and `medium_maze.txt`) into the local directory from the online repository that can be found at: `https://github.com/PacktPublishing/Hands-on-Neuroevolution-with-Python/blob/master/Chapter6/`.

Now enter this directory, and execute the following command in the Terminal application:

```
python maze_experiment.py -g 500 -t 10 -m medium --width 300 --height 150
```

Do not forget to activate the appropriate virtual environment with the following command:
`conda activate maze_ns_neat`

The preceding command runs 10 trials of the maze navigation experiment with the simple maze configuration loaded from the `medium_maze.txt` file. The neuroevolution algorithm evaluates 500 generations of maze solvers in each trial, using the NEAT configuration data loaded from the `maze_config.ini` file. The width and height parameters specify the dimensions of the maze records subplot (see the `visualize.draw_maze_records` function implementation for more details).

After 99 generations of the evolution, the successful maze solver agent is found in generation 100. There are general statistics about the population of genomes in the last generation of evolution. In the console output of the completed Python program, you will see the following for the last generation of evolution:

```
****** Running generation 100 ******

Maze solved in 391 steps
Population's average fitness: 1.28484 stdev: 0.90091
Best fitness: 13.59237 - size: (2, 8) - species 1 - id 48354

Best individual in generation 100 meets fitness threshold - complexity: (2,
8)
```

After that, we display the configuration of the winner genome and general statistics about the trial:

```
Best genome:
Key: 48354
Fitness: 13.592367006650065
Nodes:
  0 DefaultNodeGene(key=0, bias=-2.1711339938349026, response=1.0,
activation=sigmoid, aggregation=sum)
  1 DefaultNodeGene(key=1, bias=6.576480565646596, response=1.0,
activation=sigmoid, aggregation=sum)
Connections:
  DefaultConnectionGene(key=(-10, 1), weight=-0.5207773885939109,
enabled=True)
  DefaultConnectionGene(key=(-9, 0), weight=1.7778928210387814,
enabled=True)
  DefaultConnectionGene(key=(-7, 1), weight=-2.4940590667086524,
enabled=False)
  DefaultConnectionGene(key=(-6, 1), weight=-1.3708732457648565,
enabled=True)
  DefaultConnectionGene(key=(-4, 0), weight=4.482428082179011,
enabled=True)
  DefaultConnectionGene(key=(-4, 1), weight=-1.3103728328721098,
enabled=True)
  DefaultConnectionGene(key=(-3, 0), weight=-0.4583080031587811,
enabled=True)
  DefaultConnectionGene(key=(-3, 1), weight=4.643599450804774,
enabled=True)
  DefaultConnectionGene(key=(-2, 1), weight=-0.9055329546235956,
enabled=True)
  DefaultConnectionGene(key=(-1, 0), weight=-1.5899992185951817,
enabled=False)
SUCCESS: The stable maze solver controller was found!!!
```

```
Record store file: out/maze_ns/medium/0/data.pickle
Random seed: 1567086899
Trial elapsed time: 7452.462 sec
Plot figure width: 6.8, height: 7.0
Maze solved in 391 steps
Evaluated fitness of best agent: 1.000000
Plot figure width: 7.8, height: 4.0
```

The console output shows us that the winner genome that encodes the control ANN of the successful maze solver has only two node genes and eight connection genes. These genes correspond to the two output nodes in the controller ANN, with the eight connections used to establish links with the inputs. The resulting configuration of the controller ANN is shown here:

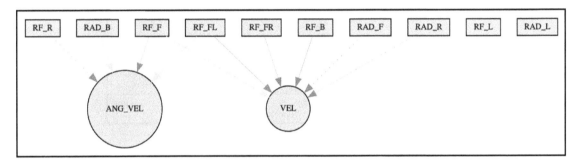

The configuration of the successful controller ANN

The configuration of the successful controller ANN is better than the configuration described in the previous chapter, which was found using the *goal-oriented* search optimization method. In this experiment, the ANN configuration omits the hidden nodes completely, and the evolutionary process takes fewer generations finding it.

Thus, we can assume that the Novelty Search optimization method is at least as effective as the goal-oriented method. This is even though the search optimization method is not based on the proximity to the final goal, but on rewarding novel behavior. The neuroevolution process produced a successful maze solver agent without any hints about the proximity to the final goal (maze exit), and that is just amazing.

Also, it is interesting to look at the speciation graph during the evolution:

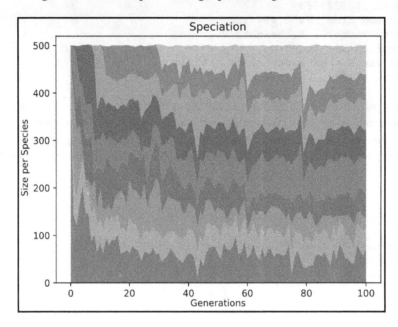

The speciation graph

In the speciation graph, we can see that the total number of species during the evolutionary process does not exceed nine. Furthermore, most of them are present from the very first generations of the evolution until a successful maze solver is found.

Agent record visualization

We used the method of visualizing agent records that was introduced in the previous chapter, and we introduced a new visualization method to visualize the path of the solver agent through the maze.

The visualization of agents records saved automatically for each completed trial as an `obj_medium_maze_records.svg` SVG file in the output directory of the corresponding experiment.

In the following image, you can look at the visualization of agents records for the experiment described in this chapter:

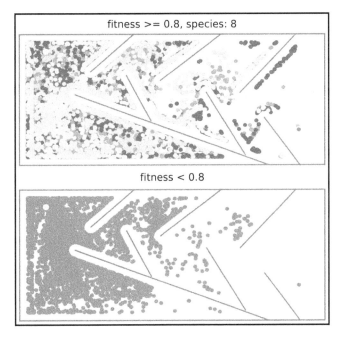

The visualization of agents records

The top subplot of the plot shows the final positions of the agents belonging to the fittest species that have a goal-oriented fitness score value above **0.8**. We were able to find eight species that explored almost all areas of the maze and were finally able to find the maze exit. At the same time, even the evolutionary losers (the bottom plot) demonstrated highly explorative behavior, evenly filling the first half of the maze area (compare this with the similar plot in the previous chapter).

Also, it is important to note that eight of the total nine species created during the evolutionary process demonstrate the highest goal-oriented fitness scores; that is, they were almost able to reach the maze exit (and one of them ultimately reached it). This achievement is in stark contrast with the experiment in the previous chapter, where only half of all species (six from twelve) achieved the same results.

However, the most exciting visualization allows us to look at the path of the successful maze solver agent that was able to find the maze exit:

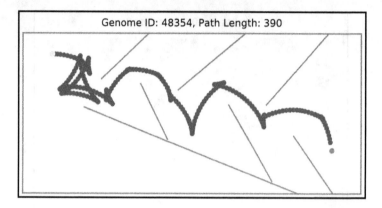

Genome ID: 48354, Path Length: 390

The path through the maze of the successful maze solver

The visualization can be found in the `output` directory of the experiment in the `best_solver_path.svg` file.

As you can see, a successful maze solver agent was able to find an almost optimal path through the maze, even though it does appear to get a little confused at the beginning.

It's just amazing that such a convoluted path through the maze can be found without any reference to the location of the maze exit but only by rewarding the novelty of each intermediate solution that is found.

Exercise 1

1. Set the population size (`pop_size`) parameter in the `maze_config.ini` file to `250`. See if the maze solver can be found in this case.
2. Change the value of the parameter specifying the probability of adding a new node (`node_add_prob`). Was the neuroevolution process able to find a solution, and is it optimal from a topological point of view?
3. Change the initial genome configuration to have zero hidden nodes at the beginning (`num_hidden`). How does this affect the algorithm's performance?
4. Try to use another novelty metric that is provided with the source code (`maze.maze_novelty_metric_euclidean`) and see what happens.

5. Change the `location_sample_rate` command-line parameter from its default value (`4000`), which allows you to include only the final position of the maze solver into its behavioral vector. Try the values that are less than `400` (the number of maze simulation steps). For example, if we set this parameter to `100`, then the behavioral vector will include coordinates a maximum of four trajectory points for each solver agent. See how this parameter can influence algorithm performance. You can provide a value for this parameter by running the following command:

```
python maze_experiment.py -g 500 -t 10 -r 100 -m medium --width 300
--height 150
```

The preceding command runs the simple maze experiment with `location_sample_rate` set to `100`.

Experimenting with a hard-to-solve maze configuration

In the next experiment, we evaluate the effectiveness of the NS optimization method in a more complex task. In this task, we try to evolve a maze solving agent that can find a path through a maze with a complex configuration.

For this experiment, we use the hard-to-solve maze configuration introduced in the previous chapter. Such an approach allows us to compare results obtained with the NS optimization method against the results obtained with the *goal-oriented* optimization method used in the previous chapter. The maze configuration is as follows:

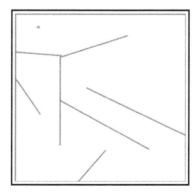

The hard-to-solve maze configuration

This maze configuration is identical to the one described in the previous chapter. Thus, you can refer to Chapter 5, *Autonomous Maze Navigation*, for a detailed description.

Hyperparameter selection and working environment setup

The hyperparameters for this experiment are the same that we used for a simple maze experiment earlier in this chapter. We decided to leave the hyperparameters unchanged to test how well the algorithm generalizes by trying to find a solution to a task within the same domain, but with a different configuration.

The working environment for this experiment is fully compatible with the environment already created for the simple maze experiment. Thus, we can use it as well.

Running the hard-to-solve maze navigation experiment

To run this experiment, we can use the same experiment runner that we developed for the simple maze experiment, with the only difference being that different command-line parameters should be provided at the start. You can start the hard maze experiment with the following command:

```
$ python maze_experiment.py -m hard -g 500 -t 10 --width 200 --height 200
```

This command starts the hard-to-solve maze experiment for 10 trials with 500 generations each. The width and height parameters determine the dimensions of the subplot to draw the maze records collected during the experiment.

Using the NEAT-Python library for the hard maze experiment, we were unable to find a successful maze solver within 10 trials, even with the NS optimization method. Nevertheless, the results obtained with the NS method are more promising than with the goal-oriented optimization method from the previous chapter. You can see this in the following plot, which depicts the final positions of the solver agents during the maze navigation simulation:

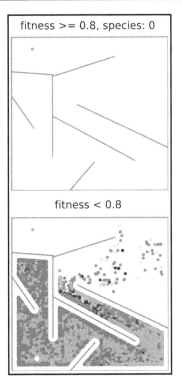

The agents records visualization

The plot that visualizes the final positions of all evaluated agents demonstrates that, during this experiment, more areas of the maze were explored with the NS optimization method than with the goal-oriented method. Also, you can see that some species were almost at the finish line, only a few steps away from reaching the maze exit.

The path of the most successful maze-solver agent is as follows:

The path through the maze of the most successful maze solver agent

The path through the maze taken by the most successful solver agent demonstrates that the agent was able to discover the crucial relations between sensor inputs and the maneuvers to perform. However, it still lacks precision in applying the control signal. Due to this flaw, some control actions lead to ineffective trajectory loops, consuming precious time steps allotted to solve the maze.

Finally, it is interesting to take a look at the topology of the control ANN of the most successful maze solver:

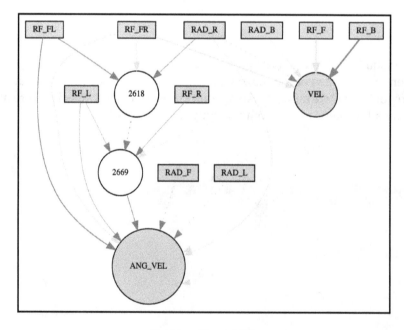

The topology of the control ANN

You can see that all sensor inputs were involved in the decision-making, in contrast with the topology of the control ANN devised in the previous experiment in this chapter. Furthermore, the network topology includes two hidden nodes, which allows the agent to implement a complex control strategy to navigate through the hard-to-solve maze environment.

Despite our failure to evolve a successful maze solver agent with the Novelty Search optimization method in this experiment using the NEAT-Python library, it is rather an issue of ineffective NEAT implementation by the library than a failure of the Novelty Search method.

 I have made an implementation of the NEAT algorithm in the GO programming language that solves a hard maze navigation task with high efficiency. You can check it out on GitHub at `https://github.com/ yaricom/goNEAT_NS`.

Exercise 2

In the source code for this chapter, we also provide the experiment runner implementation based on the MultiNEAT Python library that we introduced in `Chapter 2`, *Python Libraries and Environment Setup*.

You can try to use it to solve the hard maze task as follows:

1. Update the current Anaconda environment by installing the MultiNEAT Python library with the following command:

   ```
   $ conda install -c conda-forge multineat
   ```

2. Run the experiment runner implementation based on the MultiNEAT library:

   ```
   $ python maze_experiment_multineat.py -m hard -g 500 -t 10 --width
   200 --height 200
   ```

These commands install the MultiNEAT library in the current Anaconda environment and start 10 trials (with 500 generations each) of the hard maze experiment using an appropriate experiment runner.

Summary

In this chapter, you learned about the *Novelty Search* optimization method and how it can be used to guide the neuroevolution process in deceptive problem space environments, such as maze navigation. We conducted the same maze navigation experiments as in the previous chapter. After that, we compared the results we obtained to determine if the NS method has advantages over the goal-oriented optimization method introduced in the previous chapter.

You got the practical experience of writing source code using Python and experimented with tuning the important hyperparameters of the NEAT algorithm. Also, we introduced a new visualization method, allowing you to see the path of the agent through the maze. With this method, you can easily compare how different agents are trying to solve the maze navigation problem and whether the path through the maze that was found is optimal or not.

The next chapter introduces more advanced applications of the NEAT algorithm. We start with the task of visual discrimination and introduce you to the HyperNEAT extension of the NEAT algorithm. The HyperNEAT method allows you to work with large-scale ANNs operating over thousands or millions of parameters. This scale of operations is impossible with the classic NEAT algorithm.

3
Section 3: Advanced Neuroevolution Methods

This section discusses advanced neuroevolution methods and how to use them to solve practical problems. You will learn about advanced neuroevolution techniques and find ideas for new projects.

This section comprises the following chapters:

- Chapter 7, *Hypercube-Based NEAT for Visual Discrimination*
- Chapter 8, *ES-HyperNEAT and the Retina Problem*
- Chapter 9, *Co-Evolution and the SAFE Method*
- Chapter 10, *Deep Neuroevolution*

Hypercube-Based NEAT for Visual Discrimination

7

In this chapter, you will learn about the main concepts behind a hypercube-based NEAT algorithm and about the main challenges it was designed to solve. We take a look at the problems that arise when attempting to use direct genome encoding with large-scale **artificial neural networks** (**ANN**) and how they can be solved with the introduction of an indirect genome encoding scheme. You will learn how a **Compositional Pattern Producing Network** (**CPPN**) can be used to store genome encoding information with an extra-high compression rate and how CPPNs are employed by the HyperNEAT algorithm. Finally, you will work with practical examples that demonstrate the power of the HyperNEAT algorithm.

In this chapter, we discuss the following topics:

- The problem with the direct encoding of large-scale natural networks using NEAT, and how HyperNEAT can help by introducing the indirect encoding method
- The evolution of CPPNs with NEAT to explore geometric regularities within the hypercube, which allows us to efficiently encode connectivity patterns within the target ANN
- How to use the HyperNEAT method to detect and recognize objects in a visual field
- The definition of the objective function for a visual discrimination experiment
- A discussion of the visual discrimination experiment results

Technical requirements

The following technical requirements should be met in order to execute the experiments described in this chapter:

- Windows 8/10, macOS 10.13 or newer, modern Linux
- Anaconda Distribution version 2019.03 or newer

The code for this chapter can be found at `https://github.com/PacktPublishing/Hands-on-Neuroevolution-with-Python/tree/master/Chapter7`

Indirect encoding of ANNs with CPPNs

In the previous chapters, you learned about the direct encoding of ANNs using the nature-inspired conception of a genotype that is mapped to the phenotype in a $1:1$ ratio to represent the ANN topology. This mapping allows us to use advanced NEAT algorithm features such as an innovation number, which allows us to track when a particular mutation was introduced during the evolution. Each gene in the genome has a specific value of the innovation number, allowing fast and accurate crossover of parent genomes to produce offspring. While this feature introduces immense benefits and also reduces the computational costs needed to match the parent genomes during the recombination, the direct encoding used to encode the ANN topology of the phenotype has a significant drawback as it limits the size of the encoded ANN. The bigger the encoded ANN, the bigger the genome that is evaluated during the evolution, and this involves tremendous computational costs.

There are many tasks, primarily related to pattern recognition in images or other high-dimensional data sources, that require employing ANNs that have advanced topologies with many layers and nodes within them. Such topological configurations cannot be effectively processed by the classic NEAT algorithm due to the inefficiencies of direct encoding discussed previously.

The new method of encoding the phenotype ANN was proposed to address this drawback while still having all the benefits provided by the NEAT algorithm. We'll discuss it in the next section.

CPPN encoding

The proposed encoding scheme employs a method of representing the connectivity patterns within the phenotype ANN by querying another specialized neural network about the weights of the connections between the nodes. This specialized neural network is called a **CPPN**. Its main task is to represent the connectivity patterns of the phenotype ANN as a function of its geometry. The resulting connectivity pattern is represented as a four-dimensional hypercube. Each point of the hypercube encodes the connection between two related nodes within the phenotype ANN and is described by four numbers: the coordinates of the source node and the coordinates of the target node. The connective CPPN takes as input each point of the hypercube and calculates the weights of the connections between every node in the phenotype ANN. Also, a connection between two nodes is not expressed if the magnitude of the connection weight returned by the CPPN is less than a minimal threshold (W_{min}). Thus, we can define the connective CPPN as a four-dimensional function returning the connection weight, as given by the following formula:

$$w = CPPN(x_1, y_1, x_2, y_2)$$

The source node of the phenotype ANN is at (x_1, y_1), and the target node is at (x_2, y_2).

Another essential feature of CPPNs is that unlike conventional ANNs, which employ only one type of activation function for each node (usually from the sigmoid family of functions), CPPNs can use multiple geometric functions as node activators. Due to this, CPPNs can express a rich set of geometric motifs in the produced connectivity patterns:

- Symmetry (Gaussian function)
- Imperfect symmetry (Gaussian combined with an asymmetric coordinate frame)
- Repetition (sine function)
- Repetition with variations (sine combined with a coordinate frame that doesn't repeat)

Considering the features of the CPPN that we've discussed, we can assume that the connectivity pattern produced by it can represent any network topology for the phenotype ANN. Also, the connectivity pattern can be used to encode large-scale topologies by discovering the regularities in the training data and reusing the same set of genes within the CPPN to encode repetitions in the phenotype ANN.

Hypercube-based NeuroEvolution of Augmenting Topologies

The methodology described in the previous section was invented by Kenneth O. Stanley and was called **Hypercube-based NeuroEvolution of Augmenting Topologies (HyperNEAT)**. As its name suggests, it is an extension of the NEAT algorithm that we have already used in this book. The main difference between these two methods is that the HyperNEAT method uses an indirect encoding scheme based on the CPPN. During the evolution, the HyperNEAT method employs a NEAT algorithm to evolve a population of genomes that encode a topology of the connective CPPN. After that, each created CPPN can be used to establish the connectivity patterns within a specific phenotype ANN. Finally, the phenotype ANN can be evaluated against the problem space.

So far, we have discussed how connectivity patterns can be evolved using NEAT with a CPPN and can be applied to the nodes of the phenotype ANN. However, we have not mentioned how the geometric layout of the nodes is determined in the first place. The responsibility of defining the nodes and their positions (layout) is assigned to the human architect. The architect analyzes the problem space and utilizes the most appropriate layout.

By convention, the initial layout of the nodes of the phenotype ANN has a name: substrate. There are several types of substrate configuration (layout), and they have proven their efficiency for particular tasks:

- **Two-dimensional grid**: A regular grid of network nodes in a two-dimensional Cartesian space centered at (0,0).
- **Three-dimensional grid**: A regular grid of network nodes in a three-dimensional Cartesian space centered at (0,0,0).
- **State-space sandwich**: Two two-dimensional planar grids with corresponding source and target nodes in which one layer can only send connections in the direction of the other one.
- **Circular**: A regular radial structure suited to define regularities in radial geometry based on polar coordinates.

By arranging the ANN nodes in an appropriate layout on the substrate, it is possible to exploit regularities in the geometry of the problem space. That significantly increases the efficiency of the encoding by using the connective CPPN to draw connectivity patterns between the substrate nodes. Let's now look at the basics of a visual discrimination experiment.

For more details about the HyperNEAT method, please refer to `Chapter 1`, *Overview of Neuroevolution Methods*.

Visual discrimination experiment basics

As we have already mentioned, the main advantage of the indirect encoding employed by the HyperNEAT algorithm is the ability to encode the topology of the large-scale ANN. In this section, we will describe an experiment that can be used to test the capacity of the HyperNEAT method to train a large-scale ANN. Visual pattern recognition tasks typically require large ANNs as detectors due to the high dimensionality of the input data (the image height multiplied by the image width). In this chapter, we consider a variation of this family of computer science problems called visual discrimination tasks.

The task of visual discrimination is to distinguish a large object from a small object in a two-dimensional visual space, regardless of their positions in the visual space and their positions relative to each other. The visual discrimination task is performed by a specialized discriminator ANN, which is built on a substrate configured as a state-space sandwich with two sheets:

- The visual field is a two-dimensional array of sensors that can be in two states: on or off (black and white).
- The target field is a two-dimensional array of outputs with activation values in the [0,1] range.

The scheme of the visual discrimination task is shown here:

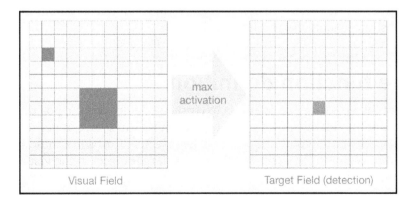

The visual discrimination task

You can see in the diagram that the objects to be detected are represented as two squares separated by an empty space. The larger object is precisely three times bigger than the other one. The algorithm we are trying to build needs to detect the center of the larger object. The detection is based on measuring the activation values of the ANN nodes in the target field. The position of the node with the highest activation value marks the center of the detected object. Our goal is to discover the right connectivity patterns between visual and target fields that align the output node with the highest activation and the center of the big object in the visual field. Also, the discovered connectivity pattern should be invariant to the relative positions of both objects.

The algorithm for the task of visual discrimination needs to evaluate a large number of inputs - the values representing the cells in the visual field. Also, the successful algorithm needs to discover the strategy that can process inputs from multiple cells simultaneously. Such a strategy should be based on the general principle that allows the detection of the relative sizes of the objects in the visual field. The visual field in our experiment is represented as a two-dimensional grid. Thus, the general geometric principle to be discovered is the concept of locality.

We can exploit the locality principle in the substrate configuration of the discriminator ANN that we have chosen by discovering a particular pattern in the scheme of the links that connect the nodes of the visual and the target fields. In this connection scheme, separate nodes of the visual field are connected to the multiple adjacent output nodes around a specific location in the target field. As a result, the more activations the output node collects, the more signals are supplied into it through connections with individual input nodes.

To effectively exploit the locality principle mentioned previously, the representation of connections should take into account the geometry of the discriminator ANN substrate and the fact that the correct connectivity pattern repeats across it. The best candidate for such a representation is a CPPN, which can discover the local connectivity pattern once and repeat it across the substrate grid at any resolution.

Objective function definition

The main task of the visual discriminator is to correctly determine the position of a larger object regardless of the relative positions of both objects. Thus, we can define the objective function to guide the neuroevolution process. The objective function should be based on the Euclidean distance between the exact position of the larger object in the visual field and its predicted position in the target field.

The loss function can be directly represented as the Euclidean distance between the actual and predicted positions as follows:

$$\mathcal{L} = \sqrt{\sum_{i=1}^{2}(G_i - P_i)^2}$$

$\mathcal{L}$ is a loss function, G_i is the ground truth coordinates of the big object, and P_i is predicted by the discriminator ANN coordinates.

With the loss function as defined previously, we can write the objective function as follows:

$$\mathcal{F}_n = 1.0 - \frac{\mathcal{L}}{D_{max}}$$

D_{max} is the maximal possible distance between the two points within the target field space. The objective function formula guarantees that the calculated fitness score ($\mathcal{F}_n$) always falls within the [0,1] range. Now that we know the basics of the visual discrimination experiment, let's start with setting it up.

Visual discrimination experiment setup

In our experiment, during the training of the discriminator ANN, we use the resolution of the visual and target fields fixed at 11 x 11. Thus, the connective CPPN must learn the correct connectivity pattern between the 121 inputs of the visual field and the 121 outputs of the target fields, which results in a total of 14,641 potential connection weights.

The following diagram shows the scheme of the substrate for the discriminator ANN:

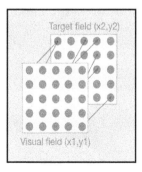

The state-space sandwich substrate of the discriminator ANN

The discriminator ANN shown in the diagram has two layers with nodes forming one two-dimensional planar grid per layer. The connective CPPN draws the connectivity patterns by connecting nodes from one layer to another.

At each generation of the evolution, each individual in the population (the genome encoding the CPPN) is evaluated for its ability to create connectivity patterns of the discriminator ANN. The discriminator ANN is then tested to see whether it can find the center of the large object within the visual field. There are a total of 75 evaluation trials for a particular ANN, in which two objects are placed at different locations in each trial. At each trial, we put a small object in one of the 25 positions uniformly distributed in the visual field. The center of a large object is five steps from the small object to the right, down, or diagonally. If a large object doesn't fit into the visual field completely, then it wraps around to the other side. Thus, considering the logic of the placement of objects relative to each other and the grid, we should be able to evaluate all possible configurations in 75 trials.

Our experiment setup has two major parts, which we will discuss in the following sections.

Visual discriminator test environment

First we need to define the test environment and provide access to the dataset, which contains all the possible visual field configurations as described in the previous section. The dataset used in this experiment is created during the test environment initialization. We will discuss dataset creation later in this section.

The test environment has two major components:

- The data structure to maintain the visual field definition
- The test environment manager, which stores the dataset and provides a means to evaluate discriminator ANNs against it

Next, we provide a detailed description of these components.

Visual field definition

We store the configuration of the visual field for each of the 75 trials discussed previously in the `VisualField` Python class. It has the following constructor:

```
def __init__(self, big_pos, small_pos, field_size):
    self.big_pos = big_pos
    self.small_pos = small_pos
    self.field_size = field_size
    self.data = np.zeros((field_size, field_size))
```

```
# store small object position
self._set_point(small_pos[0], small_pos[1])

# store big object points
offsets = [-1, 0, 1]
for xo in offsets:
    for yo in offsets:
        self._set_point(big_pos[0] + xo, big_pos[1] + yo)
```

The constructor of `VisualField` accepts as parameters the tuple with coordinates (*x, y*) of the large and small object, as well as the size of the visual field. We consider the square visual field, so the size of the visual field along each axis is equal. The visual field is internally represented as a two-dimensional binary array where ones represent positions occupied by objects, and zeros are empty spaces. It is stored in the `self.data` field, which is a NumPy array with the shape (2, 2).

The small object has a size 1 x 1, and the large object is three times bigger. The following snippet from the constructor's source code creates the representation of the big object in the data array:

```
offsets = [-1, 0, 1]
for xo in offsets:
    for yo in offsets:
        self._set_point(big_pos[0] + xo, big_pos[1] + yo)
```

The constructor of the `VisualField` class receives the coordinates of the center of the big object as a tuple, (*x, y*). The preceding code draws the big object starting from the top-left corner (x-1, y-1) and ending at the bottom-right corner (x+1, y+1).

The `_set_point(self, x, y)` function referred to in the preceding code sets the `1.0` value at the specific position in the `self.data` field:

```
def _set_point(self, x, y):
    px, py = x, y
    if px < 0:
        px = self.field_size + px
    elif px >= self.field_size:
        px = px - self.field_size

    if py < 0:
        py = self.field_size + py
    elif py >= self.field_size:
        py = py - self.field_size

    self.data[py, px] = 1 # in Numpy index is: [row, col]
```

The `_set_point(self, x, y)` function performs coordinate wrapping when the coordinate value exceeds the allowed number of dimensions per axis. For example, for the *x* axis, the source code for the coordinate value wrapping is as follows:

```
if px < 0:
    px = self.field_size + px
elif px >= self.field_size:
    px = px - self.field_size
```

The source code for coordinate wrapping along the *y* axis is similar.

After wrapping the coordinates specified as parameters of the function (if needed), we set the corresponding positions in the `self.data` field to have a value of `1.0`.

 NumPy indexes as `[row, column]`. Thus, we need to use *y* in the first position and *x* in the second position of the index.

Visual discriminator environment

The visual discriminator environment holds the generated dataset with the visual field definitions. Also, it provides methods to create the dataset and to evaluate the discriminator ANN against the dataset. The `VDEnvironment` Python class holds the definitions of all mentioned methods, as well as related data structures. Next, we'll look at all the significant parts of the `VDEnvironment` class definition:

- The class constructor is defined as follows:

```
def __init__(self, small_object_positions, big_object_offset,
        field_size):
    self.s_object_pos = small_object_positions
    self.data_set = []
    self.b_object_offset = big_object_offset
    self.field_size = field_size

    self.max_dist = self._distance((0, 0),
                        (field_size - 1, field_size - 1))

    # create test data set
    self._create_data_set()
```

The first parameter of the VDEnvironment constructor is an array with the definitions of all the possible small object positions defined as a sequence of coordinate values for each axis. The second parameter defines the offset of the coordinates of the center of the big object from the small object coordinates. We use 5 as the value of this parameter in our experiment. Finally, the third parameter is the visual field size along with both dimensions.

After all the received parameters are saved into object fields, we calculate the maximum possible distance between two points in the visual field as follows:

```
self.max_dist = self._distance((0, 0),
                    (field_size - 1, field_size - 1))
```

The Euclidean distance between the top-left and the bottom-right corner of the visual field is then stored in the self.max_dist field. This value will be used later to normalize the distances between points in the visual field by keeping them in the [0, 1] range.

- The _create_data_set() function creates all possible datasets given the specified environment parameters. The source code of this function is as follows:

```
def _create_data_set(self):
    for x in self.s_object_pos:
        for y in self.s_object_pos:
            # diagonal
            vf = self._create_visual_field(x, y,
                            x_off=self.b_object_offset,
                            y_off=self.b_object_offset)
            self.data_set.append(vf)
            # right
            vf = self._create_visual_field(x, y,
                            x_off=self.b_object_offset,
                            y_off=0)
            self.data_set.append(vf)
            # down
            vf = self._create_visual_field(x, y,
                            x_off=0,
                            y_off=self.b_object_offset)
            self.data_set.append(vf)
```

The function iterates over the small object positions along two axes and tries to create the big object at coordinates that are to the right, below, or on a diagonal from the small object coordinates.

- The `_create_visual_field` function creates the appropriate visual field configuration using the coordinates of the small object (`sx`, `sy`) and an offset of the big object's center (`x_off`, `y_off`). The following source code shows how this is implemented:

```
def _create_visual_field(self, sx, sy, x_off, y_off):
    bx = (sx + x_off) % self.field_size # wrap by X coordinate
    by = (sy + y_off) % self.field_size # wrap by Y coordinate

    # create visual field
    return VisualField(big_pos=(bx, by), small_pos=(sx, sy),
                       field_size=self.field_size)
```

If the coordinates of the big object calculated by the preceding function are outside the visual field space, we apply the wrapping as follows:

```
if bx >= self.field_size:
    bx = bx - self.field_size # wrap
```

The preceding snippet shows the wrapping along the *x* axis. The wrapping along the *y* axis is similar. Finally, the `VisualField` object is created and returned to be appended to the dataset.

- However, the most exciting part of the `VDEnvironment` definition is related to the evaluation of the discriminator ANN, which is defined in the `evaluate_net(self, net)` function as follows:

```
def evaluate_net(self, net):
    avg_dist = 0

    # evaluate predicted positions
    for ds in self.data_set:
        # evaluate and get outputs
        outputs, x, y = self.evaluate_net_vf(net, ds)

        # find the distance to the big object
        dist = self._distance((x, y), ds.big_pos)
        avg_dist = avg_dist + dist

    avg_dist /= float(len(self.data_set))
    # normalized position error
    error = avg_dist / self.max_dist
    # fitness
    fitness = 1.0 - error

    return fitness, avg_dist
```

The preceding function receives the discriminator ANN as a parameter, and returns the evaluated fitness score and the mean distance between the detected coordinates of the big object and the ground truth values calculated for all evaluated visual fields. The average distance is calculated as follows:

```
for ds in self.data_set:
    # evaluate and get outputs
    _, x, y = self.evaluate_net_vf(net, ds)

    # find the distance to the big object
    dist = self._distance((x, y), ds.big_pos)
    avg_dist = avg_dist + dist

avg_dist /= float(len(self.data_set))
```

The preceding source code iterates over all `VisualField` objects in the dataset, and uses the discriminator ANN to determine the coordinates of the big object. After that, we calculate the distance (detection error) between the ground truth and the predicted position of the big object. Finally, we find the mean of the detection errors and normalize it as follows:

```
# normalized detection error
error = avg_dist / self.max_dist
```

The maximum possible error value is `1.0`, according to the preceding code. The value of the fitness score is a complement to the `1.0` of the error value since it increases as the error decreases:

```
# fitness
fitness = 1.0 - error
```

The `evaluate_net` function returns the calculated fitness score along with the unnormalized detection error.

- The `evaluate_net_vf(self, net, vf)` function provides a means to evaluate the discriminator ANN against a specific `VisualField` object. It is defined as follows:

```
def evaluate_net_vf(self, net, vf):
    depth = 1 # we just have 2 layers

    net.Flush()
    # prepare input
    inputs = vf.get_data()
    net.Input(inputs)
    # activate
```

```
[net.Activate() for _ in range(depth)]

# get outputs
outputs = net.Output()
# find coordinates of big object
x, y = self._big_object_coordinates(outputs)

return outputs, x, y
```

The preceding function receives the discriminator ANN as the first parameter and the `VisualField` object as the second parameter. After that, it obtains the flattened input array from the `VisualField` object and uses it as input to the discriminator ANN:

```
inputs = vf.get_data()
net.Input(inputs)
```

After we set the inputs of the discriminator ANN, it must be activated to propagate input values through all network nodes. Our discriminator ANN has only two layers, as determined by the space-sandwich substrate configuration. Thus we need to activate it twice—once per each layer. After propagation of the activation signal through both layers of the discriminator ANN, we can determine the position of the big object in the target field as an index of the maximal value in the output array. Using the `_big_object_coordinates(self, outputs)` function, we can extract the Cartesian coordinates (*x*, *y*) of the big object within the target field.

Finally, the `evaluate_net_vf` function returns the raw output array along with the extracted Cartesian coordinates (*x*, *y*) of the big object in the target field space.

- The `_big_object_coordinates(self, outputs)` function extracts the Cartesian coordinates of the big object within the target field space from the raw outputs obtained from the discriminator ANN. The function's source code is as follows:

```
def _big_object_coordinates(self, outputs):
    max_activation = -100.0
    max_index = -1
    for i, out in enumerate(outputs):
        if out > max_activation:
            max_activation = out
            max_index = i

    # estimate the maximal activation's coordinates
    x = max_index % self.field_size
```

```
y = int(max_index / self.field_size)

return (x, y)
```

At first, the function enumerates through the output array and finds the index of the maximal value:

```
max_activation = -100.0
max_index = -1
for i, out in enumerate(outputs):
    if out > max_activation:
        max_activation = out
        max_index = I
```

After that, it uses the index it finds to estimate the Cartesian coordinates, taking into account the size of the target field:

```
x = max_index % self.field_size
y = int(max_index / self.field_size)
```

Finally, the function returns the tuple (*x*, *y*) with the Cartesian coordinates of the big object within the target field.

For complete implementation details, please look at `vd_environment.py` at `https://github.com/PacktPublishing/Hands-on-Neuroevolution-with-Python/blob/master/Chapter7/vd_environment.py`.

Experiment runner

As we described earlier, the solution for the visual discrimination task can be found using the HyperNEAT method. Thus, we need to use a library that provides an implementation of the HyperNEAT algorithm. The MultiNEAT Python library is the right candidate for this experiment. As such, we are implementing our experiment using this library.

Next, we discuss the most critical components of the experiment runner implementation.

For complete implementation details, please refer to `vd_experiment_multineat.py` at `https://github.com/PacktPublishing/Hands-on-Neuroevolution-with-Python/blob/master/Chapter7/vd_experiment_multineat.py`.

The experiment runner function

The `run_experiment` function allows us to run the experiment using the provided hyperparameters and the initialized visual discriminator test environment. The function implementation has the following parts.

Initializing the first CPPN genome population

In the following code, at first, we initialize the random number generator seed with the current system time. After that, we create the appropriate substrate configuration for the discriminator ANN that is able to operate over the dimensionality of the experiment's visual field. Next, we create the CPPN genome using the created substrate configuration:

```
# random seed
seed = int(time.time())
# Create substrate
substrate = create_substrate(num_dimensions)
# Create CPPN genome and population
g = NEAT.Genome(0,
                substrate.GetMinCPPNInputs(),
                0,
                substrate.GetMinCPPNOutputs(),
                False,
                NEAT.ActivationFunction.UNSIGNED_SIGMOID,
                NEAT.ActivationFunction.UNSIGNED_SIGMOID,
                0,
                params, 0)
pop = NEAT.Population(g, params, True, 1.0, seed)
pop.RNG.Seed(seed)
```

The CPPN genome created in the preceding code has the appropriate number of input and output nodes provided by the substrate. Initially, it uses the unsigned sigmoid as the node activation function. Later, during the evolution, the activation function type at each node of the CPPN will be changed, following the HyperNEAT algorithm routines. Finally, the initial population is created using the initialized CPPN genome and the HyperNEAT hyperparameters.

Running the neuroevolution over the specified number of generations

At the beginning of this part, we create the intermediate variables to hold the execution results and create the statistics collector (`Statistics`). After that, we execute the evolution loop for the number of generations specified in the `n_generations` parameter:

```
start_time = time.time()
best_genome_ser = None
```

```
best_ever_goal_fitness = 0
best_id = -1
solution_found = False

stats = Statistics()
for generation in range(n_generations):
```

Within the evolution loop, we obtain the list of genomes belonging to the population at the current generation and evaluate all genomes from the list against the test environment as follows:

```
genomes = NEAT.GetGenomeList(pop)
# evaluate genomes
genome, fitness, distances = eval_genomes(genomes,
                            vd_environment=vd_environment,
                            substrate=substrate,
                            generation=generation)
stats.post_evaluate(max_fitness=fitness, distances=distances)
solution_found = fitness >= FITNESS_THRESHOLD
```

We save the values returned by the `eval_genomes(genomes, substrate, vd_environment, generation)` function for the current generation into the statistics collector. Also, we use the fitness score returned by `eval_genomes` to estimate whether a successful solution has been found or not. If the fitness score exceeds the `FITNESS_THRESHOLD` value, we consider that a successful solution has been found.

If a successful solution was found or the current fitness score is the maximum fitness score ever achieved, we save the CPPN genome and the current fitness score:

```
if solution_found or best_ever_goal_fitness < fitness:
    best_genome_ser = pickle.dumps(genome)
    best_ever_goal_fitness = fitness
    best_id = genome.GetID()
```

Also, if a successful solution is found, we break the evolution loop and move to the reporting steps, which we will discuss later:

```
if solution_found:
        print('Solution found at generation: %d, best fitness: %f,
 species count: %d' % (generation, fitness, len(pop.Species)))
        break
```

If a successful solution was not found, we print the statistics for the current generation and advance to the next generation with the following code:

```
# advance to the next generation
pop.Epoch()
# print statistics
gen_elapsed_time = time.time() - gen_time
print("Best fitness: %f, genome ID: %d" % (fitness, best_id))
print("Species count: %d" % len(pop.Species))
print("Generation elapsed time: %.3f sec" % (gen_elapsed_time))
print("Best fitness ever: %f, genome ID: %d"
      % (best_ever_goal_fitness, best_id))
```

After the main evolution loop, the results of the experiment are reported, which uses the statistics collected in the loop.

Saving the results of the experiment

The experiment results reported and saved in textual and graphical representations (SVG files). We start by printing general performance statistics as follows:

```
print("\nBest ever fitness: %f, genome ID: %d"
      % (best_ever_goal_fitness, best_id))
print("\nTrial elapsed time: %.3f sec" % (elapsed_time))
print("Random seed:", seed)
```

The first three lines of the preceding code print the best ever fitness score obtained among all the generations of evolution to the console. After that, we print the experiment's elapsed time and the random seed value used.

If we requested to save or show visualizations, the corresponding functions are invoked:

```
# Visualize the experiment results
show_results = not silent
if save_results or show_results:
    net = NEAT.NeuralNetwork()
    best_genome.BuildPhenotype(net)
    visualize.draw_net(net, view=show_results, node_names=None,
                       directory=trial_out_dir, fmt='svg')
```

The preceding code draws the network graph of the CPPN and prints the statistics of the graph.

Next, we move to the visualization of the output of the discriminator ANN:

```
# Visualize activations from the best genome
net = NEAT.NeuralNetwork()
```

```
best_genome.BuildHyperNEATPhenotype(net, substrate)
# select random visual field
index = random.randint(0, len(vd_environment.data_set) - 1)
vf = vd_environment.data_set[index]
# draw activations
outputs, x, y = vd_environment.evaluate_net_vf(net, vf)
visualize.draw_activations(outputs, found_object=(x, y), vf=vf,
        dimns=num_dimensions, view=show_results,
        filename=os.path.join(trial_out_dir,
                        "best_activations.svg"))
```

In the preceding code, we create the discriminator ANN using the best CPPN genome found during the evolution. After that, we draw the activation outputs obtained by running the evaluation of the discriminator ANN against the test environment. We use the visual field that is randomly selected from the dataset of the experiment.

Finally, we render the general statistics collected during the experiment:

```
# Visualize statistics
visualize.plot_stats(stats, ylog=False, view=show_results,
        filename=os.path.join(trial_out_dir, 'avg_fitness.svg'))
```

The statistics plot includes the best fitness scores and the average error distances drawn over the generations of evolution.

> For implementation details of the visualization functions mentioned in this section, please refer to visualize.py
> at https://github.com/PacktPublishing/Hands-on-Neuroevolution-wit h-Python/blob/master/Chapter7/visualize.py.

The substrate builder function

The HyperNEAT method is built around the notion of the substrate that defines the structure of the discriminator ANN. Therefore, it is crucial to create an appropriate substrate configuration to be used during the experiment execution. The substrate creation routines are defined in the following two functions:

- The substrate builder function create_substrate creates the substrate object as follows:

```
def create_substrate(dim):
    # Building sheet configurations of inputs and outputs
    inputs = create_sheet_space(-1, 1, dim, -1)
    outputs = create_sheet_space(-1, 1, dim, 0)
    substrate = NEAT.Substrate( inputs, [], # hidden outputs)
```

```
        substrate.m_allow_input_output_links = True
        ...
        substrate.m_hidden_nodes_activation = \
                    NEAT.ActivationFunction.SIGNED_SIGMOID
        substrate.m_output_nodes_activation = \
                    NEAT.ActivationFunction.UNSIGNED_SIGMOID
        substrate.m_with_distance = True
        substrate.m_max_weight_and_bias = 3.0
        return substrate
```

The preceding function first creates the two grid-based Cartesian sheets that represent inputs (the visual field) and outputs (the target field) of the substrate configuration. Remember that for this experiment we selected a state-space sandwich substrate configuration. After that, the substrate instance was initialized using the created field configurations:

```
        inputs = create_sheet_space(-1, 1, dim, -1)
        outputs = create_sheet_space(-1, 1, dim, 0)
        substrate = NEAT.Substrate( inputs, [], # hidden outputs)
```

 Please note that the substrate doesn't use any hidden nodes; we provide an empty list instead of hidden nodes.

Next, we configure the substrate to only allow connections from input to output nodes and to use a signed sigmoid activation function at the output nodes. Finally, we set the maximum values for the bias and the connection weights.

- The `create_sheet_space` function invoked by the substrate builder function is defined as follows:

```
def create_sheet_space(start, stop, dim, z):
    lin_sp = np.linspace(start, stop, num=dim)
    space = []
    for x in range(dim):
        for y in range(dim):
            space.append((lin_sp[x], lin_sp[y], z))

    return space
```

The `create_sheet_space` function receives the start and end coordinates of the grid within one dimension along with the number of grid dimensions. Also, the z coordinate of the sheet is provided. Using the specified parameters, the preceding code creates the uniform linear space with coordinates starting in the [`start`, `stop`] range with a step of `dim`:

```
lin_sp = np.linspace(start, stop, num=dim)
```

After that, we use this linear space to populate the two-dimensional array with the coordinates of the grid nodes as follows:

```
space = []
for x in range(dim):
    for y in range(dim):
        space.append((lin_sp[x], lin_sp[y], z))
```

The `create_sheet_space` function returns the grid configuration in the form of a two-dimensional array.

Fitness evaluation

The genome's fitness evaluation is a significant part of any neuroevolution algorithm, including the HyperNEAT method. As you've seen, the main experiment loop invokes the `eval_genomes` function to evaluate the fitness of all genomes within a population for each generation. Here, we consider the implementation details of the fitness evaluation routines, which consists of two main functions:

- The `eval_genomes` function evaluates all genomes in the population:

```
def eval_genomes(genomes, substrate, vd_environment, generation):
    best_genome = None
    max_fitness = 0
    distances = []
    for genome in genomes:
        fitness, dist = eval_individual(genome, substrate,
                                        vd_environment)
        genome.SetFitness(fitness)
        distances.append(dist)

        if fitness > max_fitness:
            max_fitness = fitness
            best_genome = genome
    return best_genome, max_fitness, distances
```

The `eval_genomes` function takes a list of genomes, the discriminator ANN substrate configuration, the initialized test environment, and the ID of the current generation as parameters. The first lines of the function create intermediate variables, which are used to store the evaluation results:

```
best_genome = None
max_fitness = 0
distances = []
```

After that, we iterate over all the genomes in the population and collect appropriate statistics:

```
for genome in genomes:
    fitness, dist = eval_individual(genome, substrate,
                                    vd_environment)
    genome.SetFitness(fitness)
    distances.append(dist)

    if fitness > max_fitness:
        max_fitness = fitness
        best_genome = genome
```

Finally, the `eval_genomes` function returns the collected statistics as a tuple, (`best_genome`, `max_fitness`, `distances`).

- The `eval_individual` function allows us to evaluate the fitness of the individual genome as follows:

```
def eval_individual(genome, substrate, vd_environment):
    # Create ANN from provided CPPN genome and substrate
    net = NEAT.NeuralNetwork()
    genome.BuildHyperNEATPhenotype(net, substrate)

    fitness, dist = vd_environment.evaluate_net(net)
    return fitness, dist
```

In the beginning, the preceding source code creates the discriminator ANN phenotype using the CPPN genome provided as a parameter. After that, the discriminator ANN phenotype evaluated against the test environment.

The `eval_individual` function returns the fitness score and error distance obtained from the test environment during the phenotype evaluation. Now that we have completed the setup, let us start with the visual discrimination experiment.

Visual discrimination experiment

Having done all of the necessary setup steps, we are ready to start the experiment.

In the visual discrimination experiment, we use the following configuration of the visual field:

Parameter	Value
Size of the visual field	11 x 11
Positions of the small objects in the visual field along each axis	[1, 3, 5, 7, 9]
Size of the small object	1 x 1
Size of the big object	3 x 3
Offset of the center of the big object from the small object	5

Next, we need to select the appropriate values of the HyperNEAT hyperparameters, allowing us to find a successful solution to the visual discrimination problem.

 Note that the hyperparameter that we describe next determines how to evolve the connective CPPN using the neuroevolution process. The discriminator ANN is created by applying the connective CPPN to the substrate.

Hyperparameter selection

The MultiNEAT library uses the `Parameters` Python class to hold all the required hyperparameters. To set the appropriate values of the hyperparameters, we define the `create_hyperparameters` function in the experiment runner Python script. Here, we describe the essential hyperparameters that have a significant impact on the HyperNEAT algorithm performance in this experiment:

1. The `create_hyperparameters` function begins by creating a `Parameters` object to hold the HyperNEAT parameters:

```
params = NEAT.Parameters()
```

2. We decided to start with a medium-sized population of genomes to keep the computations fast. At the same time, we want to maintain a sufficient number of organisms in the population for evolutionary diversity. The population size is defined as follows:

```
params.PopulationSize = 150
```

3. We are interested in producing compact CPPN genomes that have as few nodes as possible to increase the effectiveness of indirect encoding. Thus, we set a tiny probability of adding a new node during evolution, and also keep the probability of creating a new connection quite low:

```
params.MutateAddLinkProb = 0.1
params.MutateAddNeuronProb = 0.03
```

4. The HyperNEAT method produces CPPN genomes with different types of activation functions in the hidden and output nodes. Thus, we define the probability of mutation that changes the type of the node activation. Also, in this experiment, we are interested in using only four types of activation function: signed Gaussian, signed sigmoid, signed sine, and linear. We set the likelihood of choosing any activation type among the four we just mentioned to 1.0, which effectively makes the probability of choosing each type equal. We define this in the hyperparameters as follows:

```
params.MutateNeuronActivationTypeProb = 0.3
params.ActivationFunction_SignedGauss_Prob = 1.0
params.ActivationFunction_SignedSigmoid_Prob = 1.0
params.ActivationFunction_SignedSine_Prob = 1.0
params.ActivationFunction_Linear_Prob = 1.0
```

5. Finally, we define the number of species within the population to be kept in the [5,10] range and set the value of the species stagnation parameter to 100 generations. This configuration maintains moderate species diversity, but keeps species for long enough to allow them to evolve and produce useful CPPN genome configurations:

```
params.SpeciesMaxStagnation = 100
params.MinSpecies = 5
params.MaxSpecies = 10
```

The selection of hyperparameters presented here demonstrates the high efficiency of producing successful CPPN genomes during the evolution.

Working environment setup

In this experiment, we use the MultiNEAT Python library, which provides the implementation of the HyperNEAT algorithm. Thus, we need to create an appropriate Python environment, which includes the MultiNEAT Python library and all the necessary dependencies. This can be done using Anaconda by executing the following commands in the command line:

```
$ conda create --name vd_multineat python=3.5
$ conda activate vd_multineat
$ conda install -c conda-forge multineat
$ conda install matplotlib
$ conda install -c anaconda seaborn
$ conda install graphviz
$ conda install python-graphviz
```

These commands create and activate a `vd_multineat` virtual environment with Python 3.5. After that, they install the latest version of the MultiNEAT Python library, along with the dependencies that are used by our code for the result visualization.

Running the visual discrimination experiment

To start the experiment, you need to enter the local directory that contains the `vd_experiment_multineat.py` script, and execute the following command:

```
$ python vd_experiment_multineat.py
```

> Do not forget to activate the appropriate virtual environment with the following command:
>
> ```
> $ conda activate vd_multineat
> ```

After a particular number of generations, the successful solution will be found, and you will see lines similar to the following in the console output:

```
****** Generation: 16 ******

Best fitness: 0.995286, genome ID: 2410
Species count: 11
Generation elapsed time: 3.328 sec
Best fitness ever: 0.995286, genome ID: 2410

****** Generation: 17 ******
```

```
Solution found at generation: 17, best fitness: 1.000000, species count: 11

Best ever fitness: 1.000000, genome ID: 2565

Trial elapsed time: 57.753 sec
Random seed: 1568629572

CPPN nodes: 10, connections: 16

Running test evaluation against random visual field: 41
Substrate nodes: 242, connections: 14641
found (5, 1)
target (5, 1)
```

The console output says that the solution was found at generation 17. The ID of the successful CPPN genome is 2565, and this genome has 10 nodes and 16 connections among them. Also, you can see the results of the evaluation of the discriminator ANN produced by the best CPPN genome against the randomly selected visual field.

In this case, the detected Cartesian coordinates of the big object in the target field and the actual coordinates in the visual field are the same (5, 1), which means that the solution found is capable of visual discrimination with exact precision.

Next, it is interesting to take a look at the visualization of the activation outputs of the discriminator ANN obtained during test evaluation:

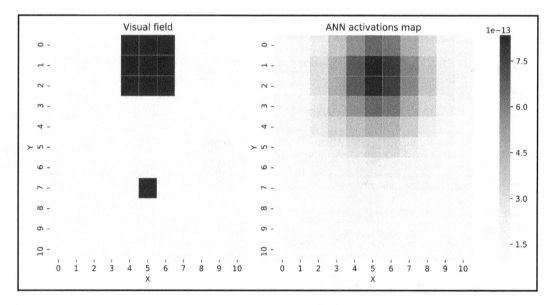

The target field activations of the discriminator ANN

The right part of the preceding plot renders the activation values of the target field (the output layer) of the discriminator ANN, which we obtained during evaluation against a random visual field. Also, in the left part of the plot, you can see the actual visual field configuration. As you can see, the maximum target field activation value (the darkest cell) is precisely at the same position as the center of the big object in the visual field, having the coordinates (5, 1).

As you can see from the preceding graph, the scale of ANN activation values is extremely low: the minimum activation is ~1e-13, and the maximum is only ~9e-13. A human-designed ANN would probably be normalized so that the output is on [0, 1], having a minimum close to zero and a maximum near one. However, we only require the activation to have a maximum in the right place, and the network is free to choose an output activation scheme that most folks would view as unusual.

Another plot allows you to study how the evolution process performed over the generations of evolution and how good the produced connective CPPNs were in creating successful discriminator ANNs:

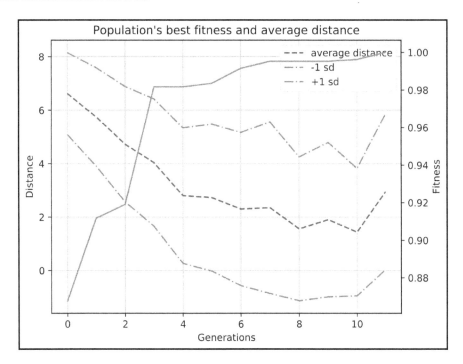

The best fitness scores and average error distances of discriminator ANNs

The preceding plot renders the change in the fitness scores (the ascending line) and the average error distances (the descending line) for each generation of the evolution. You can see that the fitness scores almost reached the maximum value in the third generation of the evolution and needed seven more generations to elaborate over the CPPN genome configurations to finally find the winner. Also, you can see that the average error distance between the detected and the ground truth position of the big object gradually decreases during the evolution process.

However, the most exciting part of this experiment is shown in the following diagram of the CPPN phenotype graph:

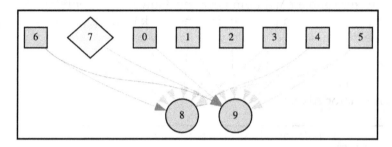

The CPPN phenotype graph of the best genome

The plot demonstrates the network topology of the CPPN phenotype that was used to draw connections over the discriminator ANN producing the successful visual discriminator. In the CPPN phenotype plot, input nodes are marked with squares, output nodes are filled circles, and the bias node is a diamond.

The two output nodes of the CPPN have the following meaning:

- The first node (8) provides the weight of the connection.
- The second node (9) determines whether the connection is expressed or not.

The CPPN input nodes are defined as follows:

- The first two nodes (0 and 1) set the point coordinates (x, y) in the input layer of the substrate.
- The next two nodes (2 and 3) set the point coordinates (x, y) in the hidden layer of the substrate (not used in our experiment).
- The next two nodes (4 and 5) set the point coordinates (x, y) in the output layer of the substrate.
- The last node (6) sets the Euclidean distance from the point in the input layer from the origin of the coordinates.

Also, you can see that the CPPN phenotype doesn't include any hidden nodes. For the visual discrimination task, the neuroevolutionary process was able to find the appropriate activation function types for the output nodes of the CPPN. This finding allows the connective CPPN to draw the correct connectivity patterns within the substrate of the discriminator ANN.

By counting the number of nodes and connections between them as presented in the preceding plot, you can feel the power of the indirect encoding method introduced by the HyperNEAT algorithm. With only 16 connections between 10 nodes, the CPPN phenotype was able to expose the connectivity pattern of the substrate, which for the visual field at 11 x 11 resolution can have up to 14,641 connections between the nodes in the visual field and the target field. So, we achieved an information compression ratio of about 0.11%, which is pretty impressive.

Such a high compression rate is possible because of the discovery of the geometric regularities within the connectivity motifs of the substrate by the connective CPPN. Using the regularities of the discovered patterns, the CPPN can store only a few patterns (local connectivity motifs) for the whole connectivity space of the substrate. After that, the CPPN can apply these local patterns multiple times at different substrate positions to draw the full connectivity scheme between the substrate layers, in our case, to draw connections between the input layer (visual field) and the output layer (target field).

Exercises

1. Try to decrease the value of the `params.PopulationSize` hyperparameter and see what happens. How did this affect the algorithm's performance?
2. Try to set zero probabilities for the values of the following hyperparameters: `params.ActivationFunction_SignedGauss_Prob`, `params.ActivationFunction_SignedSigmoid_Prob`, and `params.ActivationFunction_SignedSine_Prob`. Was a successful solution found with these changes? How did this affect the configuration of the substrate connections?
3. Print out the winning genome, try to come up with a visualization, then see how your intuition from looking at the genome matches with the visualized CPPN.

Summary

In this chapter, we learned about the method of indirect encoding of the ANN topology using CPPNs. You learned about the HyperNEAT extension of the NEAT algorithm, which uses a connective CPPN to draw connectivity patterns within the substrate of the phenotype of the discriminator ANN. Also, we demonstrated how the indirect encoding scheme allows the HyperNEAT algorithm to work with large-scale ANN topologies, which is common in pattern recognition and visual discrimination tasks.

With the theoretical background we provided, you have had the chance to improve your coding skills by implementing the solution for a visual discrimination task using Python and the MultiNEAT library. Also, you learned about a new visualization method that renders the activation values of the nodes in the output layer of the discriminator ANN and how this visualization can be used to verify the solution.

In the next chapter, we will discuss how the HyperNEAT method can be further improved by introducing an automatic way to generate the appropriate substrate configuration. We will consider the **Evolvable Substrate HyperNEAT (ES-HyperNEAT)** extension of the NEAT algorithm and see how it can be applied to solve practical tasks that require the modular topologies of the solver ANN.

ES-HyperNEAT and the Retina Problem

8

In this chapter, you will learn about the ES-HyperNEAT extension of the HyperNEAT method, which we discussed in the previous chapter. As you learned in the previous chapter, the HyperNEAT method allows the encoding of larger-scale **artificial neural network** (**ANN**) topologies, which is essential for working in areas where the input data has a large number of dimensions, such as computer vision. However, despite all its power, the HyperNEAT method has a significant drawback—the configuration of the ANN substrate should be designed beforehand by a human architect. The ES-HyperNEAT method was invented to address this issue by introducing the concept of evolvable-substrate, which allows us to produce the appropriate configuration of the substrate automatically during evolution.

After familiarizing yourself with the basics of the ES-HyperNEAT method, you will have a chance to apply this knowledge to solve the modular retina problem. During this task, we will show you how to choose an appropriate initial substrate configuration that helps the evolutionary process to discover the modular structures. Also, we will discuss the source code of the modular retina problem solver along with the test environment, which can be used to evaluate the fitness of each detector ANN.

Through this chapter, you will gain hands-on experience with applying the ES-HyperNEAT method using the MultiNEAT Python library.

In this chapter, we will cover the following topics:

- Manual versus evolution-based configuration of the topography of neural nodes
- Quadtree information extraction and ES-HyperNEAT basics
- The modular left and right retina experiment
- Discussion of the experiment results

Technical requirements

The following technical requirements should be met to execute the experiments described in this chapter:

- Windows 8/10, macOS 10.13 or newer, or modern Linux
- Anaconda Distribution version 2019.03 or newer

The code for this chapter can be found at `https://github.com/PacktPublishing/Hands-on-Neuroevolution-with-Python/tree/master/Chapter8`

Manual versus evolution-based configuration of the topography of neural nodes

The HyperNEAT method, which we discussed in `Chapter 7`, *Hypercube-Based NEAT for Visual Discrimination*, allows us to use neuroevolution methods for a broad class of problems that require the use of large-scale ANN structures to find a solution. This class of problem spreads across multiple practical domains, including visual pattern recognition. The main distinguishing feature of all these problems is the high dimensionality of the input/output data.

In the previous chapter, you learned how to define the configuration of the substrate of the discriminator ANN to solve a visual discrimination task. You also learned that it is crucial to use an appropriate substrate configuration that is aligned with the geometric features of the search space of the target problem. With the HyperNEAT method, you, as an architect, need to define the substrate configuration beforehand, using only your understanding of the spatial geometry of the problem. However, it is not always possible to learn about all the geometric regularities hidden behind a specific problem space.

If you design the substrate manually, you create an unintentional constraint on the pattern of weights drawn over it by the connective **Compositional Pattern Producing Networks (CPPNs)**. By placing nodes at specific locations in the substrate, you interfere with the ability of the CPPN to discover the geometric regularities of the natural world. The CPPN should produce a connectivity pattern that is perfectly aligned with the structure of the substrate that you provided, and connections are only possible between the nodes of this structure. This limitation leads to unnecessary approximation errors, which taints the results when you use an evolved CPPN to create the topology of the solution-solver ANN (the phenotype).

However, why are the limitations that are introduced with manual substrate configuration inflicted in the first place? Would it be better if the CPPN could elaborate on the connectivity patterns between the nodes of the substrate that are automatically positioned in the right locations in the substrate? It seems that evolving connectivity patterns in the substrate provides valuable implicit hints that help us to estimate the nodes' positions for the next epoch of the evolution. The method of substrate configuration evolution during the CPPN training got a name: **Evolvable-Substrate**.

The implicit data allowing us to estimate the position of the next node is the amount of the information encoded by the connectivity pattern in the specific substrate area. The areas with a uniform distribution of connection weights encode a small amount of information, thereby requiring only a few substrate nodes in those areas. At the same time, substrate areas with large gradients of connection weights are informationally intensive and can benefit from additional nodes placed within those areas. When you place an additional node in such areas of the substrate, you allow the CPPN to represent the much more granular encoding of the natural world. Thus, the placement of the nodes and the connectivity pattern can be mandated by the distribution of the connection weights while the CPPN produces the connection weights during the evolution.

HyperNEAT represents each connection between two nodes of the substrate as a point in the four-dimensional hypercube. The evolvable-substrate HyperNEAT algorithm extends HyperNEAT by automatically placing fewer hyperpoints in the areas of the hypercube with lower variation in the connection weights. Thus, ES-HyperNEAT uses information density as the primary guiding principle when determining the topology of the substrate during the evolution.

In the next section, we discuss the particulars of the ES-HyperNEAT algorithm.

Quadtree information extraction and ES-HyperNEAT basics

For the effective calculation of the information density within the connectivity patterns of the substrate, we need to use an appropriate data structure. We need to employ a data structure that allows an effective search through the two-dimensional substrate space at different levels of granularity. In computer science, there is a data structure that perfectly fits these requirements. This structure is the **quadtree**.

The quadtree is a data structure that allows us to organize an effective search through two-dimensional space by splitting any area of interest into four subareas. Each of these subareas consequently becomes a leaf of a tree, with the root node representing the initial region.

ES-HyperNEAT employs the quadtree data structure to iteratively look for the new connections and nodes in the substrate, starting from the input and the output nodes predefined by the data scientist. Using a quadtree to search for new connections and nodes is much more computationally effective than searching in the four-dimensional space of the hypercube.

The scheme of information extraction using the quadtree structure is shown in the following diagram:

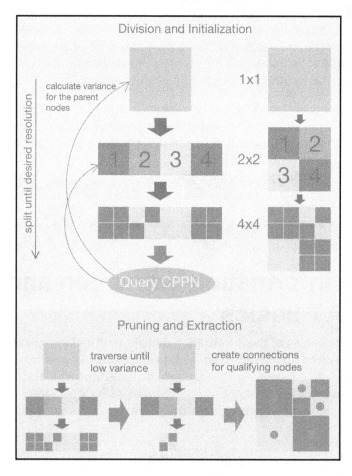

The scheme of information extraction

The information extraction method depicted in the diagram has two major parts:

1. The **division and initialization** stage is presented in the top part of the diagram. At this stage, the quadtree is created by recursively dividing the initial substrate area, which spans from (*-1, -1*) to (*1, 1*). The division stops when the desired depth of the quadtree is reached. Now we have several subspaces that are fitted into the substrate, determining the initial substrate resolution (*r*). Next, for every node of the quadtree with a center at (x_i, y_i), we query the CPPN to find a connection weight (*w*) between this node and a specific input or output neuron at coordinates (*a, b*). When we have calculated the connection weights for the *k* leaf nodes in the subtree of the quadtree, *p*, we are ready to calculate the information variance of the node, *p*, in the quadtree as follows:

$$\sigma^2 = \sum_{i=1}^{k} (\bar{w} - w_i)^2$$

$\bar{w}$ is the mean connection weight among *k* leaf nodes and w_i is a connection weight to each leaf node.

We can use this estimated variance value as a heuristic indicator of the information density in the specific subarea of the substrate. The higher this value, the higher the information density. The variance can be used to manage the information density in the specific subarea of the substrate by introducing the **division threshold** constant. If the variance is greater than the division threshold, then the division stage is repeated until the desired information density is reached.

At this stage, we create an indicative structure that allows the CPPN to decide where to make connections within the given substrate. The next stage of the processing places all necessary connections using the created quadtree structure.

2. The **pruning and extraction** stage is represented in the bottom part of the diagram. In this stage, we use the populated quadtree structure from the previous stage to find the regions with high variance and make sure that more connections are expressed among the nodes of these regions. We traverse the quadtree depth-first and stop the traversal at the node that has a variance value that's smaller than the given **variance threshold** (σ_t^2) or when the current node has no children (that is, has zero variance). For every quadtree node found by the depth-first search, we express the connection between the center of the node (x, y) and each parent node that is already determined. The parent node can either be determined by an architect (input/output nodes) or be found in the previous runs of the information extraction method, that is, from hidden nodes already created by the ES-HyperNEAT method. When this stage completes, the substrate configuration will have more nodes in the informationally intensive substrate regions and fewer nodes in the regions encoding a small amount of information.

In the following section, we will discuss how to use the ES-HyperNEAT algorithm we've just described to find a solution for the modular retina problem.

 For more details about the ES-HyperNEAT algorithm, refer to Chapter 1, *Overview of Neuroevolution Methods*.

Modular retina problem basics

The hierarchical modular structures are an essential part of the complex biological organisms and play an indispensable role in their evolution. The modularity enhances the evolvability, allowing the recombination of various modules during the evolution process. The evolved hierarchy of modular components bootstraps the evolution process, allowing operations over a collection of complex structures rather than basic genes. After that, the neuroevolutionary process does not need to spend time to evolve similar functionality from scratch again. Instead, the ready-to-use modular components can be used as building blocks to produce very complex neural networks.

In this chapter, we will implement a solution to the retina problem using the ES-HyperNEAT algorithm. The retina problem is about the simultaneous identification of valid 2x2 patterns on the left and the right side of an artificial retina that has a resolution of 4x2. Thus, the detector ANN must decide if the patterns presented on the left and the right side of the retina are valid for the corresponding side of the retina (left or right).

In the retina problem, the left and the right problem components are perfectly separated into different functional units. At the same time, some components can be present on each side of the retina, while others are unique to a specific part of the retina. Thus, to produce a successful detector ANN, the neuroevolution process needs to discover the modular structures separately for the left and the right detection zones.

The retina problem scheme is shown in the following diagram:

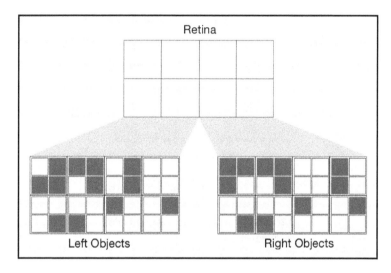

The retina problem scheme

As you can see in the preceding diagram, the artificial retina is represented as a 2D grid with a resolution of 4x2 pixels. The values of the two-dimensional array representing the patterns drawn on the retina constitute the inputs of the detector ANN. The filled pixels in the array have a value of 1.0 and the empty pixels have a value of 0.0. With the given resolution, it is possible to draw 16 different 2x2 patterns for the left and the right parts of the retina. Thus, we have eight valid patterns for the left side and eight valid patterns for the right side of the retina. Some of the patterns mentioned are valid for both sides of the retina.

The scheme of decision-making by the detector ANN in the retina problem domain is as follows:

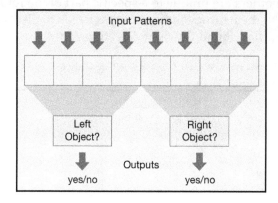

The scheme of decision making by the detector ANN

The detector ANN has eight inputs to accept input data patterns from both sides of the retina and two output nodes. Each of the output nodes produces a value that can be used to classify the pattern's validity at each side of the retina. The first output node is assigned to the left and the second node to the right side of the retina correspondingly. The activation value of the output node that is greater than or equal to 0.5 classifies the pattern for the related side of the retina as valid. If the activation value is less than 0.5, the pattern is considered not valid. To even further simplify the detection, we apply rounding to the values of the output nodes according to the rounding scheme shown in the diagram. Thus, each output node of the detector ANN serves as a binary classifier for the related part of the retina that produces a value of 0.0 or 1.0 to mark the input pattern as invalid or valid correspondingly.

Objective function definition

The task of the detector ANN is to correctly classify the inputs from the left and right sides of the retina as valid or not by producing a vector of the binary outputs with values of 0.0 or 1.0. The output vector has a length of 2, which is equal to number of the output nodes.

We can define the detection error as the Euclidean distance between the vector with ground truth values and the vector with ANN output values, as given by the following formula:

$$e^2 = \sum_{i=1}^{2}(a_i - b_i)^2$$

e^2 is the squared detection error for one trial, a is the vector with detector ANN outputs, and b is the vector with the ground truth values.

At each generation of the evolution, we evaluate each detector ANN (phenotype) against all 256 possible combinations of 4x4 retina patterns, which are produced by combining 16 different 2x2 patterns for each side of the retina. Thus, to get a final detection error value for the particular detector ANN, we calculate the sum of 256 error values obtained for each configuration of the retina patterns, as indicated by the following formula:

$$\mathcal{E} = \sum_{i=1}^{256} e_i^2$$

$\mathcal{E}$ is the sum of all errors obtained during 256 trials and e_i^2 is the squared detection error for a particular trial.

The fitness function can be defined as the inverse of the sum of the errors obtained from all 256 trials against all possible retina patterns, as shown in the following formula:

$$\mathcal{F} = \frac{1000.0}{1.0 + \mathcal{E}}$$

We add 1.0 to the sum of errors ($\mathcal{E}$) in the denominator to avoid dividing by 0 in cases when all trials produce no error. Thus, according to the fitness function formula, the maximum value of the fitness score in our experiment is 1000.0, which we will use as a fitness threshold value later.

Modular retina experiment setup

In this section, we discuss the details of an experiment aimed at creating a successful solver of the modular retina problem. In our experiment, we use this problem as a benchmark to test the ability of the ES-HyperNEAT method to discover modular topologies in the phenotype ANN.

The initial substrate configuration

As described earlier in the chapter, the retina has dimensions of 4x2, with two 2x2 areas, one on the left side and one on the right side. The particulars of the retina geometry must be represented in the geometry of the initial substrate configuration. In our experiment, we use a three-dimensional substrate, as shown in the following diagram:

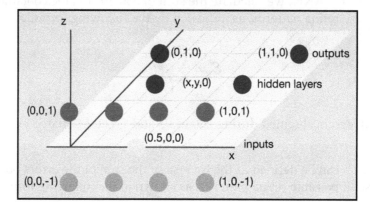

The initial substrate configuration

As you can see in the diagram, the input nodes are placed within the XZ plane, which is orthogonal to the XY plane. They are presented in two groups, with four nodes to describe the left and right sides of the retina. The two output and bias nodes are located within the XY plane, which divides the Z-plane in half with the input nodes. The evolution of the substrate creates new hidden nodes in the same XY plane where the output nodes are located. The evolved connective CPPN draws the connectivity patterns between all nodes within the substrate. Our ultimate goal is to evolve the CPPN and the substrate configuration, which produces an appropriate modular graph of the detector ANN. This graph should include two modules, each representing an appropriate configuration for the binary classifier, which we discussed earlier. Let's now look at the test environment for the modular retina problem.

Test environment for the modular retina problem

First, we need to create a test environment that can be used to evaluate the results of the neuroevolution process that aims to create a successful detector ANN. The test environment should create a dataset that consists of all possible patterns of pixels on the retina. Also, it should provide functions to evaluate the detector ANN against each pattern in the dataset. Thus, the test environment can be divided into two main parts:

- The data structure to hold visual patterns for the left-hand, the right-hand, or both sides of the retina
- The test environment storing the dataset and providing functions for detector ANN evaluation

In the following sections, we provide a detailed description of each part.

The visual object definition

Each of the allowed configurations of pixels in the specific part of the retina space can be represented as a separate visual object. The Python class encapsulating the related functionality is named `VisualObject` and is defined in the `retina_experiment.py` file. It has the following constructor:

```python
def __init__(self, configuration, side, size=2):
    self.size = size
    self.side = side
    self.configuration = configuration
    self.data = np.zeros((size, size))
    # Parse configuration
    lines = self.configuration.splitlines()
    for r, line in enumerate(lines):
        chars = line.split(" ")
        for c, ch in enumerate(chars):
            if ch == 'o':
                # pixel is ON
                self.data[r, c] = 1.0
            else:
                # pixel is OFF
                self.data[r, c] = 0.0
```

The constructor receives the configuration of a particular visual object as a string, along with a valid location for this object in the retina space. After that, it assigns received parameters to the internal fields and creates a two-dimensional data array holding the states of the pixels in the visual object.

The pixels' states are obtained by parsing the visual object configuration string as follows:

```
# Parse configuration
lines = self.configuration.splitlines()
for r, line in enumerate(lines):
    chars = line.split(" ")
    for c, ch in enumerate(chars):
        if ch == 'o':
            # pixel is ON
            self.data[r, c] = 1.0
        else:
            # pixel is OFF
            self.data[r, c] = 0.0
```

The visual object configuration string has four characters, excluding the line break, which define the state of the corresponding pixel in the visual object. If the symbol at a specific position in the configuration line is o, then the pixel at the corresponding position of the visual object is set to the ON state, and the value 1.0 is saved to the data array at this position.

The retina environment definition

The retina environment creates and stores the dataset consisting of all possible visual objects and provides functions for evaluating the fitness of the detector ANN. It has the following main implementation parts.

The function to create a dataset with all the possible visual objects

In this function, we create the visual objects for the dataset as follows:

```
def create_data_set(self):
    # set left side objects
    self.visual_objects.append(VisualObject(". .\n. .",
                                            side=Side.BOTH))
    self.visual_objects.append(VisualObject(". .\n. o",
                                            side=Side.BOTH))
    self.visual_objects.append(VisualObject(". o\n. o",
                                            side=Side.LEFT))
    self.visual_objects.append(VisualObject(". o\n. .",
                                            side=Side.BOTH))
```

```
self.visual_objects.append(VisualObject(". o\no o",
                                     side=Side.LEFT))
self.visual_objects.append(VisualObject(". .\no .",
                                     side=Side.BOTH))
self.visual_objects.append(VisualObject("o o\n. o",
                                     side=Side.LEFT))
self.visual_objects.append(VisualObject("o .\n. .",
                                     side=Side.BOTH))
```

The preceding code creates visual objects for the left side of the retina. The visual objects for the right side can be created in a similar way:

```
# set right side objects
self.visual_objects.append(VisualObject(". .\n. .",
                                     side=Side.BOTH))
self.visual_objects.append(VisualObject("o .\n. .",
                                     side=Side.BOTH))
self.visual_objects.append(VisualObject("o .\no .",
                                     side=Side.RIGHT))
self.visual_objects.append(VisualObject(". .\no .",
                                     side=Side.BOTH))
self.visual_objects.append(VisualObject("o o\no .",
                                     side=Side.RIGHT))
self.visual_objects.append(VisualObject(". o\n. .",
                                     side=Side.BOTH))
self.visual_objects.append(VisualObject("o .\no o",
                                     side=Side.RIGHT))
self.visual_objects.append(VisualObject(". .\n. o",
                                     side=Side.BOTH))
```

The created objects appended to the list of the visual objects are defined as a dataset for evaluating the fitness of the detector ANN produced by the neuroevolution process from the substrate.

The function to evaluate the detector ANN against two specific visual objects

This function evaluates the performance of the detector ANN against two given visual objects—one for each side of the retina space. For the complete source code, please refer to the `def _evaluate(self, net, left, right, depth, debug=False)` function defined at `https://github.com/PacktPublishing/Hands-on-Neuroevolution-with-Python/blob/master/Chapter8/retina_environment.py`.

The source code of the function has the following essential parts:

1. First, we prepare the inputs for the detector ANN in the order that they are defined in for the substrate configuration:

```
inputs = left.get_data() + right.get_data()
inputs.append(0.5) # the bias

net.Input(inputs)
```

The `inputs` array starts with the left-side data and continues with the right-side data. After that, the bias value is appended to the end of the `inputs` array and the array data is supplied as input to the detector ANN.

2. After a specific number of activations of the detector ANN, the outputs are obtained and rounded:

```
outputs = net.Output()
outputs[0] = 1.0 if outputs[0] >= 0.5 else 0.0
outputs[1] = 1.0 if outputs[1] >= 0.5 else 0.0
```

3. Next, we need to calculate squared detection error, which is the Euclidean distance between the outputs vector and the vector with the ground-truth values. Thus, we first create the vector with ground-truth values as follows:

```
left_target = 1.0 if left.side == Side.LEFT or \
                     left.side == Side.BOTH else 0.0
right_target = 1.0 if right.side == Side.RIGHT or \
                      right.side  == Side.BOTH else 0.0
targets = [left_target, right_target]
```

The corresponding ground-truth value is set to `1.0` if the visual object is valid for a given side of the retina, or both sides. Otherwise, it is set to `0.0` to indicate an incorrect visual object position.

4. Finally, the squared detection error is calculated as follows:

```
error = (outputs[0]-targets[0]) * (outputs[0]-targets[0]) + \
        (outputs[1]-targets[1]) * (outputs[1]-targets[1])
```

The function returns the detection error and the outputs from the detector ANN. In the next section, we will discuss the retina experiment runner implementation.

For complete implementation details, refer to the `retina_environment.py` file at `https://github.com/PacktPublishing/Hands-on-Neuroevolution-with-Python/blob/master/Chapter8/retina_environment.py`.

Experiment runner

To solve the modular retina problem, we need to use a Python library that provides an implementation of the ES-HyperNEAT algorithm. If you've read the previous chapter, you are already familiar with the MultiNEAT Python library, which also has an implementation of the ES-HyperNEAT algorithm. Thus, we can use this library to create a retina experiment runner implementation.

Let's discuss the essential components of the implementation.

For full implementation details, refer to the `retina_experiment.py` file at `https://github.com/PacktPublishing/Hands-on-Neuroevolution-with-Python/blob/master/Chapter8/retina_experiment.py`.

The experiment runner function

The `run_experiment` function runs the experiment using the provided hyperparameters and an initialized test environment to evaluate the discovered detector ANNs against the possible retina configurations. The function implementation has the following significant parts:

1. First is the initialization of the population of the initial CPPN genomes:

```
seed = 1569777981
# Create substrate
substrate = create_substrate()
# Create CPPN genome and population
g = NEAT.Genome(0,
        substrate.GetMinCPPNInputs(),
        2, # hidden units
        substrate.GetMinCPPNOutputs(),
        False,
        NEAT.ActivationFunction.TANH,
        NEAT.ActivationFunction.SIGNED_GAUSS, # hidden
```

```
        1, # hidden layers seed
        params,
        1) # one hidden layer
pop = NEAT.Population(g, params, True, 1.0, seed)
pop.RNG.Seed(seed)
```

At first, the preceding code sets the random seed value to the one that we found to be useful for generating successful solutions by sequentially running many experiment trials. After that, we create the substrate configuration that is suitable for the retina experiment, taking into account the geometry of the retina space.

Next, we create the initial CPPN genome using the substrate configuration we already have. The CPPN genome needs to have a number of input and output nodes that is compatible with the substrate configuration. Also, we seed the initial CPPN genome with two hidden nodes with a Gaussian activation function to boost the neuroevolution process in the right direction. The Gaussian hidden nodes start the neuroevolution search with a bias toward producing particular detector ANN topologies. With these hidden nodes, we introduce to the connectivity patterns of the substrate the principle of symmetry, which is precisely what we are expecting to achieve in the topology of the successful detector ANN. For the retina problem, we need to discover a symmetrical detector ANN configuration incorporating the two symmetrical classifier modules.

2. Next, we prepare the intermediary variables to hold the experiment execution results, along with the statistics collector. After that, we run the evolution loop for a set number of generations:

```
start_time = time.time()
best_genome_ser = None
best_ever_goal_fitness = 0
best_id = -1
solution_found = False

stats = Statistics()
...
```

3. Inside the evolution loop, we get the list of genomes belonging to the current population and evaluate it against the test environment as follows:

```
# get list of current genomes
genomes = NEAT.GetGenomeList(pop)

# evaluate genomes
genome, fitness, errors = eval_genomes(genomes,
```

```
                    rt_environment=rt_environment,
                    substrate=substrate,
                    params=params)
        stats.post_evaluate(max_fitness=fitness, errors=errors)
        solution_found = fitness >= FITNESS_THRESHOLD
```

The `eval_genomes` function returns a tuple that has the following components: the best-fit genome, the highest fitness score among all evaluated genomes, and the list of detection errors for each evaluated genome. We save the appropriate parameters into a statistics collector and evaluate the obtained fitness score against the search termination criterion, which is defined as a `FITNESS_THRESHOLD` constant with a value of `1000.0`. The evolutionary search terminates successfully if the best fitness score in population is greater than or equal to the `FITNESS_THRESHOLD` value.

4. If the successful solution was found, or the current best fitness score of the population is higher than the maximum fitness score ever achieved, we save the best CPPN genome and current fitness score as follows:

```
        if solution_found or best_ever_goal_fitness < fitness:
            # dump to pickle to freeze the genome state
            best_genome_ser = pickle.dumps(genome)
            best_ever_goal_fitness = fitness
            best_id = genome.GetID()
```

5. After that, if the value of the `solution_found` variable was set to `True`, we terminate the evolution loop:

```
        if solution_found:
            print('Solution found at generation: %d, best fitness:
%f, species count: %d' % (generation, fitness, len(pop.Species)))
            break
```

6. If the evolution failed to produce a successful solution, we print the statistics for the current generation and move to the next epoch:

```
        # advance to the next generation
        pop.Epoch()

        # print statistics
        gen_elapsed_time = time.time() - gen_time
        print("Best fitness: %f, genome ID: %d" %
              (fitness, best_id))
        print("Species count: %d" % len(pop.Species))
        print("Generation elapsed time: %.3f sec" %
              (gen_elapsed_time))
```

```
print("Best fitness ever: %f, genome ID: %d" %
    (best_ever_goal_fitness, best_id))
```

The rest of the experiment runner code reports the results of the experiment in different formats.

7. We report the experiment results in textual and visual formats using the statistics collected in the evolution loop. Furthermore, visualizations are also saved into the local filesystem in the SVG vector format:

```
print("\nBest ever fitness: %f, genome ID: %d" %
    (best_ever_goal_fitness, best_id))
print("\nTrial elapsed time: %.3f sec" % (elapsed_time))
print("Random seed:", seed)
```

The first three lines of the code print general statistics about experiment execution, such as the highest fitness score achieved, the time elapsed for experiment execution, and the random generator seed value.

8. The next part of the code is about visualizing the experiment results, which is the most informative part, and you should pay great attention to it. We start with visualizing the CPPN network that we create from the best genome found during the evolution:

```
if save_results or show_results:
    # Draw CPPN network graph
    net = NEAT.NeuralNetwork()
    best_genome.BuildPhenotype(net)
    visualize.draw_net(net, view=False, node_names=None,
                        filename="cppn_graph.svg",
                        directory=trial_out_dir, fmt='svg')
    print("\nCPPN nodes: %d, connections: %d" %
            (len(net.neurons), len(net.connections)))
```

9. After that, we visualize the detector ANN topology that is created using the best CPPN genome and the retina substrate:

```
net = NEAT.NeuralNetwork()
best_genome.BuildESHyperNEATPhenotype(net, substrate,
                                        params)
visualize.draw_net(net, view=False, node_names=None,
                    filename="substrate_graph.svg",
                    directory=trial_out_dir, fmt='svg')
print("\nSubstrate nodes: %d, connections: %d" %
        (len(net.neurons),
        len(net.connections)))
inputs = net.NumInputs()
```

```
outputs = net.NumOutputs()
hidden = len(net.neurons) - net.NumInputs() - \
        net.NumOutputs()
print("\n\tinputs: %d, outputs: %d, hidden: %d" %
        (inputs, outputs, hidden))
```

10. Also, we print the results of the evaluation of the detector ANN created by the preceding code against a full dataset and two randomly selected visual objects:

```
# Test against random retina configuration
l_index = random.randint(0, 15)
r_index = random.randint(0, 15)
left = rt_environment.visual_objects[l_index]
right = rt_environment.visual_objects[r_index]
err, outputs = rt_environment._evaluate(net, left,
                                        right, 3)
print("Test evaluation error: %f" % err)
print("Left flag: %f, pattern: %s" % (outputs[0], left))
print("Right flag: %f, pattern: %s" % (outputs[1], right))

# Test against all visual objects
fitness, avg_error, total_count, false_detections = \
            rt_environment.evaluate_net(net, debug=True)
print("Test evaluation against full data set [%d], fitness:
%f, average error: %f, false detections: %f" % (total_count,
fitness, avg_error, false_detections))
```

Finally, we render the statistics data collected during the experiment as follows:

```
# Visualize statistics
visualize.plot_stats(stats, ylog=False, view=show_results,
        filename=os.path.join(trial_out_dir,
'avg_fitness.svg'))
```

All visualization plots mentioned here can be found after execution of the experiment in the `trial_out_dir` directory of the local filesystem. Now, let's discuss how the substrate builder function is implemented.

The substrate builder function

The ES-HyperNEAT method runs the neuroevolution process, which includes the evolution of the CPPN genomes along with the evolution of the substrate configuration. However, even though the substrate is evolving during evolution, it is incredibly beneficial to start with an appropriate initial substrate configuration. This configuration should correspond to the geometry of the problem space.

For the retina experiment, the appropriate substrate configuration is created as follows:

1. First, we create the configuration of the input layer of the substrate. As you may remember from the *The initial substrate configuration* section, the eight nodes of the input layer are placed within the XZ plane, which is orthogonal to the XY plane. Furthermore, to reflect the geometry of the retina space, the left object's nodes need to be placed on the left side, and the right object's nodes on the right side of the plane correspondingly. The bias node should be located at the center of the input nodes plane. Thus, the input layer is created as follows:

```
# The input layer
x_space = np.linspace(-1.0, 1.0, num=4)
inputs = [
    # the left side
    (x_space[0], 0.0, 1.0), (x_space[1], 0.0, 1.0),
    (x_space[0], 0.0, -1.0), (x_space[1], 0.0, -1.0),
    # the right side
    (x_space[2], 0.0, 1.0), (x_space[3], 0.0, 1.0),
    (x_space[2], 0.0, -1.0), (x_space[3], 0.0, -1.0),
    (0,0,0) # the bias
    ]
```

    The two output nodes are located within the XY plane, which is orthogonal to the inputs plane. This substrate configuration allows natural substrate evolution by placing the discovered hidden nodes within the XY plane.

2. The output layer is created as follows:

```
# The output layer
outputs = [(-1.0, 1.0, 0.0), (1.0, 1.0, 0.0)]
```

3. Next, we define the general substrate configuration parameters as follows:

```
# Allow connections: input-to-hidden, hidden-to-output,
# and  hidden-to- hidden
substrate.m_allow_input_hidden_links = True
substrate.m_allow_hidden_output_links = True
substrate.m_allow_hidden_hidden_links = True

substrate.m_allow_input_output_links = False
substrate.m_allow_output_hidden_links = False
substrate.m_allow_output_output_links = False
substrate.m_allow_looped_hidden_links = False
substrate.m_allow_looped_output_links = False

substrate.m_hidden_nodes_activation = \
        NEAT.ActivationFunction.SIGNED_SIGMOID
```

```
substrate.m_output_nodes_activation = \
        NEAT.ActivationFunction.UNSIGNED_SIGMOID

# send connection length to the CPPN as a parameter
substrate.m_with_distance = True
substrate.m_max_weight_and_bias = 8.0
```

We allow the substrate to have connections from input-to-hidden, hidden-to-hidden, and hidden-to-output nodes. We specify that hidden nodes should use the signed sigmoid activation function, while output nodes should use the unsigned sigmoid activation function. We choose the unsigned sigmoid activation for the output nodes in order to have detector ANN output values in the range [0, 1].

In the next section, we discuss the implementation of the functions to evaluate the fitness of the solutions.

Fitness evaluation

The neuroevolution process requires a means to evaluate the fitness of the genome population at each generation of evolution. The fitness evaluation in our experiment consists of two parts, which we discuss here.

The eval_genomes function

This function evaluates the fitness of the overall population. It has the following definition:

```
def eval_genomes(genomes, substrate, rt_environment, params):
    best_genome = None
    max_fitness = 0
    errors = []
    for genome in genomes:
        fitness, error, total_count, false_detetctions = eval_individual(
                            genome, substrate, rt_environment, params)
        genome.SetFitness(fitness)
        errors.append(error)

        if fitness > max_fitness:
            max_fitness = fitness
            best_genome = genome
    return best_genome, max_fitness, errors
```

The `eval_genomes` function takes the list of CPPN genomes from the current population, the substrate configuration, the initialized test environment, and the ES-HyperNEAT hyperparameters as parameters.

At the beginning of the code, we create an intermediary object to collect the evaluation results of each specific genome:

```
best_genome = None
max_fitness = 0
errors = []
```

After that, we start the loop that iterates over all genomes and evaluates each genome against a given test environment:

```
for genome in genomes:
    fitness, error, total_count, false_detetctions = eval_individual(
                          genome, substrate, rt_environment, params)
    genome.SetFitness(fitness)
    errors.append(error)

    if fitness > max_fitness:
        max_fitness = fitness
        best_genome = genome
```

Finally, the function returns the evaluation results as a tuple that includes the best genome, the highest fitness score, and the list of all detection errors for each evaluated genome.

The eval_individual function

This function evaluates the fitness of each individual genome and has the following definition:

```
def eval_individual(genome, substrate, rt_environment, params):
    # Create ANN from provided CPPN genome and substrate
    net = NEAT.NeuralNetwork()
    genome.BuildESHyperNEATPhenotype(net, substrate, params)

    fitness, dist, total_count, false_detetctions = \
        rt_environment.evaluate_net(net, max_fitness=MAX_FITNESS)
    return fitness, dist, total_count, false_detetctions
```

It takes the CPPN genome to be evaluated, the substrate configuration, the test environment, and the ES-HyperNEAT hyperparameters as parameters. Using the provided parameters, we create the neural network configuration of the detector ANN and evaluate it against the given test environment. The function then returns the evaluation result.

Modular retina experiment

Now we are ready to start experimenting against the test environment that simulates the modular retina problem space. In the next subsections, you will learn how to select appropriate hyperparameters and how to set up the environment and run the experiment. After that, we discuss the experiment results.

Hyperparameter selection

The hyperparameters are defined as a `Parameters` Python class, and the MultiNEAT library refers to it for the necessary configuration options. In the source code of the experiment runner script, we define a specialized function called `create_hyperparameters`, which encapsulates the logic of the hyperparameter initialization. Hereafter, we describe the most critical hyperparameters and the reasons for choosing these specific values:

1. We decided to use a medium size for the CPPN genome population. This is done to intensify the evolution by providing a large space of options for the solution search from the beginning. The size of the population is defined as follows:

   ```
   params.PopulationSize = 300
   ```

2. Next, we define the number of species to be kept during evolution in the range `[5, 15]` and set the species stagnation to `100` generations. This configuration allows us to have healthy diversity among species and keep them alive for long enough to produce the solution we are looking for:

   ```
   params.SpeciesMaxStagnation = 100
   params.MinSpecies = 5
   params.MaxSpecies = 15
   ```

3. We are interested in producing an extra-compact configuration of CPPN genomes. Thus, we have very small values of probabilities that control how often new nodes and connections will be introduced into the genome:

   ```
   params.MutateAddLinkProb = 0.03
   params.MutateAddNeuronProb = 0.03
   ```

4. The ES-HyperNEAT method is an extension of the HyperNEAT method. Thus, during the evolution, it changes the types of activation functions in the hidden and output nodes. In this experiment, to produce appropriate substrate configurations, we are interested in the following activation types, selected with equal probability:

```
params.ActivationFunction_SignedGauss_Prob = 1.0
params.ActivationFunction_SignedStep_Prob = 1.0
params.ActivationFunction_Linear_Prob = 1.0
params.ActivationFunction_SignedSine_Prob = 1.0
params.ActivationFunction_SignedSigmoid_Prob = 1.0
```

5. Finally, we define the ES-HyperNEAT specific hyperparameters, which control how the substrate evolves. The following hyperparameters control the dynamics of the creation of nodes and connections within the substrate during evolution:

```
params.DivisionThreshold = 0.5
params.VarianceThreshold = 0.03
```

`params.DivisionThreshold` controls how many new nodes and connections are introduced into the substrate at each generation of evolution.
`params.VarianceThreshold` determines how many nodes and connections are allowed to remain in the substrate after the pruning and extraction phase. See the *Quadtree information extraction and ES-HyperNEAT basics* section for more details about these thresholds.

Working environment setup

In this experiment, we use the MultiNEAT Python library, which provides the implementation of the ES-HyperNEAT algorithm. Thus, we need to create an appropriate Python environment, which includes the MultiNEAT Python library and all necessary dependencies. This can be done using Anaconda by executing the following commands on the command line:

```
$ conda create --name rt_multineat python=3.5
$ conda activate vd_multineat
$ conda install -c conda-forge multineat
$ conda install matplotlib
$ conda install -c anaconda seaborn
$ conda install graphviz
$ conda install python-graphviz
```

These commands create and activate the `rt_multineat` virtual environment with Python 3.5. After that, they install the MultiNEAT Python library with the latest version, along with dependencies that are used by our code for result visualization.

Running the modular retina experiment

At this stage, we already have the experiment runner script fully defined in the `retina_experiment.py` Python script. You can start the experiment by cloning the corresponding Git repository and running the script with the following commands:

```
$ git clone
https://github.com/PacktPublishing/Hands-on-Neuroevolution-with-Python.git
$ cd Hands-on-Neuroevolution-with-Python/Chapter8
$ python retina_experiment.py -t 1 -g 1000
```

 Do not forget to activate the appropriate virtual environment with the following command:

```
conda activate rt_multineat
```

The preceding command starts one trial of the experiment for 1,000 generations of evolution. After a particular number of generations, the successful solution should be found, and you will see the following output in the console:

```
****** Generation: 949 ******

Solution found at generation: 949, best fitness: 1000.000000, species
count: 6

Best ever fitness: 1000.000000, genome ID: 284698

Trial elapsed time: 1332.576 sec
Random seed: 1569777981

CPPN nodes: 21, connections: 22

Substrate nodes: 15, connections: 28
```

As you can see in the output, the successful solution was found in generation 949. It was produced by a CPPN genome with 21 nodes and 22 connections among them. At the same time, the substrate that determines the topology of the detector ANN has 15 nodes and 28 connections between them. The successful solution was produced using random seed value 1569777981. Using other random seed values may fail to produce successful solutions, or it will require many more generations of evolution.

Next, it is interesting to look at the plot of the average fitness and error during the evolution:

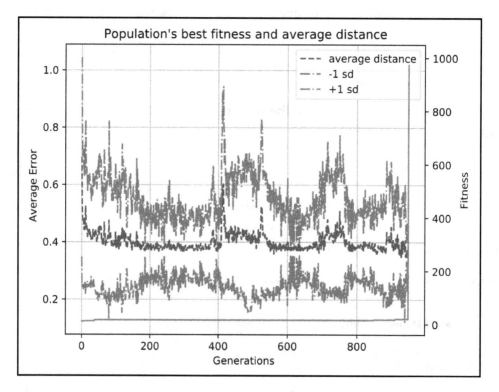

The average fitness and error per generation

You can see in the preceding plot that, during most of the evolution generations, the fitness score was very small (about 20), but suddenly, the successful CPPN genome was found, which produced an immediate evolutionary leap just in one generation.

The configuration of the successful CPPN genome is shown in the following diagram:

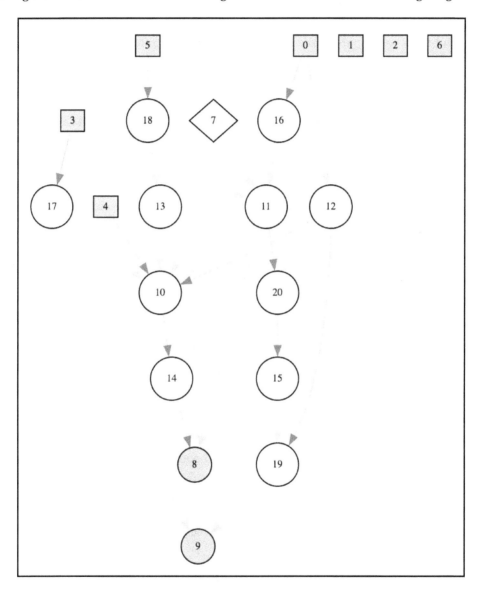

The CPPN phenotype graph of the successful genome

The diagram is extremely interesting because, as you can see, the configuration of the successful CPPN genome does not use all the available inputs (the gray squares) to produce outputs. Moreover, even more confounding is that it uses only the x coordinate of the input (node #0) and the y coordinate of the hidden (node #3) substrate nodes when deciding about exposing a connection between these substrate nodes. At the same time, both the x and y coordinates of the substrate output nodes are involved in the decision-making process (nodes #4 and #5).

When you look at the initial substrate configuration, which we presented earlier, you will see that the peculiarities we've mentioned are fully substantiated by the substrate topology. We placed the input nodes within the XZ plane. Thus, the y coordinate is not critical for them at all. At the same time, the hidden nodes located within the XY plane, with the y coordinate determining the distance from the inputs plane. Finally, the output nodes are also located within the XY plane. Their x coordinate determines the side of the retina to which each output node relates. Thus, for the output nodes, it is natural that both the x and y coordinates are included.

In the CPPN phenotype plot, the input nodes are marked with squares, the output nodes are filled circles, the bias node is a diamond, and the hidden nodes are empty circles.

Two output nodes in the CPPN diagram has the following meaning:

- The first node (8) provides the weight of the connection.
- The second node (9) determines whether the connection is expressed or not.

The CPPN's input nodes are defined as the following:

- The first two nodes (0 and 1) set the point coordinates (x, z) in the input layer of the substrate.
- The next two nodes (2 and 3) set the point coordinates (x, y) in the hidden layer of the substrate.
- The next two nodes (4 and 5) set the point coordinates (x, y) in the output layer of the substrate.
- The last node (6) sets the Euclidean distance of the point in the input layer from the origin of the coordinates.

However, you can see the most exciting part of the experiment results in the following diagram. It represents the configuration of the successful detector ANN:

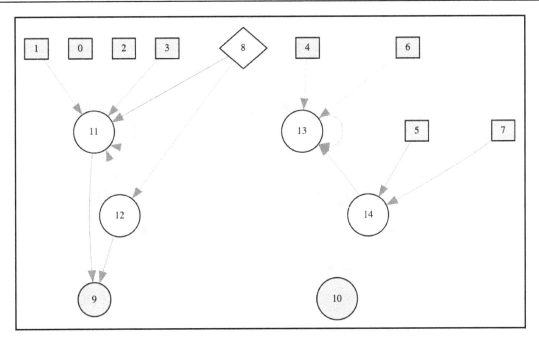

The configuration of the detector ANN

As in the previous plot, we mark the input nodes with squares, the output nodes with filled circles, the bias node as a diamond, and the hidden nodes as empty circles.

As you can see, we have two clearly separated modular structures on the left and right sides of the graph. Each module is connected to the corresponding inputs from the left (nodes #0, #1, #2, and #3) and the right (nodes #4, #5, #6, and #7) sides of the retina. Both modules have the same number of hidden nodes, which are connected to the corresponding output nodes: node #9 for the left side and node #10 for the right side of the retina. Also, you can see that connectivity patterns in the left and right modules are similar. The hidden node, #11, on the left has similar connection patterns to node #14 on the right, and the same can be said for nodes #12 and #13.

It is just amazing how the stochastic evolutionary process was able to discover such a simple and elegant solution. With the results of this experiment, we fully confirmed our hypothesis that the retina problem can be solved by the creation of modular detector ANN topologies.

More details about modular retina problem can be found in the original paper at http://eplex.cs.ucf.edu/papers/risi_alife12.pdf.

Exercises

1. Try to run an experiment with different values of the random seed generator that can be changed in line 101 of the `retina_experiment.py` script. See if you can find successful solutions with other values.

2. Try to increase the initial population size to 1,000 by adjusting the value of the `params.PopulationSize` hyperparameter. How did this affect the performance of the algorithm?

3. Try to change the number of activation function types used during the evolution by setting the probability of its selection to 0. It's especially interesting to see what happens when you exclude the `ActivationFunction_SignedGauss_Prob` and `ActivationFunction_SignedStep_Prob` activation types from selection.

Summary

In this chapter, we learned about the neuroevolution method that allows the substrate configuration to evolve during the process of finding the solution to the problem. This approach frees the human designer from the burden of creating a suitable substrate configuration to the smallest details, allowing us to define only the primary outlines. The algorithm will automatically learn the remaining details of the substrate configuration during the evolution.

Also, you learned about the modular ANN structures that can be used to solve various problems, including the modular retina problem. Modular ANN topologies are a very powerful concept that allows the reuse of the successful phenotype ANN module multiple times to build a complex hierarchical topology. Furthermore, you have had the chance to hone your skills with the Python programming language by implementing the corresponding solution using the MultiNEAT Python library.

In the next chapter, we will discuss the fascinating concept of coevolution and how it can be used to simultaneously coevolve the solver and the objective function that is used for optimization. We will discuss the method of solution and fitness evolution, and you will learn how to apply it to the modified maze-solving experiment.

Co-Evolution and the SAFE
Method

9

In this chapter, we introduce the concept of co-evolution and explain how it can be used to co-evolve the solver and the objective function that optimizes the evolution of the solver. We then discuss the **Solution and Fitness Evolution** (**SAFE**) method and provide a brief overview of different co-evolution strategies. You will learn how to use co-evolution with neuroevolution-based methods. You will also get practical experience with the implementation of a modified maze-solving experiment.

In this chapter, we will cover the following topics:

- Co-evolution basics and common co-evolution strategies
- SAFE method basics
- Modified maze-solving experiment
- Discussion about the results of the experiment

Technical requirements

The following technical requirements should be met to execute the experiments described in this chapter:

- Windows 8/10, macOS 10.13 or newer, or modern Linux
- Anaconda Distribution version 2019.03 or newer

The code for this chapter can be found at `https://github.com/PacktPublishing/Hands-on-Neuroevolution-with-Python/tree/master/Chapter9`

Common co-evolution strategies

The natural evolution of biological systems cannot be considered separately from the concept of co-evolution. Co-evolution is one of the central evolutionary drives that leads to the current state of the biosphere, with the diversity of organisms that we can perceive around us.

We can define co-evolution as a mutually beneficial strategy of the simultaneous evolution of multiple genealogies of different organisms. The evolution of one species cannot be possible without other species. During evolution, the co-evolving species mutually interact, and these inter-species relations shape their evolutionary strategy.

There are three main types of co-evolution:

- **Mutualism** is when two or more species coexist and mutually benefit each other.
- **Competitive co-evolution**:
    - **Predation** is when one organism kills another and consumes its resources.
    - **Parasitism** is when one organism exploits the resources of another but does not kill it.
- **Commensalism** is when the members of one species benefit from another species without causing harm or benefits to the other species.

Each type of co-evolution strategy has been explored by researchers, and they have pros and cons for use as guiding principles of the neuroevolution process. However, a group of researchers recently explored the commensalism strategy as a guiding principle for neuroevolution and achieved promising results. They created the SAFE algorithm, which we will discuss in this chapter.

 For more details on the SAFE algorithm, please refer to the original publication at https://doi.org/10.1007/978-3-030-16670-0_10.

Now that we have covered the common types of co-evolution, let's discuss the SAFE method in detail.

SAFE method

As the name suggests, the SAFE method is about the co-evolution of the solution and the fitness function, which guides the solution search optimization. The SAFE method is built around the *commensalistic* co-evolution strategy of two populations:

- The population of potential solutions, which evolve to solve the problem at hand
- The population of objective function candidates, which evolve to guide the evolution of the solution population

In this book, we have already discussed several search optimization strategies that can be used to guide the evolution of potential solution candidates. These strategies are objective-based fitness optimization and Novelty Search optimization. The former optimization strategy is perfect in situations when we have a plain fitness function landscape and can concentrate our optimization search on the ultimate goal. In this case, we can use the objective-based metric, which evaluates, in each epoch of evolution, how close our current solution is to the destination.

The Novelty Search optimization strategy is different. In this strategy, we are not interested in the proximity to the ultimate goal, but instead, we are concerned mostly about the path that the candidate solutions take. The central idea behind the Novelty Search method is to gradually explore the stepping stones, which finally lead to the destination. This optimization strategy is ideal for situations in which we have an intricate fitness function landscape with many deceptive dead ends and local optima.

Thus, the main idea behind the SAFE method is to benefit from both search optimization methods mentioned here. Hereafter, we will discuss the modified maze experiment, which uses both search optimization methods mentioned here to guide the neuroevolution process.

Modified maze experiment

We have already discussed in this book how to apply either the objective-based search optimization or Novelty Search optimization methods to the problem of solving a maze. In this chapter, we introduce a modified maze-solving experiment in which we try to combine both search optimization methods using the SAFE algorithm.

We introduce the co-evolution of two populations: a population of maze-solving agents and a population of objective function candidates. Following the SAFE method, we use a commensalistic co-evolution strategy in our experiment. Let's first discuss the maze-solving agent.

The maze-solving agent

The maze-solving agent is equipped with a set of sensors, allowing it to perceive the maze environment and to know the direction to the maze exit at each step. The configuration of the sensors is shown in the following diagram:

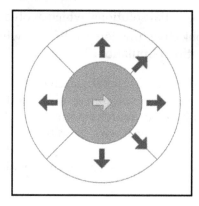

The maze-solving agent's sensor configuration

In the preceding diagram, the dark arrows define the range-finder sensors allowing the agent to perceive obstacles and find the distance to the obstacle in the given direction. The four sectors drawn around the robot's body are pie-slice radars, which detect the direction to the maze exit in each time step. The light arrow inside the robot's body determines the direction in which the robot is facing.

Also, the robot has two actuators: one to change its angular velocity (rotation) and another to change its linear velocity.

We use the same robot configuration that we used in `Chapter 5`, *Autonomous Maze Navigation*. Thus, you should refer to that chapter for more details. Now that we have covered the maze-solving agent, let's look at the maze environment.

The maze environment

The maze is defined as an area enclosed by walls from the outside. Inside the maze, multiple internal walls create multiple dead ends with local fitness optima, which makes objective-oriented optimization search not very effective. Furthermore, due to the local fitness optima, objective-based search agents can get stuck inside a particular dead end, halting the evolution process completely. The dead ends are shown in the following diagram:

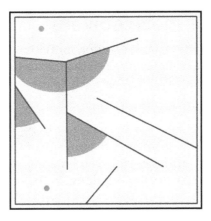

The local optima areas within the maze

In the preceding diagram, the solving agent's starting position is marked by a filled circle in the bottom-left corner, and the maze exit is marked by the filled circle in the top-left corner. The deceptive local fitness optima values are shown as filled sectors the agent's start position.

The maze environment is defined through the configuration file, and we have implemented the simulator to simulate the solving agent's traversal through the maze. We discussed the maze simulator environment implementation in `Chapter 5`, *Autonomous Maze Navigation*, and you can refer to it for the particulars.

In this chapter, we discuss the modifications that were introduced into the original experiment to implement the SAFE optimization strategy. The most critical difference is how the fitness function is defined, and we discuss that in the next section.

You can check out the complete implementation details of the maze simulator environment in the source code at `https://github.com/PacktPublishing/Hands-on-Neuroevolution-with-Python/blob/master/Chapter9/maze_environment.py`.

Fitness function definition

The SAFE method is about the co-evolution of solution candidates and the objective function candidates, that is, we have two co-evolving populations of species. Thus, we need to define two fitness functions: one for the solution candidates (maze solvers) and another for objective function candidates. In this section, we discuss both variants.

Fitness function for maze solvers

In every generation of the evolution, each solution individual (maze solver) is evaluated against all objective function candidates. We use the maximum fitness score obtained during the evaluation of a maze solver against each objective function candidate as a fitness score of the solution.

The fitness function of the maze solver is an aggregate of two metrics—the distance from the maze exit (the objective-based score) and the novelty of the solver's final position (the novelty score). These scores are arithmetically combined using a pair of coefficients obtained as an output from the particular individual in the objective function candidate's population.

The following formula gives the combination of these scores as a fitness score:

$$\mathcal{O}_i(\mathcal{S}_i) = a \times \frac{1}{D_i} + b \times NS_i$$

$\mathcal{O}_i(\mathcal{S}_i)$ is the fitness values obtained by the evaluation of the solution candidate, $\mathcal{S}_i$, against the objective function, $\mathcal{O}_i$. The pair of the coefficients used, $[a, b]$, is the output of the particular objective function candidate. This pair determines how the distance to the maze exit (D_i) and the behavioral novelty (NS_i) of the solution influence the ultimate fitness score of the maze solver at the end of the trajectory.

The distance to the maze exit (D_i) is determined as the Euclidean distance between the maze solver's final coordinates and the maze exit coordinates. This is shown in the following formula:

$$D_i = \sqrt{(x_s - x_m)^2 + (y_s - y_m)^2}$$

x_s and y_s are the final coordinates of the maze solver, and x_m and y_m are the coordinates of the maze exit.

The novelty score, NS_i, of each maze solver is determined by its final position in the maze (point x). It is calculated as the average distance from this point to the k-nearest neighbor points, which are the final positions of the other maze solvers.

The following formula gives the novelty score value at point x of the behavioral space:

$$NS_i = \frac{1}{k} \sum_{i=0}^{k} dist(x, \mu_i)$$

μ_i is the i-th nearest neighbor of x, and $dist(x, \mu_i)$ is the distance between x and μ_i.

The distance between two points is the novelty metric measuring how different the current solution (x) is from another (μ_i) produced by different maze solvers. The novelty metric is calculated as the Euclidean distance between two points:

$$dist(x, \mu) = \sqrt{\sum_{j=1}^{2} (x_j - \mu_j)^2}$$

μ_j and x_j are the values at position j of the coordinate vectors holding coordinates of the μ and x points correspondingly.

Next, we discuss how to define the fitness function for the optimization of the objective function candidates.

Fitness function for the objective function candidates

The SAFE method is based on a commensalistic co-evolutionary approach, which means that one of the co-evolving populations neither benefits nor is harmed during the evolution. In our experiment, the commensalistic population is the population of the objective function candidates. For this population, we need to define a fitness function that is independent of the performance of the maze-solver population.

A suitable candidate for such a function is a fitness function that uses the novelty score as the fitness score to be optimized. The formula to calculate the novelty score of each objective function candidate is the same as given for the maze solvers. The only difference is that in the case of the objective function candidates, we calculate the novelty score using vectors with the output values of each individual. After that, we use the novelty score value as the fitness score of the individual.

This method of novelty score estimation is a part of the modified **Novelty Search** (**NS**) method, which we discuss in the next section.

Modified Novelty Search

We presented the NS method in Chapter 6, *Novelty Search Optimization Method*. In the current experiment, we use a slightly modified version of the NS method, which we discuss next.

The modifications to the NS method that we will present in this experiment relate to a new way of maintaining the archive of novelty points. The novelty point holds the maze solver's location in the maze at the end of the trajectory, which is combined with the novelty score.

In the more traditional version of the NS method, the size of the novelty archive is dynamic, allowing the addition of a specific novel point if its novelty score exceeds a certain threshold (the novelty threshold). Also, the novelty threshold can be adjusted during runtime, taking into account how fast the new novelty points are discovered during the evolution. These adjustments allow us to control the maximum size of the archive (to some extent). However, we need to start with an initial novelty threshold value, and this choice is not an obvious one.

The modified NS method introduces the fixed-size novelty archive to address the issue of choosing the correct novelty threshold value. The new novelty points are added to the archive until it becomes full. After that, a novelty point is added to the archive only if its novelty score exceeds the current minimum score of the archive by replacing the current point with a minimal score. Thus, we can maintain the fixed size of the novelty archive and store in it only the most valuable novelty points discovered during the evolution.

The source code of the modified novelty archive implementation can be found at
`https://github.com/PacktPublishing/Hands-on-Neuroevolution-with-Python/blob/master/Chapter9/novelty_archive.py`.

Next, let's discuss the most interesting parts of the implementation.

The _add_novelty_item function

This function allows the addition of new novelty points to the archive while maintaining its size. It has the following implementation:

```
if len(self.novel_items) >= MAXNoveltyArchiveSize:
    # check if this item has higher novelty than
    # last item in the archive (minimal novelty)
    if item > self.novel_items[-1]:
        # replace it
        self.novel_items[-1] = item
else:
    # just add new item
    self.novel_items.append(item)

# sort items array in descending order by novelty score
self.novel_items.sort(reverse=True)
```

The code first checks whether the size of the novelty archive has not been exceeded yet and directly appends a new novelty point to it in this case. Otherwise, a new novelty point replaces the last item in the archive, which is the item with the smallest novelty score. We can be sure that the last item in the archive has the smallest novelty score because after adding a new item to the archive, we sort it in descending order of novelty score value.

The evaluate_novelty_score function

This function provides a mechanism to evaluate the novelty score of the novelty item against all items already collected in the novelty archive and all the novelty items discovered in the current population. We calculate the novelty score as the average distance to the $k=15$ nearest neighbors by following these steps:

1. We need to collect the distances from the provided novelty item to all items in the novelty archive:

```
distances = []
for n in self.novel_items:
    if n.genomeId != item.genomeId:
        distances.append(self.novelty_metric(n, item))
    else:
        print("Novelty Item is already in archive: %d" %
                n.genomeId)
```

2. After that, we add the distances from the provided novelty item to all items in the current population:

```
for p_item in n_items_list:
    if p_item.genomeId != item.genomeId:
        distances.append(self.novelty_metric(p_item, item))
```

3. Finally, we can estimate the average k-nearest neighbors value:

```
distances = sorted(distances)
item.novelty = sum(distances[:KNN])/KNN
```

We sort the list with the distances in ascending order to guarantee that the closest items are first in the list. After that, we calculate the sum of the first $k=15$ items in the list and divide it by the count of summed values. Thus, we obtain the value of the average distance to the *k-nearest neighbors*.

The modified NS optimization method is at the core of the fitness score evaluation for both the population of maze solvers and the population of objective function candidates. We use it extensively in the implementation of the experiment runner, which we discuss in the next section.

Modified maze experiment implementation

The implementation of the experiment runner is based on the MultiNEAT Python library, which we have used in several experiments in this book. The evolution of each co-evolving population is controlled by the basic NEAT algorithm, which was discussed in Chapter 3, *Using NEAT for XOR Solver Optimization*, Chapter 4, *Pole-Balancing Experiments*, and Chapter 5, *Autonomous Maze Navigation*.

However, in this section, we demonstrate how to use the NEAT algorithm to maintain the co-evolution of two independent populations of species: the maze solvers and the objective function candidates.

Next, we discuss the essential parts of the modified maze experiment runner.

For more details, please refer to the source code at https://github.com/PacktPublishing/Hands-on-Neuroevolution-with-Python/blob/master/Chapter9/maze_experiment_safe.py.

Creation of co-evolving populations

In this experiment, we need to create two co-evolving populations of species with different initial genotype configurations to meet the phenotypic requirements of the produced species.

The phenotype of the maze solver has 11 input nodes to receive signals from the sensors and two output nodes to produce control signals. At the same time, the phenotype of the objective function candidate has one input node receiving the fixed value (0.5), which is converted into two output values that are used as the fitness function coefficients of the maze solver.

We start with a discussion of how to create the population of the objective function candidates.

Creation of the population of the objective function candidates

The genotype encoding the phenotype of the objective function candidates must produce phenotype configurations that have at least one input node and two output nodes, as discussed previously. We implement the population creation in the `create_objective_fun` function as follows:

```
params = create_objective_fun_params()
# Genome has one input (0.5) and two outputs (a and b)
genome = NEAT.Genome(0, 1, 1, 2, False,
    NEAT.ActivationFunction.TANH, # hidden layer activation
    NEAT.ActivationFunction.UNSIGNED_SIGMOID, # output layer activation
    1, params, 0)
pop = NEAT.Population(genome, params, True, 1.0, seed)
pop.RNG.Seed(seed)

obj_archive = archive.NoveltyArchive(
                    metric=maze.maze_novelty_metric_euclidean)
obj_fun = ObjectiveFun(archive=obj_archive,
                    genome=genome, population=pop)
```

In this code, we create the NEAT genotype with one input node, two output nodes, and one hidden node. The hidden node is pre-seeded into the initial genome to boost the evolution with the pre-defined non-linearity. The activation function type of the hidden layer is selected to be hyperbolic tangent to support negative output values. This feature is essential for our task. A negative value of one of the coefficients produced by the objective function candidate can indicate that a particular component of the maze solver fitness function has a negative influence, and this sends a signal that the evolution needs to try other paths.

In the end, we create the `ObjectiveFun` object to maintain an evolving population of the objective function candidates.

Next, we discuss how the population of maze solvers is created.

Creating the population of maze solvers

The maze-solver agent needs to get inputs from 11 sensors and generate two control signals, which affect the angular and linear velocity of the robot. Thus, the genome encoding the phenotype of the maze solver must yield phenotype configurations that include 11 input nodes and two output nodes. You can see how the creation of the initial population of genomes for the maze-solver agent is implemented by taking a look at the `create_robot` function:

```
params = create_robot_params()
# Genome has 11 inputs and two outputs
genome = NEAT.Genome(0, 11, 0, 2, False,
                     NEAT.ActivationFunction.UNSIGNED_SIGMOID,
                     NEAT.ActivationFunction.UNSIGNED_SIGMOID,
                     0, params, 0)
pop = NEAT.Population(genome, params, True, 1.0, seed)
pop.RNG.Seed(seed)

robot_archive = archive.NoveltyArchive(metric=maze.maze_novelty_metric)
robot = Robot(maze_env=maze_env, archive=robot_archive, genome=genome,
              population=pop)
```

In the code, we obtain the appropriate NEAT hyperparameters from the `create_robot_params` function. After that, we use them to create an initial NEAT genotype with the corresponding number of input and output nodes. Finally, we create a `Robot` object, which encapsulates all the data related to the maze-solver population, along with the maze simulator environment.

Now, when we have created the two co-evolving populations, we need to implement the fitness score evaluation for individuals in both populations. We discuss the implementation details of the fitness score evaluation in the next section.

The fitness evaluation of the co-evolving populations

Having defined the two co-evolving populations, we need to create functions to evaluate the fitness scores of the individuals in each population. As we have already mentioned, the fitness scores of the individuals in the maze-solver population depend on the outputs produced by the population of objective function candidates. At the same time, the fitness score of each objective function candidate is wholly determined by the novelty score of that individual.

Thus, we have two different approaches to the evaluation of fitness scores, and we need to implement two different functions. Hereafter, we discuss both implementations.

Fitness evaluation of objective function candidates

The fitness score of each individual in the population of the objective function candidates is determined by its novelty score, which is calculated as we discussed previously. The implementation of the fitness score evaluation is divided between two functions: `evaluate_obj_functions` and `evaluate_individ_obj_function`.

Next, we discuss the implementations of both functions.

The evaluate_obj_functions function implementation

This function accepts the `ObjectiveFun` object, which holds the population of the objective function candidates, and uses it to estimate the fitness score of each individual in the population by following these steps:

1. First, we iterate over all genomes in the population and collect the novelty points for each genome:

```
obj_func_genomes = NEAT.GetGenomeList(obj_function.population)
for genome in obj_func_genomes:
    n_item = evaluate_individ_obj_function(genome=genome,
                                           generation=generation)
    n_items_list.append(n_item)
    obj_func_coeffs.append(n_item.data)
```

In the code, the novelty points obtained from the `evaluate_individ_obj_function` function are appended to the list of novelty points in the population. Also, we append novelty point data to the list of coefficient pairs. The list of coefficient pairs later will be used to estimate the fitness scores of the individual maze solvers.

2. Next, we iterate over the list of population genomes and evaluate the novelty score of each genome using the novelty points collected in the previous step:

```
max_fitness = 0
for i, genome in enumerate(obj_func_genomes):
    fitness = obj_function.archive.evaluate_novelty_score(
            item=n_items_list[i],n_items_list=n_items_list)
    genome.SetFitness(fitness)
    max_fitness = max(max_fitness, fitness)
```

The novelty score estimated using the novelty points are already collected in the novelty archive and the list of the novelty points created for the current population. After that, we set the estimated novelty score as the fitness score of the corresponding genome. Furthermore, we find the maximum value of the fitness score and return it, along with the list of coefficient pairs.

The evaluate_individ_obj_function function implementation

This function accepts the individual NEAT genome of the objective function candidate and returns the novelty point evaluation results. We implement it as follows:

```
n_item = archive.NoveltyItem(generation=generation, genomeId=genome_id)
# run the simulation
multi_net = NEAT.NeuralNetwork()
genome.BuildPhenotype(multi_net)
depth = 2
try:
    genome.CalculateDepth()
    depth = genome.GetDepth()
except:
    pass
obj_net = ANN(multi_net, depth=depth)

# set inputs and get outputs ([a, b])
output = obj_net.activate([0.5])

# store coefficients
n_item.data.append(output[0])
n_item.data.append(output[1])
```

We start with the creation of a `NoveltyItem` object to hold the novelty point data for a given genome. After that, we build a phenotype ANN and activate it with an input of 0.5. Finally, we use the outputs from the ANN to create the novelty point.

In the next section, we discuss the fitness score evaluation of the individuals in the maze-solver population.

Fitness evaluation of the maze-solver agents

We estimate the fitness score of each individual in the maze-solver population as a compound consisting of two components: the novelty score and the distance to the maze exit at the end of the trajectory. The influence of each component is controlled by a coefficient pair produced by the individuals from the population of the objective function candidates.

The fitness score evaluation is divided into three functions, which we are going to discuss next.

The evaluate_solutions function implementation

The `evaluate_solutions` function receives the `Robot` object as an input parameter, which maintains the population of the maze-solver agent and the maze environment simulator. Also, it receives a list of the coefficient pairs generated during the evaluation of the population of objective function candidates.

We use the input parameters of the function to evaluate each genome in the population and to estimate its fitness function. Here, we discuss the essential implementation details:

1. First, we evaluate each individual in the population against the maze simulator and find the distance to the maze exit at the end of the trajectory:

```
robot_genomes = NEAT.GetGenomeList(robot.population)
for genome in robot_genomes:
    found, distance, n_item = evaluate_individual_solution(
        genome=genome, generation=generation, robot=robot)
    # store returned values
    distances.append(distance)
    n_items_list.append(n_item)
```

2. Next, we iterate over all genomes in the population and estimate the novelty score of each individual. Also, we use the corresponding distance to the maze exit collected before and combine it with the calculated novelty score to evaluate genome fitness:

```
for i, n_item in enumerate(n_items_list):
    novelty = robot.archive.evaluate_novelty_score(item=n_item,
                                      n_items_list=n_items_list)
    # The sanity check
    assert robot_genomes[i].GetID() == n_item.genomeId

    # calculate fitness
    fitness, coeffs = evaluate_solution_fitness(distances[i],
                                      novelty, obj_func_coeffs)
    robot_genomes[i].SetFitness(fitness)
```

In the first half of the code, we use the `robot.archive.evaluate_novelty_score` function to estimate the novelty score of each individual in the population. The second half invokes the `evaluate_solution_fitness` function to estimate the fitness score of each individual using the novelty score and the distance to the maze exit.

3. Finally, we collect evaluation statistics about the performance of the best maze-solver genome in the population:

```
if not solution_found:
    # find the best genome in population
    if max_fitness < fitness:
        max_fitness = fitness
        best_robot_genome = robot_genomes[i]
        best_coeffs = coeffs
        best_distance = distances[i]
        best_novelty = novelty
elif best_robot_genome.GetID() == n_item.genomeId:
    # store fitness of winner solution
    max_fitness = fitness
    best_coeffs = coeffs
    best_distance = distances[i]
    best_novelty = novelty
```

In the end, all statistics collected during population evaluation are returned by the function.

Hereafter, we discuss how the individual maze-solver genome is evaluated against the maze environment simulator.

The evaluate_individual_solution function implementation

This is the function that evaluates the performance of a particular maze solver against the maze environment simulator. It is implemented as follows:

1. First, we create the phenotype ANN of the maze solver and use it as a controller to guide the robot through the maze:

```
n_item = archive.NoveltyItem(generation=generation,
                             genomeId=genome_id)
# run the simulation
maze_env = copy.deepcopy(robot.orig_maze_environment)
multi_net = NEAT.NeuralNetwork()
genome.BuildPhenotype(multi_net)
depth = 8
try:
    genome.CalculateDepth()
    depth = genome.GetDepth()
except:
    pass
control_net = ANN(multi_net, depth=depth)
distance = maze.maze_simulation_evaluate(
    env=maze_env, net=control_net,
    time_steps=SOLVER_TIME_STEPS, n_item=n_item)
```

In the code, we create a `NoveltyItem` object to hold the novelty point, which is defined by the robot's final position in the maze. After that, we create the phenotype ANN and run the maze simulator, using it as the control ANN for a given number of time steps (400). After a simulation completes, we receive the distance between the final position of the maze solver and the maze exit.

2. Next, we save the simulation statistics into the `AgentRecord` object that we analyze at the end of the experiment:

```
record = agent.AgenRecord(generation=generation,
                          agent_id=genome_id)
record.distance = distance
record.x = maze_env.agent.location.x
record.y = maze_env.agent.location.y
record.hit_exit = maze_env.exit_found
record.species_id = robot.get_species_id(genome)
robot.record_store.add_record(record)
```

After that, the function returns a tuple with the following values: a flag indicating whether we have found a solution, the distance to the maze exit at the end of the robot's trajectory, and the `NoveltyItem` object encapsulating information about the novelty point discovered.

In the next section, we discuss the implementation of the maze-solver fitness function.

The evaluate_solution_fitness function implementation

This function is an implementation of the maze-solver fitness function that we discussed earlier. This function receives the distance to the maze exit, the novelty score, and the list of coefficient pairs generated by the current generation of the objective function candidates. Next, it uses the received input parameters to calculate the fitness score as follows:

```
normalized_novelty = novelty
if novelty >= 1.00:
    normalized_novelty = math.log(novelty)
norm_distance = math.log(distance)

max_fitness = 0
best_coeffs = [-1, -1]
for coeff in obj_func_coeffs:
    fitness = coeff[0] / norm_distance + coeff[1] * normalized_novelty
    if fitness > max_fitness:
        max_fitness = fitness
        best_coeffs[0] = coeff[0]
        best_coeffs[1] = coeff[1]
```

First, we need to normalize the distance and the novelty score values using the natural logarithm. This normalization will guarantee that the distance and novelty score values are always on the same scale. It is essential to have these values on the same scale because the coefficient pair is always in the range [0,1]. Thus, if the values of distance and novelty score have different scales, a pair of coefficients will not be unable to influence the significance of each value when calculating the fitness score.

The code iterates over the list of coefficients pairs and, for each pair of coefficients, it calculates the fitness score by combining the distance and the novelty score values.

The ultimate fitness score of the maze solver is the maximum among all found fitness scores. This value and the corresponding pair of coefficients are then returned by the function.

The modified maze experiment runner

Now, when we have implemented all the necessary routines to create co-evolving populations and to evaluate the fitness of individuals within these populations, we are ready to start implementing the experiment runner loop.

 The complete details can be found in the `run_experiment` function in the `maze_experiment_safe.py` file at https://github.com/PacktPublishing/Hands-on-Neuroevolution-with-Python/blob/master/Chapter9/maze_experiment_safe.py.

Here, we discuss the essential details of the implementation:

1. We start with the creation of the corresponding populations of the co-evolving species:

```
robot = create_robot(maze_env, seed=seed)
obj_func = create_objective_fun(seed)
```

2. Next, we start the evolution loop and evaluate both populations as follows:

```
for generation in range(n_generations):
    # evaluate objective function population
    obj_func_coeffs, max_obj_func_fitness = \
                evaluate_obj_functions(obj_func, generation)
    # evaluate robots population
    robot_genome, solution_found, robot_fitness, distances, \
    obj_coeffs, best_distance, best_novelty = \
      evaluate_solutions(robot=robot,
        obj_func_coeffs=obj_func_coeffs, generation=generation)
```

3. After evaluating the populations, we save the results as statistics of the current generation of the evolution:

```
stats.post_evaluate(max_fitness=robot_fitness,
                    errors=distances)
# store the best genome
best_fitness = robot.population.GetBestFitnessEver()
if solution_found or best_fitness < robot_fitness:
    best_robot_genome_ser = pickle.dumps(robot_genome)
    best_robot_id = robot_genome.GetID()
    best_obj_func_coeffs = obj_coeffs
    best_solution_novelty = best_novelty
```

4. At the end of the evolution loop, we signal to both populations to advance to the next epoch if the solution has not been found in the current generation:

```
if solution_found:
    print('Solution found at generation: %d, best fitness:
%f, species count: %d' % (generation, robot_fitness,
len(pop.Species)))
    break
# advance to the next generation
robot.population.Epoch()
obj_func.population.Epoch()
```

5. After the evolution loop completes its iteration over a specified number of generations, we visualize the collected maze records:

```
if args is None:
    visualize.draw_maze_records(maze_env,
            robot.record_store.records,
            view=show_results)
else:
    visualize.draw_maze_records(maze_env,
            robot.record_store.records,
            view=show_results, width=args.width,
            height=args.height,
            filename=os.path.join(trial_out_dir,
                    'maze_records.svg'))
```

The maze records mentioned here hold the statistics of the evaluation of each maze-solver genome in the maze simulator collected during the evolution as `AgentRecord` objects. In the visualization, we render the final position of each evaluated maze solver with the maze.

6. Next, we simulate maze solving with the control ANN, which was created using the best solver genome found during the evolution. The trajectory of the maze solver during the simulation can be visualized as follows:

```
multi_net = NEAT.NeuralNetwork()
best_robot_genome.BuildPhenotype(multi_net)

control_net = ANN(multi_net, depth=depth)
path_points = []
distance = maze.maze_simulation_evaluate(
                        env=maze_env,
                        net=control_net,
                        time_steps=SOLVER_TIME_STEPS,
                        path_points=path_points)
print("Best solution distance to maze exit: %.2f, novelty:
%.2f" % (distance, best_solution_novelty))
visualize.draw_agent_path(robot.orig_maze_environment,
                    path_points, best_robot_genome,
                    view=show_results, width=args.width,
                    height=args.height,
                    filename=os.path.join(trial_out_dir,
                            'best_solver_path.svg'))
```

At first, the code creates a phenotype ANN from the best solver genome. Next, it runs the maze simulator using the created phenotype ANN as the maze solver controller. We then render the collected trajectory points of the maze solver.

7. Finally, we render the plot with the average fitness scores per generation as follows:

```
visualize.plot_stats(stats, ylog=False, view=show_results,
        filename=os.path.join(trial_out_dir, 'avg_fitness.svg'))
```

All the visualizations mentioned here are also saved into the local filesystem as SVG files and can be used later for result analysis.

In the next section, we discuss how to run the modified maze experiment and the results of the experiment.

Modified maze experiment

We are almost ready to start the experiment with co-evolution using the modified maze experiment. However, before that, we need to discuss the hyperparameter selection for each co-evolving population.

Hyperparameters for the maze-solver population

For this experiment, we choose to use the MultiNEAT Python library, which uses the `Parameters` Python class to maintain a list of all supported hyperparameters. The initialization of the hyperparameters for the population of maze solvers is defined in the `create_robot_params` function. Next, we discuss the essential hyperparameters and the reasons behind choosing particular values for them:

1. We decided to have a medium-sized population providing sufficient population diversity from the very beginning:

   ```
   params.PopulationSize = 250
   ```

2. We are interested in producing a compact genome topology during the evolution and limiting the number of species within the population. Thus, we have defined tiny probabilities for adding new nodes and connections during the evolution:

   ```
   params.MutateAddNeuronProb = 0.03
   params.MutateAddLinkProb = 0.05
   ```

3. The novelty score rewards finding unique positions in the maze. One way to achieve this is to intensify the numerical dynamics within the phenotype. Thus, we have increased the range of connection weights:

   ```
   params.MaxWeight = 30.0
   params.MinWeight = -30.0
   ```

4. To support the evolutionary process, we choose to introduce elitism by defining the ratio of the genomes to be transferred to the next generation:

   ```
   params.Elitism = 0.1
   ```

The elitism value determines that about one-tenth of the individuals will be carried to the next generation.

Hyperparameters for the objective function candidates population

We create the hyperparameters for the evolution of the population of objective function candidates in the `create_objective_fun_params` function. Here, we discuss the most critical hyperparameters:

1. We decided to start with a small population to reduce computational costs. Also, the genotypes of the objective function candidate are not expected to be very complicated. Thus, a small population should be sufficient:

   ```
   params.PopulationSize = 100
   ```

2. As with the maze solvers, we are interested in producing compact genomes. Thus, the probabilities of adding new nodes and connections are kept very small:

   ```
   params.MutateAddNeuronProb = 0.03
   params.MutateAddLinkProb = 0.05
   ```

We are not expecting a complicated topology of genomes in the population of the objective function candidates. Thus, most of the hyperparameters are set to default values.

Working environment setup

In this experiment, we use the MultiNEAT Python library. Thus, we need to create an appropriate Python environment, which includes this library and other dependencies. You can set up the Python environment with the help of Anaconda with the following commands:

```
$ conda create --name maze_co python=3.5
$ conda activate maze_co
$ conda install -c conda-forge multineat
$ conda install matplotlib
$ conda install graphviz
$ conda install python-graphviz
```

These commands create the `maze_co` virtual environment with Python 3.5 and install all necessary dependencies into it.

Running the modified maze experiment

Now, we are ready to run the experiment in the newly created virtual environment. You can start the experiment by cloning the corresponding Git repository and running the script with the following commands:

```
$ git clone
https://github.com/PacktPublishing/Hands-on-Neuroevolution-with-Python.git
$ cd Hands-on-Neuroevolution-with-Python/Chapter9
$ python maze_experiment_safe.py -t 1 -g 150 -m medium
```

 Do not forget to activate the appropriate virtual environment with the `conda activate maze_co` command.

The preceding command starts one trial of the experiment for 150 generations of evolution using the medium-complexity maze configuration. After about 100 generations of evolution, a successful solution is discovered by the neuroevolution process, and you should be able to see the following output in the console:

```
****** Generation: 105 ******

Maze solved in 338 steps

Solution found at generation: 105, best fitness: 3.549289, species count: 7


===================================
Record store file: out/maze_medium_safe/5/data.pickle
Random seed: 1571021768
Best solution fitness: 3.901621, genome ID: 26458
Best objective func coefficients: [0.7935419704765059, 0.9882050653334634]
-------------------------------
Maze solved in 338 steps
Best solution distance to maze exit: 3.56, novelty: 19.29
-------------------------
Trial elapsed time: 4275.705 sec
===================================
```

From the output presented here, you can see that a successful maze solver was found at generation 105 and was able to solve the maze in 338 steps from the allotted 400. Also, it is interesting to note that the coefficient pair produced by the best objective function candidate gives slightly more importance to the novelty score component of the maze-solver fitness function.

It is interesting to take a look at the plot of the best fitness scores per generation:

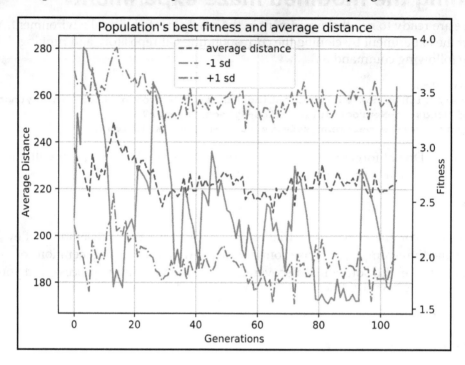

The fitness scores per generation

In the preceding plot, you can see that the best fitness score has a maximum in the early generations of evolution. This is due to the high novelty score values, which are easier to obtain at the beginning of the evolution because there are many maze areas that have not been explored. Another essential point to note is that the average distance to the maze exit remains almost at the same level for most of the generations of evolution. Thus, we can assume that the correct solution was found not by gradual improvements, but rather by a quality leap of the champion genome. This conclusion is also supported by the next plot, where we render the collected maze records per species:

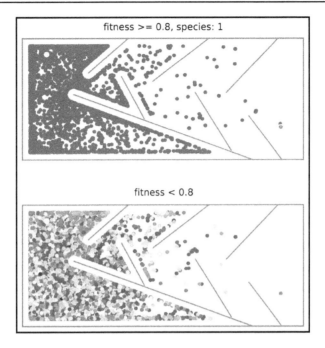

The maze records with final maze solvers positions

The preceding plot has two parts: the top for species with an objective fitness score (based on the distance from the maze exit) greater than **0.8**, and the bottom for other species. You can see that only one species produced a maze-solver genome that was able to reach the vicinity of the maze exit. Also, you can see that the genomes belonging to that species demonstrate very explorative behavior by exploring more maze areas than all other species combined.

Finally, we discuss the path of the successful maze solver through the maze, which is shown in the following diagram:

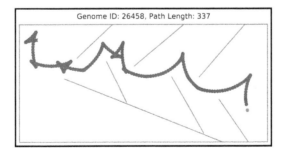

The path of the successful maze solver through the maze

The path of the successful maze solver is near-optimal for the given maze configuration.

This experiment also demonstrates the importance of the initial conditions in finding a successful solution. The initial conditions are defined by the random seed value that we choose before running the experiment.

Exercises

1. We have included the hard-to-solve maze configuration into the experiment source code at
   `https://github.com/PacktPublishing/Hands-on-Neuroevolution-with-Python /blob/master/Chapter9/hard_maze.txt`. You can try to solve the hard maze configuration by using the following command: `python maze_experiment_safe.py -g 120 -t 5 -m hard --width 200 -- height 200`.

2. We have found a successful solution using `1571021768` as a random seed value. Try to find another random seed value producing a successful solution. How many generations did it take to find it?

Summary

In this chapter, we discussed the co-evolution of two populations of species. You learned how commensalistic co-evolution can be implemented to produce a population of successful maze solvers. We introduced you to an exciting approach of implementing a fitness function of the maze solver that combines the objective-based score and the novelty score using coefficients produced by the population of the objective function candidates. Also, you have learned about the modified Novelty Search method and how it differs from the original method, which we discussed in `Chapter 6`, *Novelty Search Optimization Method*.

Using the knowledge gained in this chapter, you will be able to apply a commensalistic co-evolution approach to your work or research tasks that have no clear fitness function definition.

In the next chapter, you will learn about the deep neuroevolution method and how to use it to evolve agents that are able to play classic Atari games.

10
Deep Neuroevolution

In this chapter, you will learn about the deep neuroevolution method, which can be used to train **Deep Neural Networks** (**DNNs**). DNNs are conventionally trained using backpropagation methods based on the descent of the error gradient, which is computed with respect to the weights of the connections between neural nodes. Although gradient-based learning is a powerful technique that conceived the current era of deep machine learning, it has its drawbacks, such as long training times and enormous computing power requirements.

In this chapter, we will demonstrate how deep neuroevolution methods can be used for reinforcement learning and how they considerably outperform traditional DQN, A3C gradient-based learning methods of training DNNs. By the end of this chapter, you will have a solid understanding of deep neuroevolution methods, and you'll also have practical experience with them. We will learn how to evolve agents so that they can play classic Atari games using deep neuroevolution. Also, you will learn how to use **Visual Inspector for NeuroEvolution** (**VINE**) to examine the results of experiments.

In this chapter, we'll cover the following topics:

- Deep neuroevolution for deep reinforcement learning
- Evolving agents to play Frostbite Atari games using deep neuroevolution
- Training an agent to play the Frostbite game
- Running the Frostbite Atari experiment
- Examining the results with VINE

Technical requirements

The following technical requirements should be met so that you can complete the experiments described in this chapter:

- A modern PC with a Nvidia graphics accelerator GeForce GTX 1080Ti or better
- MS Windows 10, Ubuntu Linux 16.04, or macOS 10.14 with a discrete GPU
- Anaconda Distribution version 2019.03 or newer

The code for this chapter can be found at `https://github.com/PacktPublishing/Hands-on-Neuroevolution-with-Python/tree/master/Chapter10`

Deep neuroevolution for deep reinforcement learning

In this book, we have already covered how the neuroevolution method can be applied to solve simple **reinforcement learning** (**RL**) tasks, such as single- and double-pole balancing in `Chapter 4`, *Pole-Balancing Experiments*. However, while the pole-balancing experiment is exciting and easy to conduct, it is pretty simple and operates with tiny artificial neural networks. In this chapter, we will discuss how to apply neuroevolution to reinforcement learning problems that require immense ANNs to approximate the value function of the RL algorithm.

The RL algorithm learns through trial and error. Almost all the variants of RL algorithms try to optimize the value function, which maps the current state of the system to the appropriate action that will be performed in the next time step. The most widely used classical version of the RL algorithm uses a Q-learning method that is built around a table of states keyed by actions, which constitute the policy rules to be followed by the algorithm after training is complete. The training consists of updating the cells of the Q-table by iteratively executing specific actions at particular states and collecting the reward signals afterward. The following formula determines the process of updating a particular cell in a Q-table:

$$Q^{new}(s_t, a_t) = (1 - \alpha)Q(s_t, a_t) + \alpha(r_t + \gamma \max_a Q(s_{t+1}, a))$$

Here r_t is the reward that's received when the system state changes from state s_t to state s_{t+1}, a_t is the action taken at time t leading to the state change, α is the learning rate, and γ is a discount factor that controls the importance of the future rewards. The learning rate determines to what extent the new information overrides existing information in the specific Q-table cell. If we set the learning rate to zero, then nothing will be learned, and if we set it to 1, then nothing will be retained. Thus, the learning rate controls how fast the system is able to learn new information while maintaining useful, already-learned data.

The simple version of the Q-learning algorithm iterates over all possible action-state combinations and updates the Q-values, as we've already discussed. This approach works pretty well for simple tasks with a small number of action-state pairs but quickly fails with an increase in the number of such pairs, that is, with increased dimensionality of the action-state space. Most real-world tasks have profound dimensionality of the action-state space, which makes it infeasible for the classical version of Q-learning.

The method of Q-value function approximation was proposed to address the problem of increased dimensionality. In this method, the Q-learning policy is defined not by the action-state table we mentioned earlier but is instead approximated by a function. One of the ways to achieve this approximation is to use an ANN as a universal approximation function. By using an ANN, especially a deep ANN for Q-value approximation, it becomes possible to use RL algorithms for very complex problems, even for problems with a continuous state space. Thus, the DQN method was devised, which uses a DNN for Q-value approximation. The RL based on the DNN value-function approximation was named **deep reinforcement learning** (**deep RL**).

With deep RL, it is possible to learn action policies directly from the pixels of a video stream. This allows us to use a video stream to train agents to play video games, for example. However, the DQN method can be considered a gradient-based method. It uses error (loss) backpropagation in the DNN to optimize the Q-value function approximator. While being a potent technique, it has a significant drawback regarding the computational complexity that's involved, which requires the use of GPUs to perform all the matrix multiplications during the gradient descent-related computations.

One of the methods that can be used to reduce computational costs is **Genetic Algorithms** (**GA**), such as neuroevolution. Neuroevolution allows us to evolve a DNN for the Q-value function approximation without any gradient-based computations involved. In recent studies, it was shown that gradient-free GA methods show excellent performance when it comes to challenging deep RL tasks and that they can even outperform their conventional counterparts. In the next section, we'll discuss how the deep neuroevolution method can be used to train successful agents to play one of the classic Atari games, just by reading game screen observations.

Evolving an agent to play the Frostbite Atari game using deep neuroevolution

Recently, classic Atari games were encapsulated by the **Atari Learning Environment** (ALE) to become a benchmark for testing different implementations of RL algorithms. Algorithms that are tested against the ALE are required to read the game state from the pixels of the game screen and devise a sophisticated control logic that allows the agent to win the game. Thus, the task of the algorithm is to evolve an understanding of the game situation in terms of the game character and its adversaries. Also, the algorithm needs to understand the reward signal that's received from the game screen in the form of the final game score at the end of a single game run.

The Frostbite Atari game

Frostbite is a classic Atari game where you control a game character that is building an igloo. The game screen is shown in the following screenshot:

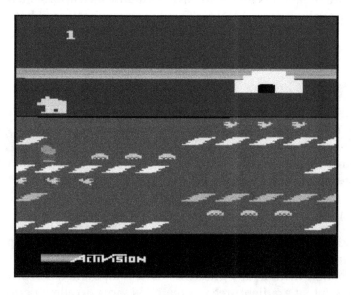

The Frostbite game screen

The bottom part of the screen is water, with floating ice blocks arranged in four rows. The game character jumps from one row to another while trying to avoid various foes. If the game character jumps on a white ice block, this block is collected and used to build an igloo on the shore in the top right of the screen. After that, the white ice block changes its color and cannot be used anymore.

To build the igloo, the game character must collect 15 ice blocks within 45 seconds. Otherwise, the game ends because the game character becomes frozen. When the igloo is complete, the game character must move inside it to complete the current level. The faster the game character completes a level, the more bonus points are awarded to the player.

Next, we'll discuss how the game screen state is mapped into input parameters, which can be used by the neuroevolution method.

Game screen mapping into actions

Deep ANNs can be trained to play Atari games if they can directly map the pixels on the screen to a system to control the game. This means that our algorithm must read the game screen and decide what game action to take to get the highest game score possible.

This task can be divided into two logical subtasks:

- The image analysis task, which encodes the state of the current game situation on the screen, including the game character's position, obstacles, and adversaries
- The RL training task, which is used to train the Q-value approximation ANN to build the correct mapping between the specific game state and actions to be performed

Convolutional Neural Networks (**CNNs**) are commonly used in tasks related to the analysis of visual imagery or other high-dimensional Euclidean data. The power of CNNs is based on their ability to significantly reduce the number of learning parameters compared to other types of ANN if they're applied to visual recognition. The CNN hierarchy usually has multiple sequential convolutional layers combined with non-linear fully connected layers and ends with a fully connected layer that is followed by the loss layer. The final fully connected and loss layers implement the high-level reasoning in the Neural Network architecture. In the case of deep RL, these layers make the Q-value approximation. Next, we'll consider the details of convolutional layer implementation.

Convolutional layers

By studying the organization of the visual cortex of higher life forms (including humans), researchers gained inspiration for the design of CNNs. Each neuron of the visual cortex responds to signals that are received from a limited region of the visual field – the neuron's receptive field. The receptive fields of various neurons overlap partially, which allows them to cover the entire visual field, as shown in the following diagram:

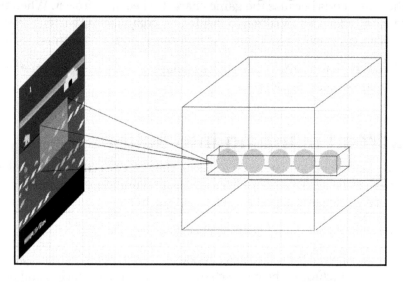

The scheme of connections between the receptive field (on the left) and neurons in the convolutional layer (on the right)

The convolutional layer consists of a column of neurons, where each neuron in a single column is connected to the same receptive field. This column represents a set of filters (kernels). Each filter is defined by the size of the receptive field and the number of channels. The number of channels defines the depth of the neurons column, while the size of the receptive field determines the number of columns in the convolutional layer. When the receptive field moves over the visual field, in each step, the new column of neurons is activated.

As we mentioned previously, each convolutional layer is usually combined with a fully connected layer with non-linear activation, such as **Rectified Linear Unit** (**ReLU**). The ReLU activation function has the effect of filtering out negative values, as given by the following formula:

$$f(x) = x^+ = \max(0, x)$$

Here, x is the input to a neuron.

In the ANN architecture, several convolutional layers are connected to a number of fully connected layers, which performs high-level reasoning. Next, we'll discuss the CNN architecture that's used in our experiment.

The CNN architecture to train the Atari playing agent

In our experiment, we'll use a CNN architecture consisting of three convolutional layers with 32, 64, and 64 channels, followed by a fully connected layer with 512 units and the output layer with the number of layers corresponding to the number of game actions. The convolutional layers have 8 x 8, 4 x 4, and 3 x 3 kernel sizes and use strides of 4, 2, and 1, respectively. The ReLU non-linearity follows all the convolutional and fully connected layers.

The source code to create the described network graph model using the TensorFlow framework is defined as follows:

```
class LargeModel(Model):
    def _make_net(self, x, num_actions):
        x = self.nonlin(self.conv(x, name='conv1', num_outputs=32,
                                  kernel_size=8, stride=4, std=1.0))
        x = self.nonlin(self.conv(x, name='conv2', num_outputs=64,
                                  kernel_size=4, stride=2, std=1.0))
        x = self.nonlin(self.conv(x, name='conv3', num_outputs=64,
                                  kernel_size=3, stride=1, std=1.0))
        x = self.flattenallbut0(x)
        x = self.nonlin(self.dense(x, 512, 'fc'))

        return self.dense(x, num_actions, 'out', std=0.1)
```

As a result of this architecture, the CNN contains about **4 million trainable parameters**. Next, we'll discuss how RL training is done in our experiment.

 For complete implementation details, refer to the dqn.py Python script at https://github.com/PacktPublishing/Hands-on-Neuroevolution-with-Python/blob/master/Chapter10/neuroevolution/models/dqn.py.

The RL training of the game agent

The RL training in our experiment was implemented using the neuroevolution method. This method is based on a simple genetic algorithm that evolves a population of individuals. The genotype of each individual encodes the vector of the trainable parameters of the controller ANN. By trainable parameters, we mean the connection weights between the network nodes. In every generation, each genotype is evaluated against a test environment by playing Frostbite and produces a specific fitness score. We evaluate each agent (genome) against 20,000 frames of the game. During the evaluation period, the game character can play multiple times, and the final Atari game score is the fitness score, which is a reward signal in terms of RL.

Next, we'll discuss the genome encoding scheme, which allows us to encode more than 4 million learning parameters of the ANN that's controlling the game-solving agent.

The genome encoding scheme

The deep RL neural network that we use as the controller of the game agent has about 4 million trainable parameters. Each trainable parameter is the weight of a connection between two nodes of the neural network. Traditionally, training neural networks is about finding the appropriate values of all the connection weights, allowing the neural network to approximate a function that describes the specifics of the modeled process.

The conventional way to estimate these trainable parameters is to use some form of error backpropagation based on the gradient descent of the loss value, which is very computationally intensive. On the other hand, the neuroevolution algorithm allows us to train ANNs using a nature-inspired genetic algorithm. The neuroevolution algorithm applies a series of mutations and recombinations to the trainable parameters to find the correct configuration of the ANN. However, to use the genetic algorithm, an appropriate scheme of encoding of the phenotype ANN should be devised. After that, the population of individuals (genomes encoding the phenotype ANN) can be created and evolved using a simple genetic algorithm, which we'll discuss later.

As we mentioned earlier, the encoding scheme should produce compact genomes that can encode values of more than 4 million connection weights between the nodes of the deep RL ANN controlling the game agent. We are looking for compact genomes to reduce the computational costs associated with genetic algorithm evaluation. Next, we'll discuss the definition of the genome encoding scheme, which can be used to encode the large phenotype ANN.

Genome encoding scheme definition

Researchers at the Uber AI lab have proposed a coding scheme that uses the seed of a pseudo-random number generator to encode the phenotype ANN. In this scheme, the genome is represented as a list of seed values, which is applied sequentially to generate the values for all the weights (trainable parameters) of connections that are expressed between the nodes of a controller ANN.

In other words, the first seed value in the list represents the policy initialization seed, which is shared between the genealogy of the descendants of a single parent. All the subsequent seed values represent the specific mutations that are acquired during the evolution process by the offspring. Each seed is applied sequentially to produce the ANN parameters vector of a specific phenotype. The following formula defines the estimation of the phenotype parameters vector for a specific individual (n):

$$\theta^n = \theta^0 + \sigma \sum_{i=1}^{n-1} \varepsilon(\tau_i)$$

Here, τ is the encoding of θ^n and consists of a list of mutation seeds; $\varepsilon(\tau_i) \sim \mathcal{N}(0, I)$ is a deterministic Gaussian pseudo-random number generator with an input seed τ_i that produces a vector of length $|\theta|$; θ^0 is an initial parameters vector that's created during initialization as follows, $\theta^0 = \phi(\tau_0)$, where ϕ is a deterministic initialization function; and σ is a mutation power that determines the strength of the influence of all the subsequent parameter vectors on the initial parameters vector θ^0.

In the current implementation, $\varepsilon(\tau_i)$ is a precomputed table with 250 million random vectors indexed using 28-bit seeds. This is done to speed up runtime processing because lookup by index is faster than the generation of new random numbers. Next, we'll discuss how to implement an encoding scheme in the Python source code.

Genome encoding scheme implementation

The following source code implements ANN parameter estimations, as defined by the formula from the previous section (see the `compute_weights_from_seeds` function):

```
idx = seeds[0]
theta = noise.get(idx, self.num_params).copy() * self.scale_by

for mutation in seeds[1:]:
    idx, power = mutation
    theta = self.compute_mutation(noise, theta, idx, power)
return theta
```

The `compute_mutation` function implements an estimation of the single step of the ANN parameter estimation, as follows:

```
def compute_mutation(self, noise, parent_theta, idx, mutation_power):
    return parent_theta + mutation_power * noise.get(idx,
                                                     self.num_params)
```

The preceding code takes the vector of the parent's trainable parameters and adds to it a random vector that's produced by a deterministic pseudo-random generator using a specific seed index. The mutation power parameter scales the generated random vector before it is added to the parent's parameters vector.

 For more implementation details, refer to the `base.py` script at `https://github.com/PacktPublishing/Hands-on-Neuroevolution-with-Python/blob/master/Chapter10/neuroevolution/models/base.py`.

Next, we'll discuss the particulars of a simple genetic algorithm that's used to train the Frostbite playing agent.

The simple genetic algorithm

The simple genetic algorithm that's used in our experiment evolves the population of N individuals over generations of evolution. As we mentioned previously, each individual genome encodes the vector of the trainable ANN parameters. Also, in each generation, we select the top T individuals to become the parents for the next generation.

The process of producing the next generation is implemented as follows. For $N-1$ repetitions, we do the following:

1. The parent is selected uniformly at random and removed from the selection list.
2. The mutation is applied to the selected parent by applying additive Gaussian noise to the parameter vector that's encoded by the individual.
3. Next, we add the new organism to the list of individuals for the next generation.

After that, the best individual from the current generation is copied in its unmodified state to the next generation (elitism). To guarantee that the best individual was selected, we evaluate each of the 10 top individuals in the current generation against 30 additional game episodes. The individual with the highest mean fitness score is then selected as an elite to be copied to the next generation.

The mutation of the parent individual is implemented as follows:

```
def mutate(self, parent, rs, noise, mutation_power):
    parent_theta, parent_seeds = parent
    idx = noise.sample_index(rs, self.num_params)
    seeds = parent_seeds + ((idx, mutation_power), )
    theta = self.compute_mutation(noise, parent_theta, idx,
                                      mutation_power)
    return theta, seeds
```

This function receives the phenotype and genotype of the parent individual, the random source, along with the precomputed noise table (250 million vectors), and the mutation power value. The random source produces the random seed number (`idx`), which is used as an index so that we can select the appropriate parameters vector from the noise table. After that, we create the offspring genome by combining the list of parent seeds with a new seed. Finally, we create the phenotype of the offspring by combining the phenotype of the parent with Gaussian noise that's been extracted from the shared noise table using a randomly sampled seed index we obtained earlier (`idx`). In the next section, we will look at an experiment we can perform in order to train an agent to play the Frostbite Atari game.

Training an agent to play the Frostbite game

Now that we have discussed the theory behind the game-playing agent's implementation, we are ready to start working on it. Our implementation is based on the source code provided by the Uber AI Lab on GitHub at `https://github.com/uber-research/deep-neuroevolution`. The source code in this repository contains an implementation of two methods to train DNNs: the CPU-based methods for multicore systems (up to 720 cores) and the GPU-based methods. We are interested in the GPU-based implementation because the majority of practitioners don't have access to such behemoths of technology as a PC with 720 CPU cores. At the same time, it is pretty easy to get access to a modern Nvidia GPU.

Next, we'll discuss the implementation details.

Atari Learning Environment

During agent training, we need to simulate actual gameplay in the Atari system. This can be done using the ALE, which simulates an Atari system that can run ROM images of the games. The ALE provides an interface that allows us to capture game screen frames and control the game by emulating the game controller. Here, we'll use the ALE modification that's available at `https://github.com/yaricom/atari-py`.

Our implementation uses the TensorFlow framework to implement ANN models and execute them on the GPU. Thus, the corresponding bridge needs to be implemented between ALE and TensorFlow. This is done by implementing a custom TensorFlow operation using the C++ programming language for efficiency. The corresponding Python interface is also provided as an AtariEnv Python class at `https://github.com/PacktPublishing/Hands-on-Neuroevolution-with-Python/blob/master/Chapter10/gym_tensorflow/atari/tf_atari.py`.

AtariEnv provides functions so that we can execute a single game step, reset the game, and return the current game state (observation). Next, we'll discuss each function.

The game step function

The game step function executes a single game step using the provided actions. It is implemented as follows:

```
def step(self, action, indices=None, name=None):
    if indices is None:
        indices = np.arange(self.batch_size)
    with tf.variable_scope(name, default_name='AtariStep'):
        rew, done = gym_tensorflow_module.environment_step(
                        self.instances, indices, action)
        return rew, done
```

This function applies the game action that's received from the controller ANN to the current game environment. Please note that this function can execute a single game step simultaneously in multiple game instances. The `self.batch_size` parameter or the length of the `indices` input tensor determines the number of game instances we'll have. The function returns two tensors: one tensor with rewards (game score) and another with flags indicating whether the current game evaluation is complete after this step (solved or failed). Both tensors have a length equal to `self.batch_size` or the length of the `indices` input tensor.

Next, we'll discuss how the game observations are created.

The game observation function

This function obtains the current game state from the Atari environment as a game screen buffer. This function is implemented as follows:

```
def observation(self, indices=None, name=None):
    if indices is None:
        indices = np.arange(self.batch_size)
    with tf.variable_scope(name, default_name='AtariObservation'):
        with tf.device('/cpu:0'):
            obs = gym_tensorflow_module.environment_observation(
                        self.instances, indices, T=tf.uint8)

        obs = tf.gather(tf.constant(self.color_pallete),
                                    tf.cast(obs,tf.int32))
        obs = tf.reduce_max(obs, axis=1)
        obs = tf.image.resize_bilinear(obs, self.warp_size,
                                    align_corners=True)
        obs.set_shape((None,) + self.warp_size + (1,))
        return obs
```

This function acquires a screengrab from the Atari environment and wraps it in a tensor that can be used by the TensorFlow framework. The game observation function also allows us to receive the state from multiple games, which is determined either by the `self.batch_size` parameter or the length of the `indices` input parameter. The function returns screengrabs from multiple games, wrapped in a tensor.

We also need to implement the function to reset the Atari environment to the initial random state, which we'll discuss next.

The reset Atari environment function

To train game agents, we need to implement a function that starts the Atari environment from a particular random state. It is vital to implement a stochastic Atari reset function to guarantee that our agent can play the game from any initial state. The function is implemented as follows:

```
def reset(self, indices=None, max_frames=None, name=None):
    if indices is None:
        indices = np.arange(self.batch_size)
    with tf.variable_scope(name, default_name='AtariReset'):
        noops = tf.random_uniform(tf.shape(indices), minval=1,
                                    maxval=31, dtype=tf.int32)
        if max_frames is None:
            max_frames = tf.ones_like(indices, dtype=tf.int32) * \
```

```
                                            (100000 * self.frameskip)
            import collections
            if not isinstance(max_frames, collections.Sequence):
                max_frames = tf.ones_like(indices, dtype=tf.int32) * \
                                        max_frames
            return gym_tensorflow_module.environment_reset(self.instances,
                            indices, noops=noops, max_frames=max_frames)
```

This function uses the `indices` input parameter to simultaneously reset multiple instances of Atari games in the random initial states. This function also defines the maximum number of frames for each game instance.

Next, we'll discuss how RL evaluation is performed on GPU cores.

RL evaluation on GPU cores

In our experiment, we'll implement an RL evaluation using the TensorFlow framework on GPU devices. This means that all the calculations related to the propagation of input signals through the controller ANN are performed on the GPU. This allows us to effectively calculate more than 4 million training parameters – the connection weights between control ANN nodes – for every single time step of the game. Furthermore, we can concurrently simulate multiple runs of the game in parallel, each controlled by a different controller ANN.

The concurrent evaluation of multiple game controller ANNs is implemented by two Python classes: `RLEvalutionWorker` and `ConcurrentWorkers`. Next, we'll discuss each class.

 For complete implementation details, refer to the `concurrent_worker.py` class at https://github.com/PacktPublishing/Hands-on-Neuroevolution-with-Python/blob/master/Chapter10/neuroevolution/concurrent_worker.py.

The RLEvalutionWorker class

This class holds the configuration and the network graph of the controller ANN. It provides us with methods so that we can create a network graph of the controller ANN, run an evaluation loop over the created network graph, and put new tasks into the evaluation loop. Next, we'll discuss how the network graph is created from a network model.

Creating the network graph

The TensorFlow network graph is created by the `make_net` function, which receives the ANN model constructor, the GPU device identifier, and the batch size as input parameters. The network graph is created as follows:

1. We'll start by creating the controller ANN model and the game evaluation environment:

```
self.model = model_constructor()
...
with tf.variable_scope(None, default_name='model'):
    with tf.device('/cpu:0'):
        self.env = self.make_env_f(self.batch_size)
```

2. Next, we'll create placeholders so that we can receive values during network graph evaluation. Also, we'll create an operator to reset the game before the start of the new game episode:

```
self.placeholder_indices = tf.placeholder(tf.int32,
                                          shape=(None, ))
self.placeholder_max_frames = tf.placeholder(
                              tf.int32, shape=(None, ))
self.reset_op = self.env.reset(
                indices=self.placeholder_indices,
                max_frames=self.placeholder_max_frames)
```

3. After that, using the context of the provided GPU device, we'll create two operators to receive game state observations and evaluate the game actions that follow:

```
with tf.device(device):
    self.obs_op = self.env.observation(
                  indices=self.placeholder_indices)
    obs = tf.expand_dims(self.obs_op, axis=1)
    self.action_op = self.model.make_net(obs,
                     self.env.action_space,
                     indices=self.placeholder_indices,
                     batch_size=self.batch_size,
                     ref_batch=ref_batch)
```

4. The `action` operator returns an array of action likelihood values, which needs to be filtered if the action space is discrete:

```
if self.env.discrete_action:
    self.action_op = tf.argmax(
                self.action_op[:tf.shape(
                self.placeholder_indices)[0]],
                axis=-1, output_type=tf.int32)
```

The code checks whether the current game environment requires discrete actions and wraps an `action` operator using the built-in `tf.argmax` operator of the TensorFlow framework. The `tf.argmax` operator returns the index of the action with the largest value, which can be used to signal that a specific game action should be executed.

 The Atari game environment is a discrete action environment, which means that only one action is accepted at each time step.

5. Finally, we create the operator to perform a single game step:

```
with tf.device(device):
    self.rew_op, self.done_op = \
                self.env.step(self.action_op,
                indices=self.placeholder_indices)
```

Here, we create a single game step operator, which returns operations to obtain rewards, `self.rew_op`, and the game completed status, `self.done_op`, after the execution of a single game step.

Next, we'll discuss how the evaluation loop is implemented.

The graph evaluation loop

This is the loop that we use to evaluate the previously created network graph over multiple games in parallel – the number of games that can be evaluated simultaneously is determined by the `batch_size` parameter.

The evaluation loop is defined in the _loop function and is implemented as follows:

1. First, we start with the creation of arrays to hold game evaluation values over multiple episodes:

```
running = np.zeros((self.batch_size,), dtype=np.bool)
cumrews = np.zeros((self.batch_size, ), dtype=np.float32)
cumlen = np.zeros((self.batch_size, ), dtype=np.int32)
```

2. Next, we start the loop and set the corresponding indices of the running array we just created to True:

```
while True:
    # nothing loaded, block
    if not any(running):
        idx = self.queue.get()
        if idx is None:
            break
        running[idx] = True
    while not self.queue.empty():
        idx = self.queue.get()
        if idx is None:
                break
        running[idx] = True
```

3. Using the indices array, we are ready to execute a single game step operator and collect the results:

```
indices = np.nonzero(running)[0]
rews, is_done, _ = self.sess.run(
        [self.rew_op, self.done_op, self.incr_counter],
        {self.placeholder_indices: indices})
cumrews[running] += rews
cumlen[running] += 1
```

4. Finally, we need to test whether any of the evaluated games are done, either by winning or by hitting the maximum game frames limit. For all the completed tasks, we apply a number of operations, as follows:

```
if any(is_done):
    for idx in indices[is_done]:
        self.sample_callback[idx](self, idx,
            (self.model.seeds[idx],cumrews[idx],
                                    cumlen[idx]))
    cumrews[indices[is_done]] = 0.
    cumlen[indices[is_done]] = 0.
    running[indices[is_done]] = False
```

The preceding code uses the indices of all the completed tasks and invokes the corresponding registered callbacks before resetting the collector variables at specific indices.

Now, we are ready to discuss how to add and run the new task using our worker.

The asynchronous task runner

This function registers a specific task to be evaluated by a worker in the GPU device context. It takes the ID of the task, the task object holder, and the callback to be executed on task completion as input. This function is defined under the name `run_async` and is implemented as follows:

1. First, it extracts the corresponding data from the task object and loads it into the current TensorFlow session:

```
theta, extras, max_frames=task
self.model.load(self.sess, task_id, theta, extras)
if max_frames is None:
    max_frames = self.env.env_default_timestep_cutoff
```

Here, `theta` is an array with all the connection weights in the controller ANN model, `extras` holds a random seeds list of the corresponding genome, and `max_frames` is the game frame's cutoff value.

2. Next, we run the TensorFlow session with `self.reset_op`, which resets a specific game environment at a specified index:

```
self.sess.run(self.reset_op, {self.placeholder_indices:[task_id],
              self.placeholder_max_frames:[max_frames]})
self.sample_callback[task_id] = callback
self.queue.put(task_id)
```

The code runs `self.reset_op` within the TensorFlow session. Also, we register the current task identifier with the `reset` operator and the maximum game frame's cutoff value for a given task. The task identifier is used in the evaluation loop to associate evaluation results of the network graph with a specific genome in the population. Next, we'll discuss how concurrent asynchronous workers are maintained.

The ConcurrentWorkers class

The `ConcurrentWorkers` class holds the configuration of the concurrent execution environment, which includes several evaluation workers (`RLEvalutionWorker` instances) and auxiliary routines to support multiple executions of concurrent tasks.

Creating the evaluation workers

One of the primary responsibilities of the `ConcurrentWorkers` class is to create and manage `RLEvalutionWorker` instances. This is done in the class constructor as follows:

```
self.workers = [RLEvalutionWorker(make_env_f, *args,
    ref_batch=ref_batch,
    **dict(kwargs, device=gpus[i])) for i in range(len(gpus))]
self.model = self.workers[0].model
self.steps_counter = sum([w.steps_counter for w in self.workers])
self.async_hub = AsyncTaskHub()
self.hub = WorkerHub(self.workers, self.async_hub.input_queue,
                        self.async_hub)
```

Here, we create the number of `RLEvalutionWorker` instances that are correlated to the number of GPU devices that are available in the system. After that, we initialize the selected ANN graph model and create auxiliary routines to manage multiple executions of asynchronous tasks. Next, we'll discuss how work tasks are scheduled for execution.

Running work tasks and monitoring results

To use the RL evaluation mechanism we described earlier, we need a method to schedule the work task for evaluation and to monitor the results. This is implemented in the `monitor_eval` function, which receives the list of genomes in the population and evaluates them against the Atari game environment. This function has two essential implementation parts, both of which we'll discuss in this section:

1. First, we iterate over all the genomes in the list and create the asynchronous work task so that each genome can be evaluated against the Atari game environment:

   ```
   tasks = []
   for t in it:
       tasks.append(self.eval_async(*t, max_frames=max_frames,
                                error_callback=error_callback))
       if time.time() - tstart > logging_interval:
           cur_timesteps = self.sess.run(self.steps_counter)
           tlogger.info('Num timesteps:', cur_timesteps,
   ```

```
'per second:',
(cur_timesteps-last_timesteps)//(time.time()-tstart),
'num episodes finished: {}/{}'.format(
sum([1 if t.ready() else 0 for t in tasks]),
len(tasks)))
tstart = time.time()
last_timesteps = cur_timesteps
```

The preceding code schedules each genome in the list for asynchronous evaluation and saves a reference to each asynchronous task for later use. Also, we periodically output the results of the evaluation process of already scheduled tasks. Now, we'll discuss how to monitor the evaluation results.

2. The following code block is waiting for the completion of asynchronous tasks:

```
while not all([t.ready() for t in tasks]):
    if time.time() - tstart > logging_interval:
        cur_timesteps = self.sess.run(self.steps_counter)
        tlogger.info('Num timesteps:', cur_timesteps, 'per
second:', (cur_timesteps-last_timesteps)//(time.time()-tstart),
'num episodes:', sum([1 if t.ready() else 0 for t in tasks]))
        tstart = time.time()
        last_timesteps = cur_timesteps
    time.sleep(0.1)
```

Here, we iterate over all the references to the scheduled asynchronous tasks and wait for their completion. Also, we periodically output the evaluation progress. Next, we'll discuss how task evaluation results are collected.

3. Finally, after the completion of all tasks, we collect the results, as follows:

```
tlogger.info(
    'Done evaluating {} episodes in {:.2f} seconds'.format(
                    len(tasks), time.time()-tstart_all))
return [t.get() for t in tasks]
```

The code iterates through all the references to the scheduled asynchronous tasks and creates a list of the evaluation results. Next, we'll discuss the experiment runner implementation.

Experiment runner

The experiment runner implementation receives a configuration of the experiment defined in the JSON file and runs the neuroevolution process for the specified number of game time steps. In our experiment, the evaluation stops after reaching 1.5 billion time steps of Frostbite. Next, we'll discuss the experiment configuration details.

Experiment configuration file

Here is the file that provides configuration parameters for the experiment runner. For our experiment, it has the following content:

```
{
    "game": "frostbite",
    "model": "LargeModel",
    "num_validation_episodes": 30,
    "num_test_episodes": 200,
    "population_size": 1000,
    "episode_cutoff_mode": 5000,
    "timesteps": 1.5e9,
    "validation_threshold": 10,
    "mutation_power": 0.002,
    "selection_threshold": 20
}
```

The configuration parameters are as follows:

- The game parameter is the name of the game, as registered in the ALE. The full list of supported games is available at https://github.com/PacktPublishing/Hands-on-Neuroevolution-with-Python/blob/master/Chapter10/gym_tensorflow/atari/tf_atari.py.
- The model parameter designates the name of the network graph model to use for the construction of the controller ANN. The models are defined at https://github.com/PacktPublishing/Hands-on-Neuroevolution-with-Python/blob/master/Chapter10/neuroevolution/models/dqn.py.
- The num_validation_episodes parameter defines how many game episodes are used for the evaluation of the top individuals in the population. After this step, we can select the true elite of the population.
- The num_test_episodes parameter sets the number of game episodes to use to test the performance of the selected population elite.
- The population_size parameter determines the number of genomes in the population.

- The `episode_cutoff_mode` parameter defines how the game evaluation stops for a particular genome. The game episode can stop either upon the execution of a particular number of time steps or by using the default stop signal of the corresponding game environment.
- The `timesteps` parameter sets the total number of time steps of the game to be executed during the neuroevolution process.
- The `validation_threshold` parameter sets the number of top individuals that are selected from each generation for additional validation execution. The population elite is selected from these selected individuals.
- The `mutation_power` parameter defines how subsequent mutations that are added to the individual influence the training parameters (connection weights).
- The `selection_threshold` parameter determines how many parent individuals are allowed to produce offspring in the next generation.

Now, we are ready to discuss the implementation details of the experiment runner.

The experiment configuration file can be found at `https://github.com/PacktPublishing/Hands-on-Neuroevolution-with-Python/blob/master/Chapter10/configurations/ga_atari_config.json`.

Experiment runner implementation

The experiment runner implementation creates the concurrent evaluation environment and runs the evolution loop over the population of individuals. Let's discuss the essential implementation details:

1. We start by setting up the evaluation environment by loading the controller ANN model and creating the concurrent workers to execute the evaluation:

```
Model = neuroevolution.models.__dict__[config['model']]
all_tstart = time.time()
def make_env(b):
    return gym_tensorflow.make(game=config["game"],
                               batch_size=b)
worker = ConcurrentWorkers(make_env, Model, batch_size=64)
```

2. Next, we create a table with random noise values, which will be used as random seeds, and define the function to create offspring for the next generation:

```
noise = SharedNoiseTable()
rs = np.random.RandomState()
```

```
def make_offspring():
    if len(cached_parents) == 0:
        return worker.model.randomize(rs, noise)
    else:
        assert len(cached_parents) ==
config['selection_threshold']
        parent = cached_parents[
                rs.randint(len(cached_parents))]
        theta, seeds = worker.model.mutate( parent, rs, noise,
            mutation_power=state.sample(
            state.mutation_power))
    return theta, seeds
```

3. After that, the main evolution loop starts. We use the previously defined function to create a population of the offspring for the current generation:

```
tasks = [make_offspring() for _ in range(
                config['population_size'])]
for seeds, episode_reward, episode_length in \
    worker.monitor_eval(tasks, max_frames=state.tslimit * 4):
    results.append(Offspring(seeds,
                [episode_reward], [episode_length]))

state.num_frames += sess.run(worker.steps_counter) - \
                frames_computed_so_far
```

Here, we create the work tasks for each offspring in the population and schedule each task for evaluation against the game environment.

4. When we finish with the evaluation of each individual in the population, we start the evaluation of the top individuals to select the elite:

```
state.population = sorted(results,
            key=lambda x:x.fitness, reverse=True)
...
validation_population = state.\
            population[:config['validation_threshold']]
if state.elite is not None:
    validation_population = [state.elite] + \
                validation_population[:-1]

validation_tasks = [
    (worker.model.compute_weights_from_seeds(noise,
    validation_population[x].seeds, cache=cached_parents),
    validation_population[x].seeds) for x in range(
                config['validation_threshold'])]
_,population_validation, population_validation_len =\
    zip(*worker.monitor_eval_repeated(validation_tasks,
```

```
            max_frames=state.tslimit * 4,
            num_episodes=config['num_validation_episodes']))
```

5. Using the evaluation results of the top 10 individuals, we select the population's elite and execute the final test runs over it to evaluate its performance:

```
population_elite_idx = np.argmax(population_validation)
state.elite = validation_population[population_elite_idx]
elite_theta = worker.model.compute_weights_from_seeds(
        noise, state.elite.seeds, cache=cached_parents)
_,population_elite_evals,population_elite_evals_timesteps=\
        worker.monitor_eval_repeated(
        [(elite_theta, state.elite.seeds)],
        max_frames=None,
        num_episodes=config['num_test_episodes'])[0]
```

The elite individual will be copied to the next generation as is.

6. Finally, we select the top individuals from the current population to become parents for the next generation:

```
if config['selection_threshold'] > 0:
    tlogger.info("Caching parents")
    new_parents = []
    if state.elite in \
        state.population[:config['selection_threshold']]:
        new_parents.extend([
            (worker.model.compute_weights_from_seeds(
            noise, o.seeds, cache=cached_parents), o.seeds)
    for o in state.population[:config['selection_threshold']]])
        else:
        new_parents.append(
            (worker.model.compute_weights_from_seeds(
            noise, state.elite.seeds, cache=cached_parents),
            state.elite.seeds))
        new_parents.extend([
            (worker.model.compute_weights_from_seeds(
            noise, o.seeds, cache=cached_parents), o.seeds)
    for o in state.population[:config['selection_threshold']-1]])
```

The preceding code collects the top individuals from the population to become the parents of the next generation. Also, it appends the current elite to the list of parents if it isn't in the parent list.

Now, we are ready to discuss how to run the experiment.

Running the Frostbite Atari experiment

Now that we have discussed all the particulars of the experiment's implementation, it is time to run the experiment. However, the first thing we need to do is create an appropriate work environment, which we'll discuss next.

Setting up the work environment

The work environment for training the agent to play Atari games assumes that a large controller ANN needs to be trained in the process. We already stated that the controller ANN has more than 4 million training parameters and requires a lot of computational resources to be able to evaluate. Fortunately, modern GPU accelerators allow the execution of massive parallel computations simultaneously. This feature is convenient for our experiment because we need to evaluate each individual against the game environment multiple times during the evolution process. Without GPU acceleration, it would either take a lot of time or require a massive number of processing cores (about 720).

Let's discuss how to prepare the working environment:

1. The working environment requires a Nvidia video accelerator (such as GeForce 1080Ti) present in the system and the appropriate Nvidia CUDA SDK installed. More details about the CUDA SDK and its installation can be found at `https://developer.nvidia.com/cuda-toolkit`.
2. Next, we need to make sure that the CMake build tool is installed, as described at `https://cmake.org`.
3. Now, we need to create a new Python environment using Anaconda and install all the dependencies that are used by the experiment's implementation:

   ```
   $ conda create -n deep_ne python=3.5
   $ conda activate deep_ne
   $ conda install -c anaconda tensorflow-gpu
   $ pip install gym
   $ pip install Pillow
   ```

   These commands create and activate a new Python 3.5 environment. Next, it installs TensorFlow, OpenAI Gym, and the Python Imaging Library as dependencies.

4. After that, you need to clone the repository with the experiment's source code:

```
$ git clone
https://github.com/PacktPublishing/Hands-on-Neuroevolution-with-Pyt
hon.git
$ cd Hands-on-Neuroevolution-with-Python/Chapter10
```

After executing these commands, our current working directory becomes the directory that contains the experiment source code.

5. Now, we need to build the ALE and integrate it into our experiment. We need to clone the ALE repository into the appropriate directory and build it with the following commands:

```
$ cd cd gym_tensorflow/atari/
$ git clone https://github.com/yaricom/atari-py.git
$ cd ./atari-py && make
```

Now, we have a working ALE environment that's been integrated with TensorFlow. We can use it to evaluate the controller ANNs that are produced from a population of genomes against an Atari game (Frostbite, in our experiment).

6. After the ALE integration is complete, we need to build an integration between OpenAI Gym and TensorFlow that is specific to our experiment implementation:

```
$ cd ../..gym_tensorflow && make
```

Now, we have a fully defined work environment and we are ready to start our experiments. Next, we'll discuss how to run the experiment.

Running the experiment

With an adequately defined work environment, we are ready to start our experiment. You can start an experiment from the Chapter10 directory by executing the following command:

```
$ python ga.py -c configurations/ga_atari_config.json -o out
```

The preceding command starts an experiment using the configuration file that was provided as the first parameter. The experiment's output will be stored in the out directory.

After completing the experiment, the console's output should look similar to the following:

```
. . .
| PopulationEpRewMax                 | 3.47e+03 |
| PopulationEpRewMean                | 839      |
| PopulationEpCount                  | 1e+03    |
| PopulationTimesteps                | 9.29e+05 |
| NumSelectedIndividuals             | 20       |
| TruncatedPopulationRewMean         | 3.24e+03 |
| TruncatedPopulationValidationRewMean | 2.36e+03 |
| TruncatedPopulationEliteValidationRew | 3.1e+03 |
| TruncatedPopulationEliteIndex      | 0        |
. . .
| TruncatedPopulationEliteTestRewMean | 3.06e+03 |
. . .
 Current elite: (47236580, (101514609, 0.002), (147577692, 0.002),
(67106649, 0.002), (202520553, 0.002), (230555280, 0.002), (38614601,
0.002), (133511446, 0.002), (27624159, 0.002), (233455358, 0.002),
(73372122, 0.002), (32459655, 0.002), (181449271, 0.002), (205743718,
0.002), (114244841, 0.002), (129962094, 0.002), (24016384, 0.002),
(77767788, 0.002), (90094370, 0.002), (14090622, 0.002), (171607709,
0.002), (147408008, 0.002), (150151615, 0.002), (224734414, 0.002),
(138721819, 0.002), (154735910, 0.002), (172264633, 0.002))
```

Here, we have the statistics output after a specific generation of evolution. You can see the following results:

- The maximum reward score that's achieved during the evaluation of a population is 3,470 (PopulationEpRewMax).
- The maximum score that's achieved among the top individuals on an additional 30 episodes of validation is 3,240 (TruncatedPopulationRewMean).
- The mean score of the top individual's evaluation is 2,360 (TruncatedPopulationValidationRewMean).
- The mean score of the elite individual that's received during an additional 200 test runs is 3,060 (TruncatedPopulationEliteTestRewMean).

The achieved reward scores are pretty high compared to other training methods if we look at the results that were published at https://arxiv.org/abs/1712.06567v3.

Also, at the end of the outputs, you can see the genome representation of the population elite. The elite genome can be used to visualize playing Frostbite by the phenotype ANN that was created from it. Next, we'll discuss how to make this visualization possible.

Frostbite visualization

Now that we have the results of the game agent's training, it will be interesting to see how the solution we've found plays Frostbite in the Atari environment. To run the simulation, you need to copy the current elite genome representation from the output and paste it into the `seeds` field of the `display.py` file. After that, the simulation can be run using the following command:

```
$ python display.py
```

The preceding command uses the provided elite genome to create a phenotype ANN and uses it as the controller of the Frostbite playing agent. It will open the game window, where you can see how the controller ANN is performing. The game will continue until the game character doesn't have any lives left. The following image shows several captured game screens from the execution of `display.py` in an Ubuntu 16.04 environment:

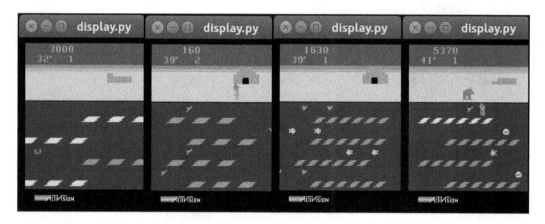

Frostbite screenshots, all of which have been taken from the elite genome game-playing session

It is pretty amazing to see how the trained controller ANN can learn the game rules solely from visual observations and is able to demonstrate such smooth gameplay.

Next, we'll discuss an additional visualization method that allows us to analyze the results.

Visual inspector for neuroevolution

During the neuroevolution process, we are evolving a population of individuals. Each of the individuals is evaluated against the test environment (such as an Atari game) and reward scores are collected per individual for each generation of evolution. To explore the general dynamics of the neuroevolution process, we need to have a tool that can visualize the cloud of results for each individual in each generation of evolution. Also, it is interesting to see the changes in the fitness score of the elite individual to understand the progress of the evolution process.

To address these requirements, the researchers from Uber AI developed the VINE tool, which we'll discuss next.

Setting up the work environment

To use the VINE tool, we need to install additional libraries into our virtual Python environment with the following commands:

```
$ pip install click
$ conda install matplotlib
$ pip install colour
$ conda install pandas
```

These commands install all the necessary dependencies into a virtual Python environment that we have created for our experiment. Next, we'll discuss how to use the VINE tool.

Don't forget to activate the appropriate virtual environment with the following command before running the preceding commands: conda activate deep_ne.

Using VINE for experiment visualization

Now, when we have all the dependencies installed on the Python virtual environment, we are ready to use the VINE tool. First, you need to clone it from the Git repository with the following commands:

```
$ git clone https://github.com/uber-research/deep-neuroevolution.git
$ cd visual_inspector
```

Here, we cloned the deep neuroevolution repository into the current directory and changed the directory to the `visual_inspector` folder, where the source code of the VINE tool is present.

Let's discuss how VINE can be used to visualize the results of the neuroevolution experiment using the results of the Mujoco Humanoid experiment provided by the Uber AI Lab. More details about the Mujoco Humanoid experiment can be found at `https://eng.uber.com/deep-neuroevolution/`.

Now, we can run the visualization of the Mujoco Humanoid experiment results, which is supplied in the `sample_data` folder, using the following command:

```
$ python -m main_mujoco 90 99 sample_data/mujoco/final_xy_bc/
```

The preceding command uses the same data that was supplied by Uber AI Lab from their experiment for training humanoid locomotion and displays the following graphs:

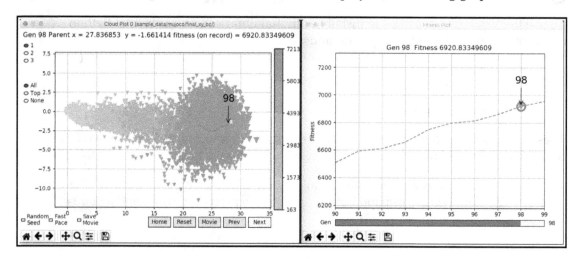

The VINE tool's visualization of Humanoid locomotion results

On the left-hand side of the graph, you can see the cloud of results for each individual in the population, starting from generation 90 and ending at generation 99. On the right-hand side of the graph, you can see the fitness score of the population's elite per generation. In the right-hand graph, you can see that the evolutionary process demonstrates the positive dynamics from generation to generation as the fitness score of the elite is increasing.

Each point on the left-hand side graph demonstrates the behavioral characterization points for each individual in a population. The behavioral characterization for the Humanoid locomotion task is the final position of the Humanoid at the end of the trajectory. The farther it is from the origin coordinates $(0, 0)$, the higher the fitness score of the individual. You can see that, with the progress of evolution, the results cloud is moving away from the origin coordinates. This movement of the results cloud is also a signal of the positive learning dynamics because each individual was able to stay balanced for a more extended period.

For more details about the Mujoco Humanoid locomotion experiment, please refer to the article at `https://eng.uber.com/deep-neuroevolution/`.

Exercises

1. Try to increase the `population_size` parameter in the experiment and see what happens.
2. Try to create the experiment results, which can be visualized using VINE. You can use the `master_extract_parent_ga` and `master_extract_cloud_ga` helper functions in the `ga.py` script to do this.

Summary

In this chapter, we discussed how neuroevolution can be used to train large ANNs with more than 4 million trainable parameters. You learned how to apply this learning method to create successful agents that are able to play classic Atari games by learning the game rules solely from observing the game screens. By completing the Atari game-playing experiment that was described in this chapter, you have learned about CNNs and how they can be used to map high-dimensional inputs, such as game screen observations, into the appropriate game actions. You now have a solid understanding of how CNNs can be used for value-function approximations in the deep RL method, which is guided by the deep neuroevolution algorithm.

With the knowledge that you've acquired from this chapter, you will be able to apply deep neuroevolution methods in domains with high-dimensional input data, such as inputs that have been acquired from cameras or other image sources.

In the next chapter, we'll summarize what we have covered in this book and provide some hints about where you can continue your self-education.

4
Section 4: Discussion and Concluding Remarks

In this section, we provide a summary of what you've learned in this book and direct you to resources you can use to learn more about neuroevolution-based algorithms.

This section comprises the following chapters:

- Chapter 11, *Best Practices, Tips, and Tricks*
- Chapter 12, *Concluding Remarks*

11
Best Practices, Tips, and Tricks

In this chapter, we provide some advice on best practices, tips, and tricks for writing and analyzing neuroevolution algorithms. By the end of this chapter, you will know how to start working with the problem at hand, how to tune the hyperparameters of the neuroevolution algorithm, how to use advanced visualization tools, and what metrics can be used to the analyze the algorithm's performance. Also, you will learn about the best coding practices for Python, which will help you in the implementation of your projects.

In this chapter, we will cover the following topics:

- Starting with problem analysis
- Selecting the optimal search optimization method
- Using advanced visualization tools
- Tuning hyperparameters and knowing what should be tuned
- Understanding which performance metrics to collect
- Python coding tips and tricks

Starting with problem analysis

Starting with a proper analysis of the problem space is a recipe for success. Neuroevolution is lenient with programmer errors. Such mistakes are a part of the environment, and the evolution process can adapt to them. However, there is a particular category of mistakes that can hinder the evolution process from finding a successful solution: the numerical stability of the evolution process. Most types of activation function are designed to operate in a range of inputs between zero and one. As a result, too large or negative values do not have much influence on the evolution process.

Thus, you may need to preprocess the input data to avoid these numeric issues. Do not skip the analysis of the input data samples and data preprocessing steps.

Next, we discuss how to preprocess the input data.

Preprocessing data

Always examine the range of possible data inputs and check for outliers. If you find that the scale of one input parameter differs from another by an order of magnitude, you need to preprocess the input data samples. Otherwise, the input data features with higher magnitude will have such a significant impact on the training process that they will ultimately outweigh the contribution of the other input data features. However, the small signals produced by the data inputs with small magnitude are often crucial to finding a successful solution. Delicate input signals can characterize subtle but valuable traits in the underlying process.

Data standardization

Most machine learning algorithms greatly benefit from input data that is normally distributed; that is, it has a mean and unit variance of zero. The common approach to scaling input data to have a zero mean and unit variance is given by the following formula:

$$z = \frac{x - u}{s}$$

Note that z is a scaled input score, x is the input data sample, u is the mean of training samples, and s is the standard deviation of the training samples.

You can use the Scikit-learn Python library to apply standard scaling to your input data samples. The following source code is an example of this:

```
>>> from sklearn.preprocessing import StandardScaler
>>> data = [[0, 0], [0, 0], [1, 1], [1, 1]]
>>> scaler = StandardScaler()
>>> print(scaler.fit(data))
StandardScaler(copy=True, with_mean=True, with_std=True)
>>> print(scaler.mean_)
[0.5 0.5]
>>> print(scaler.transform(data))
[[-1. -1.]
 [-1. -1.]
 [ 1.  1.]
 [ 1.  1.]]
```

In the code, we first create the input data samples. After that, `StandardScaler` is used to center and scale the input samples. The results of the data transformation are shown in the last lines of the code.

Another method of data preprocessing is scaling features to fit into a specific range, which we discuss next.

Scaling inputs to a range

Scaling inputs to fit into a specific range is another method of data preprocessing. This method is an alternative to standardization. Range scaling produces data samples that lie within a given range between the minimum and maximum values. Often, this method is used to scale input data in a range between zero and one. You can use `MinMaxScaler` of the Scikit-learn Python library to scale data in a range, as shown in the following example:

```
>>> import sklearn.preprocessing
>>> X_train = np.array([[ 1., -1., 2.],
... [ 2., 0., 0.],
... [ 0., 1., -1.]])
...
>>> min_max_scaler = preprocessing.MinMaxScaler()
>>> X_train_minmax = min_max_scaler.fit_transform(X_train)
>>> X_train_minmax
array([[0.5 , 0. , 1. ],
       [1. , 0.5 , 0.33333333],
       [0. , 1. , 0. ]])
```

The code starts with the creation of a sample dataset and transforms it using the `MinMaxScaler` class. In the final output, you can see the results of the range-scaling transformation.

Sometimes, you need to have data samples with the same units. This type of preprocessing is called **normalization**. We discuss it in the next section.

Data normalization

Often, your input data features have different units of measurement. For example, in the pole-balancing experiment, the cart position was measured in meters, the linear speed was in meters per second, and the angular speed was in radians per second. It is beneficial to normalize input data to simplify the comparison between input data features.

The process of normalization effectively eliminates the units of measurement from the input data samples. After that, all the samples will be in the range between zero and one.

There are different types of normalization in statistics. We already mentioned two methods: data standardization and data range scaling. Additionally, Scikit-learn provides a specialized transformer to perform data normalization, which scales individual samples to what is known as a unit norm. The following code demonstrates how to use it:

```
>>> import sklearn.preprocessing
>>> X = [[ 1., -1., 2.],
... [ 2., 0., 0.],
... [ 0., 1., -1.]]
>>> X_normalized = preprocessing.normalize(X, norm='12')
>>> X_normalized
array([[ 0.40..., -0.40..., 0.81...],
       [ 1. ..., 0. ..., 0. ...],
       [ 0. ..., 0.70..., -0.70...]])
```

The code creates the test data sample and applies normalization to it using the `12` norm and outputs the results.

The Scikit-learn library provides the implementation of many other data preprocessing methods. It would be useful for you to get familiar with them. You can find an excellent tutorial at `https://scikit-learn.org/stable/modules/preprocessing.html`.

Understanding the problem domain

In this book, some of the experiments we have discussed have been related to real processes in the physical world. To find successful solutions for such processes, you need to understand the underlying physical laws and principles. For example, the problem of balancing the cart-pole apparatus requires us to define a full set of equations of motion to write an accurate simulator of the task.

Also for most tasks in the field of robotics, you need to write a simulator that uses the correct physical model and equations of the underlying apparatus. You need to fully comprehend the physics of the process to implement the simulator correctly. And even if you use a ready-made simulator, understanding the physical principles implemented in it is incredibly beneficial for you because understanding the dynamics of the real-world process allows you to tune the hyperparameters of the training algorithm appropriately.

Writing good simulators

When working on a specific problem, it is crucial to write an appropriate simulator that correctly implements the specifics of the simulated process. If you use such a simulator, you will be able to run long episodes of training, which is impossible when using direct inputs from physical devices.

A good simulator should allow you to control the duration of the single time step of the simulated process. During neuroevolution, you need to evaluate each individual in the population against the given simulator. Thus, it makes sense during training to make the duration of a single time step as small as possible to increase the execution speed. On the other hand, when a solution has been found and you need to test it by hand, it would be beneficial if you could run the simulator at normal execution speed.

Also, you can use the existing mature simulators for your projects, which can save you a lot of time. Familiarize yourself with well-established open source simulator packages. They often provide advanced physics simulation as well as a collection of premade building blocks for your virtual robots and environments. You can start your search at `https://github.com/cyberbotics/webots`.

Next, we discuss how to select the right search optimization method for your experiment.

Selecting the optimal search optimization method

In this book, we have presented you with two basic search optimization methods: goal-oriented search and Novelty Search. The former method is more straightforward to implement and easier to understand. However, Novelty Search is handy in cases where the fitness function has a deceptive landscape with many local optima traps.

In the next section, we briefly discuss both methods to remind you of the details and to help you choose which one to use in a given situation. We start with goal-oriented search.

Goal-oriented search optimization

Goal-oriented search optimization is based on measuring the proximity of the solution to the ultimate goal. To calculate the average distance to the goal, it often uses a metric such as the mean squared error. Next, we discuss the particulars of the mean squared error metric.

Mean squared error

The mean squared error is the average squared difference between the obtained results and the actual values. It's given by the following formula:

$$MSE = \frac{1}{n} \sum_{i=1}^{n} (y_i - \bar{y}_i)^2$$

Here y_i is the estimated value, and $\bar{y}_i$ is the actual value.

We used a variation of the mean squared error to define an objective function for the XOR experiment. Next, we discuss goal-oriented metrics for problems related to positioning in Euclidean space.

Euclidean distance

Euclidean distance is an appropriate metric for tasks related to navigation through the Euclidean problem space. In the Euclidean problem space, we define the problem goal as a point with particular coordinates.

Using the Euclidean distance, it is easy to calculate the distance between the position of the navigational agent and the target point it is trying to reach. The following formula calculates the Euclidean distance between two vectors:

$$\mathcal{D} = \sqrt{\sum_{i=1}^{2} (a_i - b_i)^2}$$

Here $\mathcal{D}$ is the Euclidean distance between the vector with agent position a_i and the vector with the ultimate goal of the agent, b_i. We used this metric to define the objective function of an agent navigating through the maze in Chapter 5, *Autonomous Maze Navigation*.

However, the problem of autonomous maze navigation is caused by the deceptive fitness function landscape, which makes goal-oriented search optimization inefficient. Next, we discuss the Novelty Search optimization method, which is able to address this inefficiency.

Novelty Search optimization

As we have mentioned, navigation through the maze is a deceptive problem that requires a different approach to define the fitness function. In `Chapter 5`, *Autonomous Maze Navigation*, we presented you with a particular maze configuration that produces areas with strong local optima of goal-oriented fitness scores. As a result, the training process can be trapped inside these areas and will fail to produce a successful solution. The Novelty Search optimization method was devised to address issues with deceptive fitness function landscapes.

Novelty Search rewards the novelty of a solution rather than its proximity to the ultimate goal. Furthermore, the novelty metric, which is used to calculate the fitness score of each solution, completely ignores the proximity of the solution to the ultimate goal. There are two popular approaches to calculate the novelty score:

- The novelty score is calculated from differences in the architectures of the solutions.
- The novelty is calculated using the unique variations in the behavior of the solutions in the common behavioral space.

The former calculates a difference between the encoding of the current solution and all the previous solutions. The latter compares the result produced by the current solution in the behavioral space to results produced by other solutions.

We used novelty scores based on the uniqueness of the exposed behavior to define the fitness function of the maze solvers. The trajectory of the maze solver through the maze entirely determines the behavioral space of the agent and can be used to calculate the novelty score. In this case, the novelty score is the Euclidean distance between the trajectory vectors of the current solution and all other solutions.

Now that we have discussed the importance of choosing an appropriate search optimization method, we can move on to the discussion of another important aspect of a successful experiment. You need to have a good visualization of the results of the experiment to get insights into its performance. Next, we discuss the visualization of results.

Advanced visualization

Almost always, proper visualization of inputs and results is crucial to the success of your experiment. With proper visualization, you will get intuitive insights about what has gone wrong and what needs to be fixed.

Always try to visualize the simulator execution environment. Such visualization can save you hours of debugging when you get an unexpected result. Usually, with adequate visualization, you can see that something has gone wrong at a glance, such as a maze solver that got stuck up in a corner.

With neuroevolution algorithms, you also need to visualize the performance of the genetic algorithm execution per generation. You need to visualize speciation from generation to generation to see whether the evolutionary process has stagnated. Stagnated evolution fails to create enough species to maintain healthy diversity among solvers. On the other hand, too many species hinder evolution by reducing the chances of reproduction between different organisms.

Another important visualization allows us to see the topology of the produced phenotype **artificial neural network (ANN)**. It is useful to visually inspect the topologies of the produced solution to check whether it satisfies our expectations. For example, when we discussed the modular retina problem in `Chapter 8`, *ES-HyperNEAT and the Retina Problem*, it was beneficial to see that modular structures evolved in the topology of the successful solutions.

You need to familiarize yourself with the standard Python scientific plotting libraries to create adequate visualizations for the results of your experiments. It is essential to develop good practical skills with such visualization libraries as Matplotlib (`https://matplotlib.org`) and Seaborn (`https://seaborn.pydata.org`).

Next, we discuss the importance of hyperparameter tuning for the performance of the neuroevolution process.

Tuning hyperparameters

With proper tuning of the hyperparameters, you can make tremendous improvements in the training speed and efficiency of the neuroevolution process. Here are some practical tips:

- Do short runs with different seed values of the random number generator and note how the algorithm performance changes. After that, choose the seed value that gives the best performance and use it for the long runs.
- You can increase the number of species in the population by decreasing the compatibility threshold and by slightly increasing the value of the disjoint/excess weight coefficient.

- If the process of neuroevolution has stumbled while trying to find a solution, try to decrease the value of the NEAT survival threshold. This coefficient maintains the ratio of the best organisms within a population that got the chance to reproduce. By doing this, you increase the quality of the individuals allowed to reproduce based on their fitness score.

- By increasing the maximum stagnation age, you can guarantee that species survive long enough to have a chance to introduce beneficial mutations in the later stages of evolution. Sometimes, such an operation can help to revitalize the neuroevolution process that stalls. However, you should always try with the small stagnation age values (15-20) to initiate a quick rotation of the species, and only increase this parameter significantly if all other tweaks fail.

- After hyperparameter adjustments, do a short run for a few tens of generations to see the performance change dynamics. Pay special attention to the number of species—there should be at least more than one species in the population. Too many species is also a bad sign. Usually, 5 to 20 species is a good range.

- Use the visualization of the experiment results to get quick insights into the performance of the experiment. Never pass up the chance to visualize the ANN topology of the discovered solutions. These visualizations can give you priceless insights on how to tune up the neuroevolutionary process.

- Don't waste your time on long evolutionary runs. If the experiment fails to find a successful solution in 1,000 generations, there's a good chance that something is wrong with your code or the library you are using. For most simple problems, a successful solution can be found even in 100 generations.

- The population size is a critical parameter of the evolutionary process. With large populations, you get great diversity from the very beginning of the process, which boosts the process. However, large populations are hard to compute. Thus, there is always a trade-off between population size and computational cost. As a rule of thumb, if you struggle to find other suitable hyperparameters, try to increase the population size and see if it helps. But be ready to wait extra time for the neuroevolution process to complete.

- Always print the debug information, allowing you to restart the experiment from any stage of evaluation. It is always painful when you find a solution after two days of computation, but due to some programming mistakes your program crashes when trying to output the congratulations message. You need to output at least the random seed value at the beginning of each trial. This can guarantee that you can accurately recreate all the generations of the evolution in case of failure.

Do not underestimate the importance of hyperparameter tuning. Even taking into account that the neuroevolution process can handle many programming mistakes, choosing the right hyperparameters can significantly improve the efficiency of the process. As a result, you will be able to find a successful solution in hundreds of generations instead of thousands or more.

To compare the performance of the different solutions, you need to use appropriate performance metrics, which we discuss next.

Performance metrics

After a successful solution is found, it is crucial to compare it with other solutions to estimate how good it is. There are many important statistical metrics that compare different models.

Become familiar with concepts such as precision score, recall score, F1 score, ROC AUC, and accuracy. Understanding these metrics will help you to compare the results produced by different models in various classification tasks. Next, we give a brief overview of these metrics.

Precision score

The precision score attempts to answer the question of how many among the positive identifications are actually correct. The precision score can be calculated as follows:

$$precision = \frac{TP}{TP + FP}$$

TP is the true positives, and FP is the false positives.

Recall score

The recall score answers the question of how many actual positives were identified correctly. The recall score can be given with the following formula:

$$recall = \frac{TP}{TP + FN}$$

TP is the true positives, and FN is the false negatives.

F1 score

The F1 score is a weighted average between the precision and recall scores. The best value of the F1 score is one, and the worst is zero. The F1 score allows measuring classification accuracy specific to a particular class. It can be defined as follows:

$$F_1 = 2 \frac{precision * recall}{precision + recall}$$

Here $precision$ is the precision score, and $recall$ is the recall score relative to a specific positive class.

In the next section, we will look at the **Receiver Operating Characteristic** (**ROC**) curve and **Area Under the Curve** (**AUC**).

ROC AUC

We create the ROC by plotting true positive rates against false positive rates at different thresholds. It shows the performance of the classification model at different thresholds.

The **true positive rate** (**TPR**) is a synonym of recall, which we discussed earlier. It can be given by this formula:

$$TPR = \frac{TP}{TP + FN}$$

The false positive rate is calculated as follows:

$$FPR = \frac{FP}{FP + TN}$$

TN is the true negatives.

The AUC allows us to estimate the discrimination power of the classification model, that is, the ability of the model to correctly rank the random positive points more highly than the random negative points. Here is an example of an ROC curve:

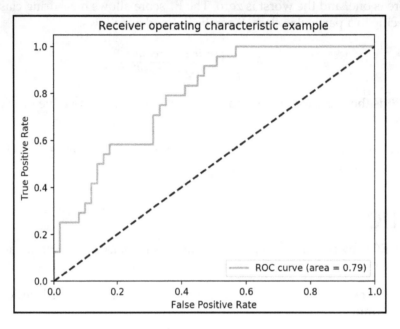

The ROC curve example

In the graph, you can see the ROC curve example. The larger the AUC is, the more accurate the classifier model. The dashed line shows the worst classifier accuracy. In general, the closer the ROC curve is to the upper-left corner, the better the performance of the classification model.

Accuracy

Accuracy is a metric measuring how many correct predictions our model was able to produce. The accuracy is given by the following formula:

$$accuracy = \frac{TP + TN}{TP + TN + FP + FN}$$

FP is the false positives, and FN is the false negatives.

More details about described metrics can be found at `https://scikit-learn.org/stable/auto_examples/model_selection/plot_precision_recall.html`.

Next, we discuss Python coding tips.

Python coding tips and tricks

Having decided to work with Python, it is vital to learn the best coding practices of the language. Here, we provide you with some tips and give you directions to continue with self-learning.

Coding tips and tricks

The following coding tips and tricks will help you master Python:

- You should learn how to use the popular machine learning libraries, such as NumPy (`https://numpy.org`), pandas (`https://pandas.pydata.org`), and Scikit-learn (`https://scikit-learn.org/stable/`). Mastering these libraries will give you tremendous power in data manipulation and analysis. This will help you to avoid many mistakes, and enable easy debugging of the results collected from the experiments.
- Learn about the object-oriented coding paradigm. This will allow you to write a clean and maintainable source code that is easy to understand. You can start at `https://www.datacamp.com/community/tutorials/python-oop-tutorial`.
- Do not write everything into one huge function. Break your code into smaller reusable blocks implemented as functions or classes that can be reused in multiple projects and easily debugged.
- Print the relevant debug output to understand what is going on in your implementation. Having enough debugging outputs allows you to understand what is going wrong with the execution.
- Write comments related to the functions, classes, and intricate places in your source code. Good comments can significantly help in code understandability. Writing the comments before starting the implementation also helps you to clarify your thoughts.
- When writing comments to the function, describe all the input and output parameters and their default values, if any exist.

- If you decide to continue with Python, spend some time learning about the Python standard libraries. Python is a mature programming language with many utility functions embedded into its standard libraries. It also has many functions allowing advanced data manipulations, which can be used in machine learning tasks. More details about standard Python libraries can be found at `https://docs.python.org/3/library/index.html`.

- Follow the standard Python source code conventions when giving names to variables and classes. Adhering to the standard naming conventions makes your code more readable and easy to understand for anyone experienced with Python. You can find more details at `https://docs.python-guide.org/writing/style/` and `https://www.python.org/dev/peps/pep-0008/`.

- Make yourself familiar with modern version control systems, such as Git. A **Version Control System** (**VCS**) is a potent tool at your disposal that may save you hours and even days of attempts to recover your lost work caused by a hard drive crash. You can learn about Git at `https://github.github.com/training-kit/downloads/github-git-cheat-sheet.pdf` and `https://www.atlassian.com/git/tutorials`.

- Learn about online code repositories such as GitHub (`https://github.com`) and Bitbucket (`https://bitbucket.org`), where you can share your source code and study the source code of other data scientists.

Another important aspect of writing good implementations is setting up the working environment correctly and using adequate programming tools.

Working environment and programming tools

It is always a good idea to use one of the mature Python package managers, such as the Anaconda Distribution, to set up your working environment properly. As an additional benefit, you will get a lot of free scientific and machine learning packages that are ready to be installed with a single command. Furthermore, the Anaconda Distribution handles the management of all indirect dependencies and helps you keep all your packages up to date. You can find the Anaconda Distribution at `https://www.anaconda.com/distribution/`.

Always create a new virtual Python environment for each of your experiments. After that, if something goes wrong with dependencies, you will be able to clean everything with one command and start from scratch. The new Python environment can be created with the Anaconda Distribution as follows:

```
$ conda create --name <name>
$ conda activate <name>
```

When creating a new environment, always specify the exact Python version you are planning to use in it. Providing the exact version will help you to avoid many surprises caused by incompatibility. The Python version can be defined for the new environment as follows:

```
$ conda create --name <name> python=3.5
```

If you need to use a new dependency in your project, first check that the appropriate installation package exists in Anaconda Cloud. By using libraries from Anaconda Cloud, you can avoid the problems of indirect dependency installation. Furthermore, some frameworks, such as TensorFlow, require the installation of additional system drivers and headers. This task can be very cumbersome and require additional expertise.

Use a good code editor that supports code completion, documentation browsing, and maintaining virtual Python environments. A good editor to start with is Visual Studio Code—a free editor provided by Microsoft. You can find it at `https://code.visualstudio.com`.

Make yourself familiar with modern Linux systems, such as Ubuntu. Most machine learning libraries are much easier to use with Linux. This is especially true for libraries that use GPU acceleration. More details about Ubuntu and its installation can be found at `https://ubuntu.com`.

Summary

In this chapter, we provided you with practical tips that we hope will make your life easier. You learned about the standard methods of data preprocessing and about conventional statistical metrics that can be used to evaluate the performance of the models you created. Finally, you learned how to improve your coding skills and where to look for additional information about Python and machine learning topics.

In the next chapter, we will look at a few concluding remarks based on what we have learned in the book and where we can use the concepts we have learned in the future.

12
Concluding Remarks

In this chapter, we will summarize everything we have learned in this book and will provide further information so that you can continue your self-education. This chapter will help us revise the topics we have covered in a chapter-wise format and then provide a roadmap by sharing some details on Uber AI Labs, alife.org, and open-ended evolution at Reddit. We will also have a quick overview of the NEAT Software Catalog and the NEAT Algorithm Paper.

In this chapter, we will cover the following topics:

- What we learned in this book
- Where to go from here

What we learned in this book

Now that we have finished with the experiments, I hope that you have gained a solid understanding of the neuroevolution method of training artificial neural networks. We used neuroevolution to find solutions to a variety of experiments, from classic computer science problems to the creation of agents that are capable of playing Atari games. We also examined tasks related to computer vision and visual discrimination.

In this section, we will summarize what we learned in each chapter of this book.

Overview of the neuroevolution methods

In this chapter, we learned about the core concepts of genetic algorithms, such as genetic operators and genome encoding schemes.

We discussed two major genetic operators that allow us to maintain the evolutionary process:

- The mutation operator implements random mutations of the offspring, which introduces genetic diversity into the population.
- The crossover operator generates offspring by sampling genes from each parent.

After that, we continued with a discussion about the importance of choosing the right genome encoding schema. We considered two major encoding formats that exist: direct and indirect genome encoding. The former introduces a one-to-one relationship between the genome and the encoded phenotype ANN. Usually, direct encoding is applied to encode small ANNs, which has a limited number of connected nodes. The more advanced indirect encoding scheme allows us to encode the evolving ANN topology of large networks, often with millions of connections. Indirect encoding allows us to reuse repeating encoding blocks, thus significantly reducing the size of a genome.

Once we were familiar with existing genome encoding schemes, we proceeded to discuss the neuroevolution method, which uses different encoding schemes. We started with an introduction to the NEAT algorithm, which uses the direct genome encoding scheme and enhances it with the concept of the innovation number. The innovation number associated with each gene of the genotype provides a means to precisely track when a particular mutation was introduced. This feature makes crossover operations between two parents straightforward and easy to implement. The NEAT method emphasizes the importance of starting from a very basic genome that gradually becomes more complex during evolution. In this manner, the evolutionary process has an excellent chance of finding the optimal solution.

Furthermore, the concept of speciation was introduced, which keeps useful mutations by isolating them in particular species (niches). The species within one niche are only allowed to cross over with each other. Speciation is the great moving force behind natural evolution, and it was shown to have a high impact on neuroevolution as well.

Having discussed the basic NEAT algorithm, we proceeded to a discussion of its derivatives to address the limitations of the original algorithm. One of the significant drawbacks of the NEAT algorithm is caused by using a direct genome encoding scheme. This scheme, while easy to visualize and implement, only encodes small topologies of the phenotype ANNs. With an increase in the phenotype ANN size, the size of the genome increases in linear proportion. This linear increase in genome size eventually makes it hard to maintain. Thus, to address these drawbacks, a series of extensions based on the indirect genome encoding schemes, such as HyperNEAT and ES-HyperNEAT, were introduced.

The HyperNEAT method uses an advanced format to represent connections between nodes of the phenotype ANN in the form of four-dimensional points in the hypercube. The chosen hypercube's dimensionality is based on the fact that connections between two nodes within an ANN can be encoded by the coordinates of connection endpoints in a medium called the substrate. The substrate topology provides a framework that draws connections between the nodes of the phenotype ANN. The strength of a connection that's drawn between two particular nodes in a substrate is estimated by the auxiliary neural network known as the **Compositional Pattern Producing Network** (**CPPN**). The CPPN receives the coordinates of the hyper-point (the coordinates of the connection endpoints) as input and calculates the strength of the connection. Also, it computes the value of the flag, which indicates whether a connection should be expressed or not. The experimenter defines the substrate configuration in advance. It is defined by the geometric properties of the problem to be solved. At the same time, the topology of the CPPN is evolved during the neuroevolution process using the NEAT algorithm. Thus, we have the best of both worlds. The power of the NEAT algorithm allows us to evolve the optimal CPPN configurations. At the same time, the indirect encoding scheme is maintained by the CPPN and allows us to represent large phenotype ANNs.

The ES-HyperNEAT method introduces a further enhancement to the original NEAT and HyperNEAT methods by proposing an advanced method of substrate evolution that's on par with the evolution of the connectivity CPPN. The substrate evolution is built around the notion of information density, which allows more dense node placement in the areas with higher information variability. This approach allows the neuroevolution process to discover substrate configurations that precisely follow the geometrical regularities that are exposed by the problem to be solved.

We finished the first chapter with a discussion about the fascinating search optimization method known as **Novelty Search** (**NS**). This method is based on the concept of guiding the evolutionary search by criteria that have been estimated using the novelty of the solutions found. Conventionally, search optimization is based on goal-oriented fitness criteria, which measure how close we are to the goal. But there is a whole area of real-world problems that have deceptive fitness function landscapes, which introduce strong local optima traps. The goal-oriented search has a good chance of getting stuck in one of these traps and failing to find the ultimate solution. At the same time, the search optimization method, which rewards the novelty of the solution found, allows us to avoid these traps by completely ignoring the proximity to the final goal. The NS method was shown to be effective in tasks of autonomous navigation through deceptive maze environments; it outperformed the objective-based search methods.

In the next chapter of this book, we discussed how to set up a working environment correctly and what Python libraries can be used to experiment with neuroevolution.

Python libraries and environment setup

In this chapter, we started by discussing the practical aspects of the neuroevolution methods. We discussed the pros and cons of popular Python libraries that provide implementations of the NEAT algorithm and its extensions.

Along with the highlights of each Python library, we also provided small code snippets, giving you a feel of how to use each specific library in your experiments.

After that, we proceeded to discuss how to correctly set up the working environment. The working environment must have the necessary dependencies installed to allow the usage of the mentioned Python libraries. The installation can be done using several methods. We considered the two most common ones – the standard **package installer for Python (PIP)** utility and the Anaconda Distribution. Another critical aspect of the working environment's preparation is the creation of isolated virtual Python environments for each specific experiment. The virtual environments provide the benefits of having different dependency configurations for varying combinations of experiments and the NEAT Python libraries that are used in them.

Having dependencies isolated in a virtual environment also allows easy management of all the installed dependencies as a whole. The environment can be quickly deleted from your PC with everything installed into it, thus freeing disk space. You can also reuse a specific virtual environment for different experiments, which depends on the same NEAT implementation library.

This chapter should have got you familiar with every tool you need in order to start with neuroevolution experiments. In the next chapter, we proceeded to discuss the XOR solver experiment using the basic NEAT algorithm.

Using NEAT for XOR solver optimization

This was the first chapter in which we started experimenting with the NEAT algorithm. We did this by implementing a solver for one of the classic computer science problems. We started by building a solver for the XOR problem. The XOR problem solver is a computer science experiment in the field of reinforcement learning. The XOR problem cannot be linearly separated and thus requires a solver to find the non-linear execution path. However, we can find the non-linear execution path by introducing hidden layers into the ANN structure.

We discussed how the NEAT algorithm perfectly fits this requirement due to its inherent ability to evolve ANNs from a very simple or a complex topology by gradual complexification. In the XOR experiment, we started with an initial ANN topology that consisted of the two input nodes and a single output node. During the experiment, the relevant topology of the solver ANN was discovered, and it introduced an additional hidden node representing the non-linearity, as we expected.

Also, we explained how to define an appropriate fitness function to guide the evolutionary search and to understand how to implement it in the Python script. We put great attention into describing the hyperparameters that fine-tune the performance of the NEAT-Python library for the XOR experiment.

In this chapter, we acquired the skills that are necessary in order to implement basic solvers for essential computer science experiments and were ready to move on to more advanced experiments.

Pole-balancing experiments

In this chapter, we continued with experiments related to the classic problems of computer science in the field of reinforcement learning. We started with a discussion of how to implement an avoidance control optimization method using the NEAT algorithm, allowing us to balance a cart-pole apparatus (or an inverted pendulum). We began with a single pole-balancing system and provided all the necessary equations of motion that allow us to numerically approximate real-world physical apparatus.

We learned how specific control actions could be applied to the cart-pole apparatus in the form of the bang-bang controller. The bang-bang controller is a unique form of control system that is designed to apply a series of actions with equal force but in different directions continuously. To manage a bang-bang controller, the control's ANN needs to continuously receive and analyze the state of the cart-pole apparatus and produce the relevant control signals. The input signals of the system are defined by the horizontal position of the cart on the track, its linear speed, the current angle of the pole, and the angular speed of the pole. The output of the system is a binary signal indicating the direction of a control action that needs to be applied.

The neuroevolution process uses the cart-pole apparatus' simulation for the trial and error process characteristic of every RL-style training algorithm. It maintains the population of the genomes that evolve from generation to generation until a successful solver is found. During their evolution, each organism in the population is tested against a simulation of the cart-pole apparatus. At the end of the simulation, it receives a reward signal in the form of the number of time steps during which it was able to keep the apparatus balanced within the track's bounds. The received reward signal defines the fitness of the organism and determines its fate during the neuroevolution process.

Then, we discussed how the objective function could be defined using the mentioned reward signal. After that, you learned how to implement an objective function using Python.

Having finished with a single pole-balancing experiment, we looked at a modified version of this experiment. The modified version comprised two poles with different lengths connected to the moving cart that needed to be balanced. This experiment had more complicated physics and required the discovery of a much more sophisticated controller during the experiment.

Both experiments that were presented in this chapter highlighted the importance of keeping a well-balanced population of solvers with a moderate number of species. Too many species in the population may hinder the neuroevolution process by reducing the chance of reproduction between the two organisms belonging to different species. Furthermore, taking into account that the population size is fixed, the more species you have within the population, the less populated they become. Sparsely populated species reduce the chance of discovering useful mutations. On the other hand, separate species allow us to maintain useful mutations within each speciation niche and exploit each mutation further in the next generations. Thus, too few species are also harmful to evolution. At the end of the pole-balancing experiment, you gained some practical skills that relate to keeping the number of species balanced by tweaking the corresponding hyperparameters of the NEAT algorithm (such as the compatibility threshold).

Another essential feature of the neuroevolution process that was highlighted in the pole-balancing experiment is related to the selection of the right initial condition of the stochastic process that guides the evolutionary process. The neuroevolution method's implementation is built around a pseudo-random number generator, which provides the likelihood of genome mutations and crossover rates. In the pseudo-random number generator, the sequence of numbers that will be produced is solely determined by the initial seed value that is supplied to the generator at the beginning. By using the same seed value, it is possible to produce the same random number sequences using the pseudo-random generator.

As a result of the experiment with the evolving controller's ANN for the cart-pole balancers, we discovered that the probability of finding a successful solution strongly depends on the value of the random number generator seed.

Mastering the pole-balancing experiments allowed you to be prepared to solve more complex problems associated with autonomous navigation, which were discussed in the next chapter.

Autonomous maze navigation

In this chapter, we continued our experiments with neuroevolution as an attempt to create a solver that can find an exit from a maze. Maze solving is a fascinating problem as it allows us to study a new search optimization method called Novelty Search. In Chapter 5, *Autonomous Maze Navigation*, and Chapter 6, *Novelty Search Optimization Method*, we explored a series of the maze navigation experiments using the goal-oriented search optimization and the Novelty Search optimization method.

In this chapter, you learned how to implement a simulation of a robot that has an array of sensors that detect obstacles and monitor its position within the maze. Also, we discussed how to implement a goal-oriented objective function to guide the evolutionary process. The mentioned objective-function implementation is calculated as Euclidean distance between the robot's final position and the maze's exit.

Using the maze navigation simulator and the defined objective function, we conducted two experiments with simple and hard maze configurations. The results of the experiments give us insights into the impact of the deceptive fitness function landscape on the performance of the evolutionary process. In local optima areas, neuroevolution tends to produce fewer species, which hinders its ability to explore novel solutions. In extreme cases, this leads to the degeneration of the evolutionary process. This can result in having only a single species in the entire population.

At the same time, you learned how to avoid such misfortunes by adjusting NEAT hyperparameters such as the compatibility disjoint coefficient. This parameter controls how strong topological differences in the compared genomes affect the compatibility factor, which is used to determine whether genomes belong to the same species. As a result, we were able to boost speciation and increase population diversity. This change had a positive impact on the search for a successful maze solver, and we were able to find it for a simple maze configuration. However, a hard maze configuration with more extreme local optima areas resisted all our attempts to find a successful maze solver using the goal-oriented objective function.

Thus, we were ready to learn about the Novelty Search optimization method, which was devised to overcome the limitations of the goal-oriented search.

Novelty Search optimization method

In all the experiments preceding this chapter, we defined an objective function as a derivative based on its proximity to the final goal of the problem. However, the maze-solving problem posed challenges that could not be solved by a goal-oriented objective function. Specific maze configurations can introduce strong local optima in which a goal-oriented objective search may become stuck. In many cases, a deceptive fitness function landscape such as this effectively blocks a goal-oriented objective search from finding a successful solution.

Thus, using the practical experience we gained during the creation of a maze solver in the previous chapter, we embarked on the path of creating a more advanced solver. Our brand new solver used the Novelty Search optimization method to guide the evolutionary process. However, first of all, we needed to define the appropriate metric to estimate the novelty score of each solution in each generation. The novelty score that was produced by this metric was going to be used as a fitness value that would be assigned to the genomes in the population of solvers. Thus, the novelty is integrated into the standard neuroevolution process.

The novelty metric should measure how novel each solution is compared to the solutions we found in the past and all the solutions from the current generation. There are two ways to measure solution novelty:

- The genotypic novelty is the novelty score and shows how the genotype of the current solution differs from the genotypes of all the other found solutions.
- The behavioral novelty demonstrates how the behavior of the current solution differs within the problem space compared to all the other solutions.

For the problem of solving a maze, a good choice is to use a behavioral novelty score because, in the end, we are interested in reaching the maze exit, which can be facilitated by exposing a certain behavior. Furthermore, the behavioral novelty score is much easier to calculate than the genotypic novelty score.

The trajectory of a particular solver through the maze defines its behavioral space. Thus, we can estimate the novelty score by comparing the trajectory vectors of the solvers. Numerically, the novelty score can be estimated by calculating the Euclidean distance between trajectory vectors. To further simplify this task, we can use only the coordinates of the last point of the solver trajectory to estimate the novelty score.

Having defined the novelty metric, you learned how to implement it in the source code using Python and integrate it into the maze simulator you created in `Chapter 5`, *Autonomous Maze Navigation*. After that, you were ready to repeat the experiments from the previous chapter and compare the results.

The experiment with a simple maze solver demonstrated an improvement in the topology of the produced control ANN. The topology became optimal and less complicated.

Unfortunately, the experiment with hard maze configuration also failed to produce a successful solver, the same as it did in `Chapter 5`, *Autonomous Maze Navigation*. The failure seems to be caused by the inefficiency of a particular implementation of the NEAT algorithm used in the experiment. I have implemented the NEAT algorithm in Go so that it solves the hard maze configuration with ease using the Novelty Search optimization. You can find it on GitHub at `https://github.com/yaricom/goNEAT_NS`.

In `Chapter 6`, *Novelty Search Optimization Method*, you learned that the Novelty Search optimization method allows you to find a solution, even when the fitness function has a deceptive landscape with many local optima traps scattered inside. You have learned that the stepping stones forming the way to the solution are not always obvious. Sometimes, you need to step back to find the correct way. That is the main idea behind the Novelty Search method. It tries to find a solution by completely ignoring the proximity to the final goal and rewarding the novelty of each intermediate solution that is found on the way.

In this chapter, we got acquainted with the standard NEAT algorithm, and we were ready to begin experimenting with its more advanced extensions.

Hypercube-based NEAT for visual discrimination

This chapter was the first of four chapters in which we discussed advanced neuroevolution methods. In this chapter, you learned about the indirect genome encoding scheme, which uses the **Compositional Pattern Producing Network** (**CPPN**) to aid with the encoding of large phenotype ANN topologies. The CPPN encoding scheme introduced by the NEAT extension is named **HyperNEAT**. This extension is built around the concept of the connectivity substrate that represents the phenotype ANN topology. At the same time, connections between nodes in the substrate are expressed as four-dimensional points within the hypercube. In the HyperNEAT method, the topology of the CPPN is the part that is evolving and guided by the NEAT algorithm. We had already discussed the particulars of HyperNEAT, so we skipped the rest of the details of HyperNEAT for brevity.

In this chapter, we presented you with the interesting task of visual discrimination, which highlights the ability of the HyperNEAT algorithm to distinguish patterns in the visual field. You learned that the HyperNEAT method could find a successful visual pattern discriminator due to its inherent ability to reuse the successful connectivity patterns it found multiple times in the substrate that encodes the phenotype ANN of the solver. This was possible because of the power of the CPPN, which can discover the right strategy by passing signals from the input nodes (the perceiving image) to the output nodes (representing results).

You learned how to choose the correct geometry of a substrate to effectively employ the capabilities of the CPPN to find the geometric regularities. After that, you had a chance to apply your acquired knowledge in practice by implementing the visual discriminator that was trained using the HyperNEAT algorithm.

Also, having completed the visual discriminator experiment, you were able to verify the effectiveness of the indirect encoding scheme. We did this by comparing the topology of the produced CPPN with the maximum possible number of connections in the discriminator ANN substrate. The results of the visual discriminator experiment were pretty impressive. We were able to achieve an information compression ratio of 0.11% by encoding the connectivity pattern among 14,641 possible connections of the substrate, with only 16 connections between 10 nodes of the CPPN.

Visual tasks expose a high demand for the discriminator ANN architecture due to the high dimensionality of the input signal. Thus, in Chapter 8, *ES-HyperNEAT and the Retina Problem*, we proceeded with a review of another class of visual recognition problems.

ES-HyperNEAT and the retina problem

In this chapter, you learned how to select the substrate configuration that is best suited for a specific problem space. However, it is not always obvious what configuration to choose. If you select the wrong configuration, you can significantly impact the performance of the training process. As a result, the neuroevolution process can fail to produce a successful solution. Also, particular substrate configuration details can only be discovered during the training process, and cannot be known in advance.

The problem with finding an appropriate substrate configuration was solved using the ES-HyperNEAT method. In this chapter, you learned how the neuroevolution process could automatically handle the evolution of the substrate configuration among the evolution of connectivity CPPNs. We introduced you to the concept of the quadtree data structure, which allows effective traversal through the substrate topology and the detection of areas with high information density. We learned that it is beneficial to automatically place new nodes into these areas to create more subtle connectivity patterns, which describe hidden regularities that can be found in the real world.

After you became familiar with the details of the ES-HyperNEAT algorithm, you learned how to apply it to solve the visual recognition task known as the retina problem. In this task, the neuroevolution process needs to discover a solver that can recognize valid patterns simultaneously in two separate visual fields. That is, the detector ANN must decide if patterns presented in the right and left visual fields are valid for each field. The solution of this task can be found by introducing the modular architecture to the topology of the detector ANN. In such a configuration, each ANN module is responsible only for pattern recognition in the related side of the retina.

In this chapter, we implemented a successful retina problem solver using the ES-HyperNEAT method. We were able to visually confirm that the produced topology of the detector ANN included the modular structures. Furthermore, from the experiment's results, you learned that the resulting detector ANN structure has near-optimal complexity. Once again, this experiment demonstrated the potential of neuroevolution-based methods to discover efficient solutions by method of gradual complexification.

All the experiments, including the one described in this chapter, used a particular form of the fitness function that is defined in advance before the experiments started. However, it would be interesting to explore how the performance of the neuroevolution algorithm changes if the fitness function is allowed to co-evolve along with the solution it tries to optimize.

Co-evolution and the SAFE method

In this chapter, we discussed how the co-evolution strategy is widely found in nature and can be transferred into the realm of neuroevolution. You learned about the most common co-evolutionary strategies that can be found in nature: mutualism, competition (predation or parasitism), and commensalism. In our experiment, we explored the commensalistic type of evolution, which can be defined in commensalistic relationships as follows: the members of one species gain benefits without causing harm or giving benefits to other participating species.

Having learned about evolution strategies in the natural world, you were ready to understand the concepts behind the SAFE method. The abbreviation **SAFE** means **Solution And Fitness Evolution**, which suggests that we have two co-evolving populations: the population of potential solutions and the population of the fitness function candidates. At each generation of evolution, we evaluate each potential solution against all the objective function candidates and choose the best fitness score, which is observed as the fitness of the genome encoding solution. At the same time, we evolve the commensalistic population of the fitness function candidates using the Novelty Search method. Novelty Search uses the genomic novelty of each genome in the population as a novelty metric to estimate the individual's fitness score.

In this chapter, you learned how to implement a modified maze solving experiment based on the SAFE method to evaluate the performance of the co-evolution strategy. Also, you learned how to define the objective function to guide the evolution of the population of potential solutions. This objective function includes two fitness metrics: the first is the distance from the maze exit, while the second is the behavioral novelty of the solution that was found. These metrics are combined using the coefficients that are produced by a population of the fitness function candidates.

As in all the previous chapters, you continued to improve your Python skills by implementing the SAFE method using the MultiNEAT Python library. In the next chapter, you continued by studying even more advanced methods, thereby allowing you to use neuroevolution to train Atari game solvers.

Deep Neuroevolution

In this chapter, we presented you with the concept of deep neuroevolution, which can be used to train **Deep Artificial Neural Networks** (**DNNs**). You learned how deep neuroevolution can be used to train Atari game-playing agents using the deep reinforcement learning algorithm.

We started with a discussion of the basic concepts behind reinforcement learning. We paid special attention to the popular Q-learning algorithm, which is one of the classic implementations of reinforcement learning. After that, you learned how a DNN could be used to approximate the Q-value function for complex tasks that cannot be approximated by a simple action-state table with Q-values. Next, we discussed how the neuroevolution-based method could be used to find the trainable parameters of the DNN. You learned that neuroevolution evolves a DNN for Q-value function approximation. As a result, we can train the appropriate DNN without using any form of error backpropagation that is common in conventional methods of DNN training.

Having learned about deep reinforcement learning, you were ready to apply your knowledge in practice by implementing the Atari game solver agent. To train an agent to play the Atari game, it needs to read the pixels of the game screen and derive the current state of the game. After that, using the extracted game state, the agent needs to select an appropriate action to be executed in the game environment. The ultimate goal of the agent is to maximize the final reward that will be received after completion of a particular game episode. Thus, we have classic trial and error learning, which is the essence of reinforcement learning.

As we mentioned, the game-playing agent needs to parse game screen pixels. The best way to do this is to use a **Convolutional Neural Network** (**CNN**) to process the inputs that are received from the game screen. In this chapter, we discussed the essentials of the CNN architecture and how it can be integrated into the game-playing agent. You learned how to implement CNN in Python using a popular TensorFlow framework.

Also, you learned about a unique genome encoding scheme that was designed specifically for tasks related to deep neuroevolution. This scheme allows us to encode the phenotype ANNs with millions of trainable parameters. The proposed scheme employs the seeds of the pseudorandom number generator to encode the connection weights of the phenotype ANN. In this encoding scheme, the genome was represented as a list of the random generator seeds. Each seed is used consequentially to generate all the connection weights from a source of pseudorandom numbers.

After learning about the details of genome encoding, you were ready to start an experiment that aimed to create an agent that was able to play the Frostbite Atari game. Furthermore, you learned how to employ a modern GPU to accelerate the computations involved in the training process. At the end of this chapter, we also presented an advanced visualization tool (VINE) that allows us to study the results of the neuroevolution experiments.

With this chapter, we finished our brief acquaintance with the most popular neuroevolution methods that exist at the time of writing this book. However, there are still many things that you can learn in the fast-growing field of applied artificial intelligence and neuroevolution methods.

Where to go from here

We hope that your journey through the neuroevolution methods that were presented in this book was pleasant and insightful. We have done our best to present you with the most recent achievements in the field of neuroevolution. However, this field of applied computer science is developing rapidly, and new achievements are announced almost every month. There are many laboratories in universities, as well as in corporations around the globe, working on applying neuroevolution methods to solve tasks that are beyond the strength of mainstream deep learning algorithms.

We hope that you have become fond of the neuroevolution methods we discussed and are eager to apply them in your work and experiments. However, you need to continue your self-education to keep pace with the next achievements in the area. In this section, we will present some places where you can continue your education.

Uber AI Labs

The core of Uber AI Labs is built around the Geometric Intelligence startup that was co-founded by Kenneth O. Stanley – one of the prominent pioneers in the field of neuroevolution. He is the author of the NEAT algorithm, which we have used often in this book. You can follow the works of Uber AI Labs
at https://eng.uber.com/category/articles/ai/.

alife.org

The **International Society for Artificial Life** (**ISAL**) is a well-established community of researchers and enthusiasts from all around the world who are interested in scientific research activities related to artificial life. Genetic algorithms and neuroevolution, in particular, are among the areas of interest of this society. ISAL publishes the Artificial Life journal and sponsors a variety of conferences. You can find out more about ISAL activities
at http://alife.org.

Open-ended evolution at Reddit

The concept of open-ended evolution is directly related to genetic algorithms and neuroevolution in particular. Open-ended evolution assumes the creation of an evolutionary process that is not bound by any particular goal. It is inspired by the natural evolution of biological organisms, which produced us, humans. There is a dedicated subreddit where all of those who are interested discuss the research. You can find it at https://www.reddit.com/r/oee/.

The NEAT Software Catalog

The University of Central Florida maintains the list of software libraries that implement the NEAT algorithm and its extensions. The software is moderated by Kenneth O. Stanley, the author of the NEAT algorithm. My implementation of the NEAT and Novelty Search in Go language is also present in this catalog. You can find it at http://eplex.cs.ucf.edu/neat_software/.

arXiv.org

arXiv.org is a well-known service that publishes preprints of papers in many areas of science. It is generally an excellent source of cutting-edge information in the area of computer science. You can search through it for neuroevolution-related papers using the following search query: http://search.arxiv.org:8081/?query=neuroevolution&in=grp_cs.

The NEAT algorithm paper

The original dissertation written by Kenneth O. Stanley describing the NEAT algorithm is a very enlightening read and is recommended for everyone interested in neuroevolution. It is available at http://nn.cs.utexas.edu/downloads/papers/stanley.phd04.pdf.

Summary

In this chapter, we briefly summarized what we learned in this book. You also learned about the places where you can search for further insights and continue your self-education.

We are happy to live in an era where the future becomes a reality at such a pace that we completely fail to notice the tremendous changes that happen in our life. Humanity is rapidly moving on a path to mastering the marvels of gene editing and synthetic biology. We continue to conquer the deep mysteries of the human brain, which opens the way for an ultimate understanding of our consciousness. Our advanced experiments in cosmology allow us to zoom closer and closer to the very first moments of the Universe.

We have built an advanced piece of mathematical apparatus that allows us to describe such mysteries as a neutrino that, on its path, can become an electron and after that, a neutrino again. Our technological achievements can't be easily distinguished from magic, as Arthur C. Clark stated.

Life is about feeling its beauty. Keep your mind sharp, and always be curious. We are standing on the edge, where sparks from the research of synthetic consciousness will ignite the evolution of novel life forms. And who knows – maybe you will be the one who will start this.

Thank you, my dear reader, for your time and effort. I look forward to seeing what you will create using the knowledge you've gained from this book.

Other Books You May Enjoy

If you enjoyed this book, you may be interested in these other books by Packt:

Hands-On Deep Learning Algorithms with Python
Sudharsan Ravichandiran

ISBN: 978-1-78934-415-8

- Implement basic-to-advanced deep learning algorithms
- Master the mathematics behind deep learning algorithms
- Become familiar with gradient descent and its variants, such as AMSGrad, AdaDelta, Adam, and Nadam
- Implement recurrent networks, such as RNN, LSTM, GRU, and seq2seq models
- Understand how machines interpret images using CNN and capsule networks
- Implement different types of generative adversarial network, such as CGAN, CycleGAN, and StackGAN
- Explore various types of autoencoder, such as Sparse autoencoders, DAE, CAE, and VAE

Python Deep Learning - Second Edition

Gianmario Spacagna, Daniel Slater, Ivan Vasilev, Peter Roelants

ISBN: 978-1-78934-846-0

- Grasp the mathematical theory behind neural networks and deep learning processes
- Investigate and resolve computer vision challenges using convolutional networks and capsule networks
- Solve generative tasks using variational autoencoders and Generative Adversarial Networks
- Implement complex NLP tasks using recurrent networks (LSTM and GRU) and attention models
- Explore reinforcement learning and understand how agents behave in a complex environment
- Get up to date with applications of deep learning in autonomous vehicles

Leave a review - let other readers know what you think

Please share your thoughts on this book with others by leaving a review on the site that you bought it from. If you purchased the book from Amazon, please leave us an honest review on this book's Amazon page. This is vital so that other potential readers can see and use your unbiased opinion to make purchasing decisions, we can understand what our customers think about our products, and our authors can see your feedback on the title that they have worked with Packt to create. It will only take a few minutes of your time, but is valuable to other potential customers, our authors, and Packt. Thank you!

Index

G

genetic algorithms (GA) 47, 279
genetic operators
  about 11
  crossover operator 13
  mutation operator 12
genome encoding schemes
  about 14, 284
  defining 285
  direct genome encoding 14, 15
  implementing 285, 286
  indirect genome encoding 16
genome's fitness evaluation 211, 212
goal-oriented search optimization
  about 315
  Euclidean distance 316
  mean squared error 316

H

hard-to-solve maze configuration experiment
  about 149, 183, 184
  executing 148, 184, 185, 187
  hyperparameter selection 149, 184
  working environment setup 149, 184
hard-to-solve maze configuration
  experiment runner implementation 149
hard-to-solve maze navigation experiment
  executing 150, 151, 152
  exercises 152
hierarchy 17
hypercube-based NEAT
  about 23, 24
  Compositional Pattern Producing Networks
    (CPPNs) 24, 25
  for visual discrimination 335, 336
  substrate layout configurations 25
Hypercube-based NeuroEvolution of Augmenting
  Topologies (HyperNEAT) algorithm
  about 16, 24, 194, 335
  evolving 26, 27
hypercube
  information patterns 28, 29
HyperNEAT method 222
hyperparameter selection

about 63
  DefaultGenome section 65, 66
  DefaultReproduction section 65
  DefaultSpeciesSet section 65
  DefaultStagnation section 64
  NEAT section 63, 64
hyperparameters
  tuning 318, 320

I

indirect genome encoding 16
individual fitness evaluation function 167, 169,
  170
information extraction
  with quadtree 224
inputs
  scaling, to range 313
International Society for Artificial Life (ISAL) 340

M

manual configuration, versus evolution-based
  configuration
  topography of neural nodes 222, 223
Matplotlib
  URL 318
maze configuration experiment
  about 138, 170, 171
  executing 135, 136
  exercises 148
  experiment runner function 174, 175
  hyperparameter selection 136, 137, 171, 172
  working environment setup 139, 172
maze configuration, experiment runner
  implementation
  about 139, 140, 141, 172
  genome fitness evaluation 141
  trials cycle 173, 174
maze navigation experiment
  agent record visualization 146, 147
  executing 142, 144, 145, 146
  executing, with NS optimization 177, 179, 180
maze navigation problem 122, 123
maze simulation environment, implementation
  about 126, 127
  agent position update 129, 130, 131

PyTorch NEAT 42
Python
    programming tools 324, 325
    working environment 324
PyTorch NEAT library
    about 42
    reference link 44
    usage example 43, 44, 45

Q

quadtree information extraction
    about 224
    division and initialization stage 225
    pruning and extraction stage 226
quadtree
    about 223
    as effective information extractor 29, 31

R

recall score 320
Receiver Operating Characteristic (ROC) 321, 322
Rectified Linear Unit (ReLU) 282
reinforcement learning (RL) 278
reinforcement signal 105
retina problem 336, 337
RL evaluation, on GPU cores
    about 290
    ConcurrentWorkers class 295
    RLEvalutionWorker class 290
RL training, of game agent
    about 284
    genome encoding schemes 284
    simple genetic algorithm 286, 287
RLEvalutionWorker class
    about 290
    asynchronous task runner 294
    graph evaluation loop 292, 293
    network graph, creating 291, 292

S

SAFE method 253, 337, 338
Seaborn
    URL 318
simulators
    writing 315

single-pole balancing experiment
    about 93
    cart-pole apparatus simulation 89, 90
    environment setup, working 95
    executing 98, 100, 101
    exercises 101
    genome fitness evaluation 92, 93
    genomes, evaluating in population 96
    hyperparameter selection 93, 94
    objective function 88, 89
    simulation cycle 90, 92
single-pole balancing problem
    about 84
    equations of motion 85, 86
    experiment runner function 97
    experiment runner implementation 95
    solver and simulator, interactions between 87, 88
    state equations and control actions 86
six rangefinder sensors 124
Solution and Fitness Evolution (SAFE) 16, 252
speciation algorithm 22
speciation graph 180
structural mutations 19, 20
substrate configuration, types
    circular 194
    state-space sandwich 194
    three-dimensional grid 194
    two-dimensional grid 194
substrate layout configurations 25
substrate layout configurations, examples
    circular 26
    State-Space Sandwich 26
    three-dimensional grid 26
    two-dimensional grid 26

T

topography, of neural nodes
    manual configuration, versus evolution-based configuration 222, 223

U

Uber AI Labs
    about 340
    reference link 340

V

X

www.ingramcontent.com/pod-product-compliance
Lightning Source LLC
Chambersburg PA
CBHW080614060326
40690CB00021B/4689